# JUST CAUSE

# JUST CAUSE

The Real Story of America's High-Tech
Invasion of Panama

## Malcolm McConnell

St. Martin's Press

New York

*Editor: Jared Kieling*
*Production Editor: Mark H. Berkowitz*
*Copyeditor: W.L. Broecker*
*Design by Susan Hood*

Library of Congress Cataloging-in-Publication Data
McConnell, Malcolm.
Just Cause: the real story of America's high-tech invasion of Panama.
p.  cm.
ISBN 0-312-06383-0
1. United States—Foreign relations—Panama. 2. Panama—Foreign relations—United States. 3. Panama—History—American invasion, 1989.
I. Title.
E183.8.P2M35  1991    327.7307287—dc20     91-18121

First Edition: November 1991

1  3  5  7  9  10  8  6  4  2

TO THE MEN AND WOMEN OF THE AMERICAN ARMED FORCES

# Contents

# JUST CAUSE

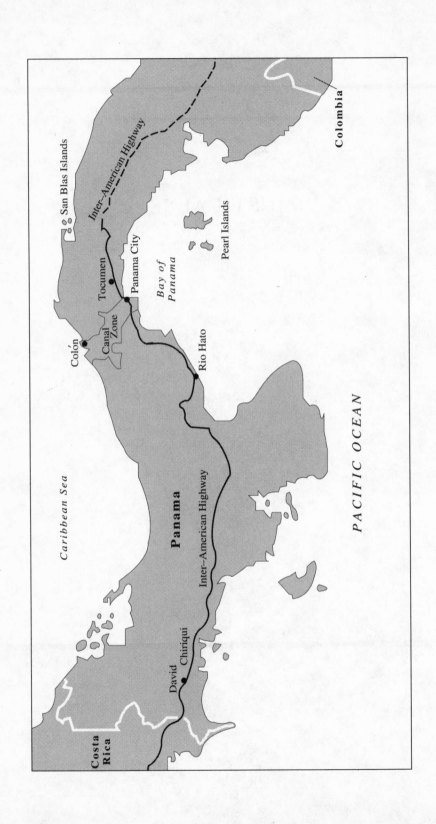

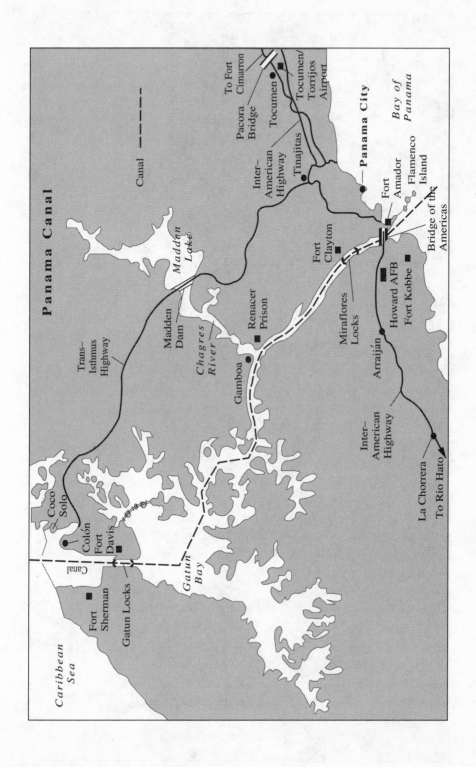

# Panama Canal

Caribbean Sea

Canal ----

Fort Sherman ■
Gatun Locks
Coco Solo
Colón
Fort Davis ■
Gatun Bay

Trans–Isthmus Highway

Madden Lake

Madden Dam
Renacer Prison ■
Chagres River
Gamboa ●

Inter–American Highway
Tinajitas ●
Pacora Bridge
To Fort Cimarron
Tocumen ●■
Tocumen/Torrijos Airport

Panama City
Bay of Panama

Fort Clayton ■
Miraflores Locks
Fort Amador
Flamenco Island
Bridge of the Americas

Arraiján ●
Howard AFB ■
Fort Kobbe ■

Inter–American Highway
La Chorrera ●
To Río Hato

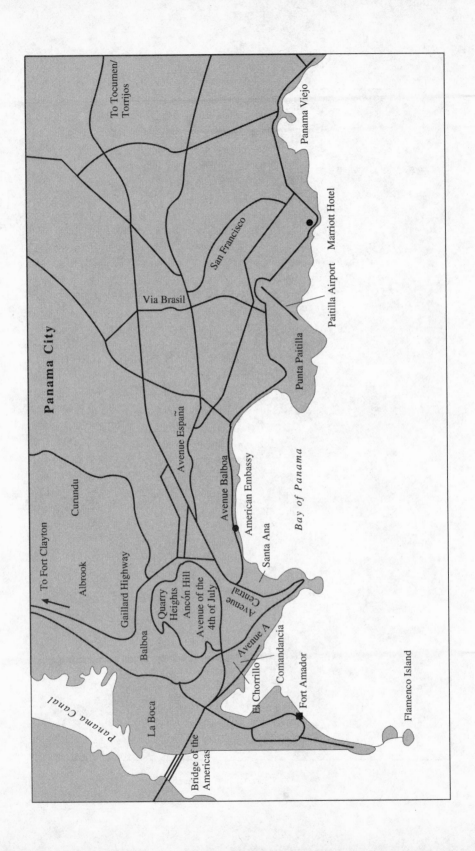

# Prologue

## Lessons Learned

*0736 Hours, 3 October 1989*

The familiar convoy swept along Avenida Balboa, past the gleaming phalanx of high-rise banks and office towers that had sprung up around Punta Paitilla during the previous two decades of affluence. Along the esplanade, the harsh tropic sun was softened by the blue expanse of Panama Bay; the morning sea breeze rattled the fronds of the old royal palms that graced this seaside boulevard.

A white Toyota Land Cruiser with smoked-glass windows preceded two customized, steel-blue Mercedes 380S sedans, riding low on their reinforced springs under the burden of armor plate. Fifty meters behind the sedans, an open pickup truck carried four young soldiers of the Panama Defense Forces (PDF), armed with assault rifles and an evil-looking M-60 machine gun. As the convoy roared past the wrought-iron gates of the American Embassy, the driver of the pickup hit his warbling siren, a taunting reminder that the lone passenger in the second Mercedes, General Manuel Antonio Noriega, was still a free man and the absolute master of his own and his country's destiny.

Shielded from the rising heat of the morning by the car's powerful air-conditioning, Noriega sat comfortably in the leather upholstered back seat, sipping his first heavily watered Old Parr whiskey of the day and leafing through the computer printout of the overnight intelligence summary. He had adopted the morning habit of a dilute whiskey after reading that one of his heroes, Winston Churchill, always began his day with a long warm bath and a tall whiskey-and-soda while he read the London newspapers.

General Noriega did not read newspapers. He had an assistant who did that for him, because reading the lies written in the press was too upsetting. But he certainly did enjoy the relaxing whiskey while he read his morning intelligence report. There was nothing new.[1] Military forces of the U.S. Southern Command were still conducting their harassment provocations, forcing columns of armored vehicles and truckloads of heavily armed troops into Panamanian sovereign territory within the old Panama Canal Zone. By a strictly legalistic interpretation of the Panama Canal Treaties of 1978—the Carter-Torrijos Accord—the gringo forces were to be granted access to such areas. And they always claimed to be merely exercising these treaty rights, according to Southcom's barking dog public relations officers up on Ancon Hill.[2] But Noriega and every Panamanian above the age of reason knew better. The yanquis were using the treaties as a pretext to intimidate the PDF with their superior firepower in order to undercut the troops' loyalty to their leader, General Noriega. For months now, George Bush, that hypocritical moralist who hid his bloody CIA past in a mantle of democratic sermons, had been openly calling for the Panamanian military to overthrow Noriega.

And, once the leader had been toppled, the shit-eating coup-makers would supposedly either murder him or turn him over to Southcom. They'd arrest and extradite him on the eleven counts of drug trafficking that the kangaroo grand jury in Miami had handed down almost two years before.

Noriega sipped his weak whiskey and gazed through the tinted car windows at Cerro Ancon—Ancon Hill—hulking massively above the jumble of mildewed concrete shops and wooden tenements that marked Panama City's old barrios of Santa Ana and El Chorrillo. The gringos insisted on calling the tree-clad granite monolith Quarry Heights, a mocking, anachronistic reference to the building of the Canal, when they had used indentured black Caribbean contract labor and

Panamanian *campesinos* to hew the stone for the roads and railbeds of the Gaitan Cut.

But Cerro Ancon was the only valid name for this mountain fortress. Panama was a sovereign nation, not the last colony in Central America. From here on Avenida Balboa he could see the largest flag in the world, the red-blue-and-white banner of the Republic of Panama, which the late and lamented General Omar Torrijos-Herrera had ordered raised on Ancon Hill after his treaty victory over Jimmy Carter. Now that flag, half the size of a soccer field, bore tangible proof—all the sunlit day and floodlit night—that the gringos' holdings, even their precious Quarry Heights, would revert to the people of Panama at midnight on December 31, 1999.

Noriega liked to watch private vehicles pull quickly to the curb to allow him free passage. Each car and pickup truck bore the same lemon-yellow license plate, emblazoned with the patriotic slogan he had written with his own hand: *Ano 2000. . . Soberena Total* (Year 2000. . . Total Sovereignty). This was a message the people understood, and they knew that the only route to that total sovereignty lay along the path of *Torrijisma* pioneered by the legitimate guardians of the national honor, the Panama Defense Forces. In fact, Noriega had recently delivered a long and spirited television address on this very matter, and the response of the people had been magnificent.

Of course the *rabiblancos* had mocked him in La Prensa, as they always did. But, as he had noted to the general staff immediately following the speech, that scorn had simply been the defensive reaction of a defeated class of parasites. They all claimed pure, untainted Castillian, Basque, or Italian bloodlines, but half of the blue-eyed redheads chasing their silly tennis balls at the Club Union were Jews. And the blood of the other half was so thinned by inbreeding that they kept entire wards of Miami hospitals filled with their harelipped and idiot offspring. And yet they sneered at *his* mestizo ancestry.

Manuel Noriega hated Panama's wealthy rabiblancos—named for the local White Tail Warbler—almost as much as he hated the gringos. In reality, he often told his officers, the Guillermo "Billy" Fords, Calderóns, and Guillermo Endaras were merely extensions of North American imperialism, not a distinct class or community. And when the gringos were finally expelled from Panama, the pampered brokers, bankers and "publishers" of Punta Paitilla and Alto del Golf would all depart with them, colonial Quislings following their masters. They would no doubt take their stolen wealth with them. It was interesting to note that the North American economic sanctions that Bush imposed after the drug indictments had all but ruined the economy and driven thousands of already poor families into hungry destitution, yet the rabiblancos still managed to drive their BMWs and take their ski trips to Vail and St. Moritz. But their day of reckoning would come.

In the interim, of course, there were problems. Ancon Hill stood like Gibraltar, a tangible symbol of insult to the sovereign people. And, like that British fortress—a cancer in the breast of Spain—Southcom and its network of bases possessed serious military potential. Only a fool would openly provoke such military power. And Noriega was no fool.

But this certainly did not mean the Defense Forces and their leader had to genuflect to the gringos, then drop their drawers and smear their asses with butter, as he often told his loyal officers. No, certainly not. The task of the military was to thwart the gringos at every turn, to use cunning and nerve to smash their plots. And then, if the North Americans persisted in their intent to destroy the Revolution of Torrijos, it would be the duty of every honorable soldier of Panama to sacrifice himself for the homeland. As he had proclaimed after the CIA tried to rig the so-called free elections in May, the people would not be driven one step further from the path of total sovereignty. After that bogus election, Noriega had himself written yet another unifying political slogan. *Una Vida por la Patria, Ni un Paso Atras* (One Life for the Homeland, Not One Step Further).

Manuel Noriega's small convoy turned down the narrow canyon of Avenida A, then left onto the even narrower Calle 17. He had been raised on Calle 12, here in Santa Ana, a neighborhood of mildewed, crumbling stucco and rusty iron balconies, a barrio of poor whites and mestizos, just a paycheck above the abject poverty of El Chorrillo, the predominantly black and Creole slum of two-story wooden tenements that lay on the far side of La Comandancia, the defense force headquarters.

This thick-walled fortress rose with comforting solidity at the end of Calle 17. The Comandancia occupied an entire city block. Within the encircling wall stood a dozen separate buildings, barracks for the Security Force Company, a motor pool, mess halls for officers and men, even an attractive little Catholic chapel that Noriega had ordered built the year of his gringo indictment. The complex was dominated by the curved concrete buttresses of the general staff headquarters, which had once housed the entire National Guard staff, when that precursor of the defense forces had merely been a token gendarmerie, subservient in every way to the American masters of the Zone. Now the Comandancia was a headquarters worthy of a true national army.

In many ways, the prominent landmarks of Panama City mapped a moral and political terrain that transcended geography. Punta Paitilla, with the rabiblanco bankers' glass-and-steel towers and the Club Union (which had never even considered admitting a dusky parvenu like Noriega), was one corner of Panama's power triangle. The gringos' Gibraltar on Ancon Hill, nerve center of the base network literally straddling Panama, was the nexus of America's geopolitical grip on the nation. And the Comandancia, poised between the shabby respectability of Santa Ana and the squalor of El Chorrillo, the headquarters of a military complex that had grown to grotesque proportions for a country of only 2.3 million inhabitants, epitomized Noriega's concerted effort to meld his personal ambitions with the nationlist aspirations of Panama's dispossessed. As he so often shouted at mass rallies of his Dignity Battalions (citizens he had recently had armed and trained as a PDF auxiliary militia), "I know you perfectly"—he would use the singular familiar *tu* pronoun to a crowd of *campesinos*—"You are me, and I am you."

\*     \*     \*

The moment Noriega's convoy entered the steel double gates of the Comandancia, he realized something was very wrong. He saw soldiers of the PDF's 4th Infantry Company, the "Urraca" reconnaissance unit (named for a Panamanian Indian tribe) deployed in obvious combat formations, carrying shoulder weapons and extra ammunition. And troops of the Security Company, the "Dobermans" in their black berets—so feared by the cowardly rabiblanco protesters—were grouped near the important doorways, their Uzi submachine guns unslung.

Noriega squared his high-prowed officer's hat, an adornment worthy of either an SS *Sturmbanfuehrer* or a Soviet Red Army Marshal, and stepped briskly from the car. His personal bodyguards were already out of the lead Mercedes, their hands on their pistol holsters. The steel gates slammed shut, excluding the trailing pickup.

An Urraca captain strode forward, fumbling with his German 9 mm submachine gun. Noriega's bodyguard moved close to him, their pistols drawn.

"What is all this?" Noriega demanded.[3]

"General," the captain stammered, "it's a training exercise."

Noriega saw the man was lying. He also saw that there was no escape from this well-guarded courtyard. If the second coup attempt in seventeen months were actually unfolding, the plotters had not yet deployed troops in the surrounding streets. His only chance to rally loyal forces lay inside the General Staff headquarters, where he had a secure multichannel communications system in his private office.

"Stay close," he whispered to Captain Ivan Castillo, the commander of his personal escort.

In the anteroom of Noriega's second-floor office, the group encountered Major Moises Giroldi Vega, one of Noriega's most stalwart officers, a young professional soldier who had led the troops that had smashed the ill-fated and tragicomic May 1988 coup attempt. Giroldi was clearly shocked by their sudden arrival. Noriega had personally promoted Giroldi from captain to major and assigned him to command the PDF Security Force Company, a sinecure that carried with it the assurance of generous gratuities from grateful members of the business community who owed their prosperity to Noriega. Now, it appeared, Major Giroldi was turning on the very source of all his good fortune. But Giroldi did not seem completely committed, otherwise he simply would have shot Noriega and ended the dangerous confusion. Certainly, had Noriega been in Giroldi's position, he would not have hesitated to explain circumstances that were blatant.

Giroldi raised his weapon, then lowered it and gestured toward the windows above the courtyard. *"General mio,"* he began respectfully, "for the good of the nation, the corps of company-grade and field-grade officers has decided . . ." He was stammering like the Urraca captain in the courtyard. ". . . All senior officers with more than twenty-five years service shall be retired, honorably retired . . ."

"You, Major," Noriega said, jabbing his finger at Giroldi's chest, "are fucking crazy."

Noriega turned to Castillo. "Shoot out the windows. Sound the alarm."

The bodyguards bundled Noriega into the office and fired their Uzis and pistols through the thermopane glass. But instead of rushing to their commander's aid, the soldiers below fired back, a volley of assault rifle rounds that pocked the walls and ceiling and ricocheted around the office, sending everyone scurrying for the anteroom again.

Noriega now understood that his fate depended on his ability to cajole and dominate Major Giroldi and his small group of plotters, to stall for time long enough to muster support from loyal units. If he did not succeed, he was a dead man.


General Maxwell R. Thurman, USA, was beginning his second full day as Commander in Chief (CINC), United States Southern Command, when Major Giroldi's coup attempt took place. Thurman's direct superior, General Colin Powell, had also been sworn in on October 1, 1989. This fluke of timing, as much as any other circumstance, influenced the course of events over the coming hours, days, and weeks. In Army parlance, Generals Powell and Thurman were expected to act decisively when they had not yet been fully "read-in" on the problems of Noriega's Panama.

Thurman had been handpicked for Southcom by Defense Secretary Dick Cheney (himself a relative newcomer to the Bush administration). Cheney wanted a CINC who could be relied upon to act with prudence when required and with disciplined audacity should direct military intervention be required. Max Thurman had the personal attributes and the experience to command either course of action. At fifty-eight, he had been about to retire when he was named to replace General Frederick Woerner as CINC in Panama. A tall, somewhat scholarly looking southerner, Thurman, like most of his staff, was a product of the ROTC system rather than the cookie cutter of West Point. His degree from North Carolina State was in chemical engineering, an exacting and precise discipline that epitomized his approach to duty during his thirty-seven-year Army career.

Max Thurman had never married. He was a devout Catholic with a nostalgia for the traditional Latin High Mass (one brother was a priest), who had served as an altar boy in decidedly Baptist High Point, North Carolina, which might have explained his adult aloofness. The only times he enjoyed away from duty were Sunday mass and vigorous contests on the tennis court. His career had included service in the Airborne Artillery—he had remained airborne qualified with over 200 jumps—Military Intelligence, and command of the Army's Training and Doctrine Command. Thurman had taught at West Point and led an artillery battalion during the Tet offensive in Vietnam. In the early 1980s, he had been deputy Chief of Staff of the Army, and often represented the Army at meetings of the Joint Chiefs of Staff (JCS). To many, Max Thurman was the ideal blend of combat leader, scholar and staff officer. To others, perhaps less well-motivated officers, Thurman was a relentless taskmaster. The men who served under him tended to either love Thurman or view him with fearful distaste. "Intense" was the most common epithet heard at the Officers' Club bar after Thurman took over on Quarry Heights.

By noon on Tuesday, October 3, 1989, General Max Thurman was in a state of controlled outrage. He had been briefed on Major Giroldi's planned coup just two days before. From the first briefing, Thurman had been skeptical. Giroldi was a member of Noriega's inner clique, a man who owed his entire career to Noriega. It was highly unlikely that this young major, who had led the force that had rescued Noriega in the previous coup attempt, would now turn on the leader of the PDF. Moreover, Thurman was deeply suspicious of the timing. Why plan a coup so early in the tenure of both Powell, the JCS chairman, and the new Southcom CINC? General Thurman, who had spent a year as a corps intelligence adviser in Vietnam during the endless and convoluted military coup and countercoup plotting of the immediate post-Diem years, had learned to look for the political motives behind seemingly straightforward military actions.

Giroldi had made contact with Southcom through his wife, who had friends among the American community. On the advice of the Southcom J-2 (intelligence officer), Brigadier General Mike Schneider, Thurman had agreed to send a CIA and a Military Intelligence officer from Southcom's J-2 shop to listen to Giroldi's proposal. What Thurman heard only deepened his suspicion that the planned coup was actually an elaborate trap meant to ensnare the new Southcom CINC and further discredit the United States in Latin America. Giroldi merely intended to "retire" Noriega, not to topple his corrupt and illegal regime and install the government of Guillermo Endara, which had been freely elected in May. Further, Giroldi requested direct American intervention in the coup—the blocking of access routes to the Comandancia that could be used by pro-Noriega reinforcements—intervention that was both blatant and nonthreatening to the PDF, including, of course, Noriega himself. Giroldi had rationalized this seemingly irrational request, stating he did not want to "taint" his coup with direct gringo support. The entire enterprise stank of deception.

General Max Thurman recognized that deception—often involving double- and even triple-dealing of Byzantine complexity—was Manuel Noriega's forte. Moreover, Noriega had a long record of manipulative intrigues in his relations with the United States. At various times over the previous twenty years, he had been an "asset" of U.S. Military Intelligence, the CIA, the Drug Enforcement Administration (DEA), and the National Security Council (NSC). Noriega had often successfully played one of these agencies against the other for personal gain and to insure his political survival. He might betray some minor drug trafficker to the DEA, then turn around and arrange a new partnership with a Colombian cocaine baron. Noriega had proved capable of simultaneously supporting the anti-Communist Nicaraguan Contras and serving as an anti-Contra intelligence link between the Nicaraguan Sandinistas and Fidel Castro. From the convoluted history of Manuel Noriega's dealings with the United States one undeniable fact emerged: *nothing* about Noriega was ever clear-cut or straight forward; there was always some hidden motive, some secret agenda.[4]

On Monday, when the originally planned coup date came and went with no action by Giroldi, Thurman was positive the Giroldi plot had actually been one of Noriega's famous double-cross deception operations. On the afternoon of Monday, October 2, Thurman had advised the Pentagon that the planned coup was a hoax.

Then the coup attempt was made on Tuesday morning. But Thurman's guidance from the JCS had been vague and slow in coming. It was not until mid-morning, when officers allied with Giroldi came to Fort Clayton and announced they wanted to negotiate turning Noriega over to Southcom, that Thurman received authorization to use American forces to block key reinforcement routes to the Comandancia. But this was as much a stalling tactic as it was decisive action. Southcom had not yet received any clear guidance on how to "process" Noriega, should the rebels actually deliver him to American control.

U.S. Marines eventually sealed off the Bridge of the Americas, which spanned the Pacific entrance to the Canal, thus blocking access to Panama City by the 6th and 7th PDF Mechanized Infantry companies—the "Macho de Monte"—the fiercest Noriega loyalists in the PDF. American soldiers from the 87th Infantry blocked the gates of Fort Amador, the joint

U.S.–PDF base on the green peninsula flanking the eastern approaches to the Canal near the bridge. Noriega's other loyal allies, the 5th "Cholo" Infantry Company inside Amador, chose not to challenge the Americans.

But those actions had only blocked two of the four major routes into Panama City and the Comandancia, where Noriega apparently had managed to gain control of the tense standoff between the coup plotters and the general's bodyguard. A little after 11:00 A.M., a civilian Panamanian Boeing 727 landed at the PDF's Tocumen Air Base, located on the same complex as Torrijos International Airport, eighteen miles east of the city. On board were the 7th Company of the Macho de Monte from Rio Hato, led by their commander, a tough Cuban-trained commando captain named Gonzalo Charlo Gonzales. There was no mistaking who they were: only the 6th and 7th companies wore black T-shirts and let their beards grow in a fierce tangle, a subtle tribute to their spiritual mentor, Che Guevara. They trotted off the plane and into waiting trucks, bearing a variety of AK assault rifles, machine guns, and grenade launchers.

Near the airport, they linked up with a mechanized column of Battalion 2000 from nearby Fort Cimarron, which had just swept across the unguarded choke point of the Pacora River Bridge. Within forty minutes of landing, the 7th Company trucks, trailed by the V-150 and V-300 armored personnel carriers of Battalion 2000, rumbled past the American Embassy on Avenida Balboa, en route to rescue Noriega at the Comandancia.

As the world watched through the live television eye of Cable News Network, the combined 7th Company force and the Battalion 2000 armor surrounded the Comandancia. The troops inside did not resist. Ten minutes after they had arrived in the narrow streets around the Comandancia, the Macho de Monte had disarmed the Doberman security troops and the hapless soldiers of the Urraca Company. Up on Quarry Heights, Southcom officers had no need for CNN. The south flanks of Ancon Hill dominated the Comandancia, only 500 meters below. Major Donald Jones led a small group from the

J-2 shop to the parking lot near the back gate, where they had an unobstructed view of the action below.[5]

"Goddamn it," Jones swore. "It's over. It's fucking well over." He knew this latest fiasco would be labeled yet another American "intelligence failure." When in doubt, dump on the Intel people.

He turned in disgust to trudge back through the midday heat to the Southcom Operations Building. One of his colleagues waved to him. "Hey, Don," the officer called. "Hang on. We can't be sure what the hell's going down."

"I can," Jones said. "It's clear as hell to me."

By two that afternoon, it was clear to the world as well. CNN's unblinking eye recorded the lines of Urraca troops and the once fierce Dobermans, their empty hands clasped atop their bare heads, being marched through the open gates of the Comandancia toward brutal interrogation and captivity. What the CNN camera could not record was the drama inside the General Staff headquarters.

Giroldi had never even managed to disarm Noriega's bodyguard squad, who had barricaded themselves inside the bullet-riddled inner office with their leader. There Noriega, cut off from his high-technology secure communications system, had used an open civilian line to alert political allies, who in turn had contacted Captain Charlo Gonzales at Rio Hato and the loyal elements of Battalion 2000 at Fort Cimarron. Now it was time to face down Giroldi and *his* bodyguard.

Flanked by two loyal soldiers holding their MP-5 submachine guns at high port, Noriega confronted the rebel group in the outer office. "A true commander of men," he shouted directly into Giroldi's face, "has balls, *cojones*." He sneered openly at the major's stricken expression. "If you have any balls," Noriega added, "you will shoot me now."

Giroldi watched the flat mestizo faces of Noriega's two bodyguards. "*General mio . . .*" he tried to reason.

But there was no longer time for reasonable discourse. The door of the outer office burst open and a loyal officer of Battalion 2000 rushed in, brandishing his assault rifle. In the ensuing confused scuffle, Noriega displayed the deceptive intrigue that was his hallmark. He convinced Giroldi that the major had been "misled" by sinister superior officers. When Giroldi wavered, Noriega urged him warmly to simply put down the gun and reenter the fold of honorable Panamanian officers.

Major Giroldi lowered his weapon. The loyal troops from the courtyard now filled the wide, echoing staircase and the outer office. Noriega pushed his way to one of Giroldi's subordinate officers, who had just been disarmed. Stating that he was "shit tired" of traitors, Manuel Noriega shot the rebel officer in the side of the head with the man's own pistol. Then he offered the gun to Giroldi, urging him to show his "honor" by killing himself. Major Giroldi wavered and was clubbed to the floor by troops from the 7th Compnay.[6]

The Macho de Monte swept Noriega into the headquarters courtyard, where loyal troops saluted him with volleys from their assault rifles, the only prolonged fire of the entire confrontation.

Late that night at Fort Cimarron, General Manuel Antonio Noriega took part in the final torture of Major Moises Giroldi Vega. By then, the major's naked, violated body was a swollen and shattered travesty of a human form. He had been tormented with electrodes, burnt, beaten, and raped. His interrogators had extracted all the useful information he possessed on his fellow conspirators. Yet Noriega reportedly insisted the torture continue. In recent months his appetite for sadism had grown baser and more persistent. And this diversion was much more satisfying than the sadistic "snuff" videos supplied Noriega by his diplomats in North America.[7]

But finally, the game was over. Noriega tested the loyalty of several officers by ordering them to join him in firing their pistols into Major Giroldi's body.

Over the next several days, while the firestorm of media and congressional criticism about the thwarted coup flared around the Bush White House, Secretary Cheney and General Powell's Pentagon, and above all, around U.S. Southcom and its new

CINC, General Maxwell Thurman kept his own counsel. Major Don Jones saw Thurman on several occasions early in the cool mornings, walking with a lone MP guard along the drive to the back gate of Quarry Heights. Ironically, the coup that Thurman had feared was a provocation Noriega had contrived to embarrass him had in fact been genuine, but had nevertheless humiliated Thurman more painfully than if it had actually been another of Noriega's elaborate intrigues.

The general would pause on the paved overlook and gaze down at the Comandancia. Often Noriega's distinctive blue Mercedes stood in its parking slot beneath the curved flanks of the General Staff headquarters. The bullet-pitted walls of the Comandancia had been patched within twenty-four hours of the attempted coup. And the squat fortress lying in the shadow of America's tropical Gibraltar was seemingly intact. But Major Jones could see in the expression of thoughtful contempt on Thurman's face that the final act in the dramatic conflict between the two generals had not yet been written.

Jones also realized that Thurman was far too professional to allow his obvious personal disgust for Noriega to color his judgment concerning the now apparently inevitable military conflict between America and Panama. Instead, Thurman fell back on his long experience in training and doctrine commands. No matter whether a force enjoyed success or suffered a reverse in an engagement, American military doctrine held, there were always "lessons learned," which could be applied to a future encounter. And now Max Thurman was studying those lessons. Jones's section in J-2 was working overtime, supplying the CINC with detailed background material on Noriega's strengths and weaknesses—personal, political, and military.

Jones found the CINC's exercise fascinating. There were probably few occasions in history when such absolute opposites had been pitted against each other in a political-military contest. Max Thurman was a devout Catholic whose Christian faith was rock solid; there were no cracks, no deviation from Church doctrine. He was personally abstemious, a one beer or one cocktail man at the occasional formal dinner or reception he had attended since arriving in Panama. He was rigorously self-disciplined, a man who routinely spent fourteen-hour workdays. In the current crisis, he demanded such an effort from his staff, yet he made allowances for men to spend some time with their families. Thurman could focus his energy and intelligence on the matter at hand. He made a point of telling his staff that Panama was only one country in Southcom's area of responsibility. They couldn't let Noriega make them lose sight of Nicaragua, El Salvador, and the war to interdict the flow of drugs from South America. That was typical of Thurman; he thought like a four-star general had to in order to do his job well.

As the J-2 staff added to the CINC's detailed portrait of Manuel Noriega, Thurman's distaste became more evident. Noriega was a pagan. Although he gave lip service to Roman Catholicism, Noriega was not only a devotee of Caribbean Santeria, an animist cult of African origin, he also employed at least three Brazilian sorceresses, whom he maintained in comfort in two "witch houses" at Fort Amador, hard by his Building 8 office and the granite tomb of General Omar Torrijos. Noriega was also a bisexual satyr. He often relieved the stress of his precarious grasp on power by partaking in orgies, replete with whores, cocaine, and free-flowing liquor. Agent reports indicated that Noriega sometimes enjoyed dressing in perfumed drag on these occasions and performing oral sex on his favorite young officers. Even more distasteful to Thurman was the evidence that Noriega had increasingly turned to torture and sadistic sexual abuse of prisoners for his gratification. And, of course, the mounting, irrefutable evidence that Noriega was deeply involved with the Colombian drug cartels, that he had formed a de facto alliance with them (as well as their Nicaraguan Sandinista and Cuban confederates) was a direct threat to Thurman's stated mission as Southcom CINC.

If Max Thurman were the Christian Knight on the white charger, one of Jones's colleagues commented, then the Big Central Casting in the sky couldn't have invented a more appropriate adversary for him than Manuel Noriega.

## *2110 Hours, 16 December 1989*

The lobby of the Caesar Park Marriott Hotel was a gaudy parody of a gringo sugarplum Christmas. A tree of snowy vinyl bows studded with blinking lights and ornaments the size of melons rose high in the atrium. Muzak carols echoed.

But the four young Marine officers skirting the edges of the Southcom curfew were not here to gawk at the decorations. They were drawn to the Mio Rincon Bar, where single rabiblanco girls could sometimes be found. The Marines just had time for one drink, maybe a quick meeting with the promise of a future date, and then they'd have to make tracks for Fort Clayton to meet the 2200 hours Personnel Movement Limitation, Level C ("PML Charlie") restrictions imposed after the October coup attempt. But this Saturday night the bar was half-deserted. Even the more liberated young Panamanian women would not risk harassment and perhaps unpleasant detention at the dozens of roadblocks that Noriega's Dignity Battalions had thrown up on the streets of the capital.

In the previous twenty-four hours Noriega had increased his antigringo rhetoric to alarming levels. His handpicked national assembly had rubber-stamped the order proclaiming him "Maximum Leader," a position of unlimited extraconstitutional power. And they had also endorsed a second proclamation that a state of war existed between Panama and the United States.[8] Noriega was trying to bypass his now-shaky power base in the PDF by appealing directly to the masses of urban poor and dispossessed campesinos. The ranks of the Dignity Battalions (Digbats) had been swollen with new recruits in recent weeks.

One of the Marines, Captain Dick Haddad, worked in General Schneider's J-2 Intel shop. Haddad had seen the reports that Noriega hoped to solidify the Cuban and Nicaraguan military support he was already receiving for the Digbats by provoking a clumsy and blatant Southcom military response to intensified harassment of American troops or civilians. Hence the PML Charlie and the steady exodus of dependent families and nonessential personnel. The Marines gulped their Coors and left in Haddad's rusty old Impala.

But they never made it to Fort Clayton.

Instead of battling the congested crosstown streets to the Gaitan Highway, Haddad chose to move with the fast traffic along Avenida Balboa, then cut through the warren of narrow lanes feeding into the Avenida Central shopping area at the eastern base of Quarry Heights. As so often happened, the young Americans became confused in the skein of one-way, dim, cobblestone streets thronged with local barrio people escaping the heat of their tenements. The Americans found their car jammed into a line of vehicles on Avenida A, stalled by a Digbat roadblock ahead. To their chagrin, they realized they were only a hundred meters from the Comandancia.

They agreed that First Lieutenant Bob Paz, a Marine of Colombian descent who spoke native Spanish, would do the talking when they were confronted by the Digbats. As the line of cars ground slowly ahead, however, they saw bearded PDF soldiers in black T-shirts, brandishing AK-47 assault rifles with folding stocks and long banana-shaped magazines.

"Shit," one of the Marines said, "it's the fucking Machos."

There was no way to avoid the roadblock. When the PDF soldiers spotted the Impala, they ostentatiously snapped back the cocking levers of their AK-47s and leveled the weapons at the car.

"They just locked and loaded," Haddad shouted. "Let's get the hell out of here!" He hit the gas and sped past the startled PDF soldiers.

But the Americans could not escape the volley of 7.62 mm assault rifle rounds that snapped and ricocheted after them. The car was struck by at least six bullets. One entered the trunk, struck a steel molding and was deflected up to pierce the back seat and slash into Lt. Bob Paz's lower back. His left renal artery was severed. Haddad was hit in the right shin, but managed to keep control as the hulking old Chevrolet careened down the lanes of El Chorrillo. Paz was slumped over, moaning softly. They had to get him to Gorgas Army Hospital, halfway up Heights Drive on the hill. But again, Haddad lost his way in the web of narrow slum lanes.

When they finally reached the steep ramp of the hospital's

emergency entrance, Lt. Bob Paz was no longer moaning. The internal hemorrhage had killed the young officer.

Back at the roadblock on Avenida A, the PDF's 7th Company troops seized an American Navy lieutenant and his attractive young wife, who had also stopped at the roadblock and had seen the unprovoked shooting. They were manhandled into an unmarked van, handcuffed, blindfolded with duct tape, and driven to a nearby station of the National Department of Investigation (DENI), a formerly civilian police agency that had been completely taken over by Noriega's PDF loyalists.

In a stuffy, windowless interrogation room, the Navy couple, still blindfolded, were jammed face to the wall, while an unseen PDF officer speaking excellent colloquial English examined the Navy officer's ID card and his wife's passport. She had arrived in Panama only that day on a brief Christmas visit. What the PDF did not know was that her husband was a member of the elite Navy SEALs (special operations forces named for their Sea-Air-Land fighting skills). He was not in Panama as a tourist; his unit had deployed as the advance party of a SEAL Special Warfare group preparing the way for an American invasion, should that eventually prove necessary.

The SEAL lieutenant refused to answer the Panamanian's questions. "Please call the Duty Officer at Quarry Heights," he said, trying to keep his voice calm. "You have no right to hold us."

The guards spun the lieutenant around and kicked him savagely in the groin, three times. Then they cuffed his head and punched him in the stomach. He had been through much worse in the SEALs' thorough Survival, Evasion, Rescue, and Escape (SERE) training. He refused to answer the questions.

But his wife had never been prepared for this type of treatment. The PDF interrogator pulled up her knit cotton jumper and thrust his hand inside. "Nice tits," he said. The young woman shuddered and tried to pull away.

"I'll fuck her tonight," he added. "You won't have a chance to do that for a while."

The PDF soldiers proceeded to knee and karate kick the American officer in the groin until he passed out on the floor.

But they did not follow through on their threat to rape his wife.

By midnight, the couple had been released to American MPs from Fort Clayton.


The next afternoon, General Maxwell Thurman was in his office in the Quarry Heights headquarters building (having flown back from Washington in the middle of the night), reviewing a thick loose-leaf binder with a scarlet Top Secret cover, emblazoned OPERATION BLUE SPOON. This was the ambitious contingency operations plan that he had been refining for the previous nine weeks. That morning he had telephoned JCS Chairman General Colin Powell with the recommendation that the Blue Spoon OPLAN be executed.

The rust-orange NRC-13 secure satellite phone buzzed twice.

"Max," Colin Powell said slowly, "I've just come from the president's office."

"Yes, sir," Thurman replied. He hoped that the operation had been approved.

"The president said I should be sure to tell you that enough is enough," General Powell said. "Execute Blue Spoon."

"Roger, sir."

"D-day," Powell continued, reading from notes, "twenty December. H-hour, oh-one-hundred."

"Yes, sir," Max Thurman said. "I understand my orders."

The United States of America was about to invade Panama to crush Manuel Noriega and his army.

# I

# The First Night

# 1

# 19–20 December 1989

—

# Don't Forget Nothing

*2215 Hours, 19 December*

On the single most important night of his life, General Manuel Antonio Noriega, newly proclaimed Maximum Leader of the Republic of Panama, Commanding Officer of the Panama Defense Forces, world-class master of espionage and deception, indicted drug trafficker and bisexual satyr with an affinity for sadomasochism, was drunk. Noriega slouched in the soft, wide-winged CEO's chair at the head of his polished mahogany conference table. All the chairs in the conference room were upholstered with smooth camouflage polyester, and there was a collection of rare small arms mounted on the silk brocade wall behind him, which clashed with the Louis Quatorze chandelier above the table, typical of the many ironic dichotomies about the room. As always, his private office suite in Building 8 at Fort Amador was air conditioned to a chill seventeen degrees Celsius (63°F). Noriega adored starched, tightly tailored uniforms. Sweat ruined starched creases. It was hard not to sweat in Panama, unless you had access to an unusually powerful air-conditioning system. General Manuel Antonio Noriega had access to virtually anything he wanted. On his own turf, Noriega did not sweat.

But he did drink. Captain Ivan Castillo, the general's chief bodyguard, responded instantly to Noriega's indignantly cocked eyebrow. The captain refilled the crystal tumbler at

Noriega's elbow with Old Parr Scotch whiskey and added three ice cubes with a silver tongs. Noriega's momentary irritation seemed to have passed. He thanked Castillo with ponderous courtesy, a sure sign that the *Jefe* was very drunk.

Castillo tried to judge the extent and quality of his superior's intoxication in order to better predict the course of the evening. They had been on the road all day, attending mass political rallies meant to bolster the morale of the Dignity Battalions. For the past twelve hours they had traveled by helicopter and limousine around the city, by Learjet to Colon on the Atlantic coast, and finally back to this office in a small convoy of vehicles, which included a closed white van for Noriega, followed by a maroon Mercedes decoy car and a Toyota Land Cruiser jammed with bodyguards. Noriega had sat in the back seat of the white van, his hat off and uniform hidden by a cheap windbreaker, when the vehicle had swept past the joint U.S.–PDF guard post at Amador's front gate. The decoy vehicles had gone to ground elsewhere in the city, hopefully taking the U.S. Delta Force with them.

During the long day of emotional speeches—punctuated with wild flourishes of the gold-plated campesino's machete that had become the symbol of his *Torrijista* legitimacy since the October treachery—Noriega had changed uniforms six times, and had consumed the best part of two bottles of Old Parr.

Now he seemed bored, vaguely irritated, which could be the precursor to either yet another tirade against the gringos and their traitorous rabiblanco allies, or just a sign that the general was struggling to stay awake and would soon pass out. But the irritation could also be a deception, masking his true intentions. Since the events of October, Castillo found it increasingly difficult to judge Noriega's moods.

The telephone console chirped and Noriega punched the speaker button. It was Major Gonzalo Charlo Gonzales who commanded the task group of the 7th Company that had guarded the Comandancia since October.

"General," Charlo Gonzales said in his habitual grave manner, "all the indictions I'm receiving point to a major military action by the gringos sometime tonight."

Noriega listened, his head reclined in the shadows of the

enveloping chair. He was stroking one of his office mascots, a fuzzy teddy bear decked out like a paratrooper, replete with miniature jump boots and a red beret.[1] In a handsome antique China cabinet near him resided his collection of porcelain and ceramic *sopas*, toads. There were some who said the General loved toads because of their squat appearance and warty hides, which reflected his physique and acne-pocked complexion. But those who knew him well understood the true significance of the toads; in Spanish the word *sopa* was slang for informant. Manuel Noriega had climbed to power on the backs of informants and a small army of these toads helped him maintain his control of the country.

"Source?" Noriega asked. His voice was no longer slurred. He had instantly reverted to the professional military intelligence officer.

Major Gonzales paused to rustle some notes. "Our observers at Albrook, Fort Clayton, and Howard Air Force Base all report increased vehicle traffic." They heard Gonzales flip back a page of computer paper. "Flights are landing at Howard every five minutes. A convoy of armored personnel carriers, trucks and Humvees departed Clayton front gate at 2130 and traveled to a holding point across the Miraflores swing bridge. There are other convoys assembling at the Curundu Elementary School, and they've doubled the guard at Clayton back gate."

"What is the unit of the armored tracks?" Now the general seemed disinterested, bored once again.

"Fourth Battalion, Sixth Infantry of the 5th Mechanized Division," Gonzales recited, the consummate professional.

"The *entire* battalion, Major?" Noriega yawned. His eyes slid shut.

"No, General, but several companies."

Noriega drained his glass and rattled the ice cubes. "It's just another of their damned provocation exercises, Charlo."

"General," Major Gonzales protested, "this is . . ."

"We'll look into the matter, Charlo," Noriega said, "of that you have my word."

He clicked off the speaker phone and extended his arm for Castillo to refill the whiskey tumbler.

"Marcelita," Noriega called, summoning his personal secretary, Marcela Tason, from the outer office. "Make some phone calls, find out what's happening tonight."

Through family connections, Marcela had excellent and discrete contacts in the influential rabiblancos circles. If this was invasion night, someone among the country's business leaders was certain to know it.

Noriega rose and paced the thick carpet before his huge 1-to-25,000 scale tactical map of Panama, which, ironically, had been a gift of a long-departed U.S. Southcom general during the halcyon years when Colonel Manuel Noriega had been viewed as a pillar of anticommunist resolve in the Red morass of Latin America. Then he turned decisively to Ivan Castillo.

"Call my driver."

Sergeant First Class Carlos Cortillo trotted in and saluted smartly.

Noriega grinned. "Go pick up Gloria. I'll meet her at the Ceremi guest house."

Captain Castillo was not happy with this unexpected turn of events, which meant another trip on the dangerous roads of the city. Gloria was one of Noriega's regular girlfriends, a buxom woman in her thirties, estranged from her husband. Noriega had bragged of her penchant for unusual sex. He often entertained her in his suite at the Ceremi senior officers' guest house, located near Tocumen Air Base, thirty kilometers east of the city. The general rose unsteadily from his splendid chair. He obviously did not intend to wait for Marcela to complete her phone calls.

Captain Castillo grabbed his FM radio to call ahead to the bodyguard detail to prepare the small convoy. As he lowered the radio set, he saw Noriega actually pouring another drink by himself. It was, Castillo knew, going to be a long night.

## 2340 Hours

Lieutenant Colonel Jerry Murguia had been in Southcom's provisional Operations Center for only five hours, but already the unfolding campaign had acquired a grinding sense of timelessness, as if he'd always been in the cramped, brightly lit, and decidedly stuffy room, jostled by departing and arriving officers, surrounded by ringing telephones and softly purring computer printers. The site General Max Thurman had chosen to oversee Operation Blue Spoon was not the regular Southcom Current Operations room in the Quarry Heights headquarters building. Instead, Thurman picked the briefing room, located at the far end of the tunnel and guarded by MPs, a secure "exclusion area" that had been hewn from the solid granite of Ancon Hill in the later 1940s and converted into a modern hardened command facility thirty years later.

As with all his decisions, Thurman had carefully considered his options. Above all, he wanted to be assured of direct, unbroken communications both upward to General Colin Powell in the Pentagon's National Command Center, and downward to Joint Task Force South commander, Lieutenant General Carl Stiner, whose headquarters were in Building 95 at Fort Clayton. To guarantee the integrity of this vital command chain and to be certain that potential civilian "field marshals" in the Defense Department or the National Security Council did not succeed in micromanaging the operation, Thurman had to place himself and his Southcom crisis staff as a buffer between Stiner, his field commander, and Chairman Powell and Defense Secretary Dick Cheney.

The briefing room and its adjacent communications center offered exactly the facilities he needed; Thurman made sure it was the sole nexus of the secure voice and data network connecting the American military in Panama and the national command authority in the United States. Thurman had an alternate command post across the Canal at Howard Air Force base, to be activated should Quarry Heights become untenable. But this tunnel had been built to ride out a nuclear attack, so the PDF probably wouldn't succeed in driving Max Thurman from it. And the tunnel was also "tempest hardened," absolutely electronically secure; no matter how hard Noriega's G-2 electronic intelligence people tried, they would never penetrate the room's security.

He had told General Powell and the Secretary that he did not want Carl Stiner or his staff unnecessarily disturbed during the first critical twenty-four hours of the operation. The chairman and the secretary were in full concurrence. The plan was sound, they'd said, let the professionals get on with it. President George Bush also fully concurred. Unlike Lyndon Johnson and Jimmy Carter, he felt no compulsion to prove himself as a combat leader.

Unfortunately, this small room, the size of a Holiday Inn family suite, was hardly adequate for the assembled staff of twenty officers from the four services and their supporting communications technicians. The briefing room also had notoriously bad ventilation, being located near the air-conditioner exhausts of a computerized cryptographic operations vault and the communications center. Some officers among the "tunnel rats" had taken to calling the room the "gas chamber," when it was used for post-lunch briefings. Jerry Murguia anticipated that conditions would only get worse during the course of the operation.

But he certainly had not anticipated the actual execution of this operation when he'd been called to the tunnel just after dark that evening. Murguia had been up to his neck helping his family unpack in their new quarters at Fort Amador. Despite the tensions of the previous three days, Jerry Murguia, the chief of Southcom's Current Operations A-Team, had no idea what was about to take place. He had entered the Op Room and found General Thurman, dressed in freshly pressed, camouflaged battle dress uniform (BDU), seated calmly at a long T-shaped folding table next to Brigadier General Bill Hartzog, Southcom's Operations Officer. Brigadier General Mike Schneider, Southcom's intelligence officer (J-2), sat to Hartzog's right talking on the orange scrambler phone with soft-spoken intensity.

"Hi, Jerry," General Thurman had called casually, "how's your tennis game?" Max Thurman managed to keep fit playing tennis with wiry younger officers like Jerry. But neither officer had managed much time on the courts in recent weeks.

Jerry Murguia took his place at the Ops crisis management table, near the unused slide screen facing the command table. Thurman's chief of staff, Rear Admiral David Chandler, was the senior man on this side of the room. As far as Murguia knew, this was just another surprise command post exercise, designed to shake up the PDF and keep them guessing about American intentions following the shooting of Lieutenant Paz.

"What's up?" Jerry Murguia asked his J-2 colleague, Colonel Bill Bratten.

Bratten glanced at Jerry over his reading glasses and paused. "Full Blue Spoon."

Murguia felt an electric pulse of adrenaline. The United States was about to invade Panama in the biggest military operation since the Vietnam War. He swallowed hard, opened the ring-binder marked with a scarlet Top Secret cover and set about reviewing the long execution checklist.

Jerry Murguia was a methodical Field Artillery officer who had a habit of carefully studying data before he took action. As he slowly reviewed the meticulously structured Blue Spoon operations plan (OPLAN) and its execution checklist—which contained such minute details as the distance from an intersection the lead driver of a convoy was to extinguish his headlights—he was carried back over the past months of exhausting preparation and through the complex evolution of the plan.

In February 1988, a federal grand jury had indicted Manuel Noriega for drug trafficking, following testimony by former key PDF associates of his. The already tense relations between Panama and the United States suddenly soured badly. For the first time, the Pentagon had to consider the Panama Defense Forces, not just Noriega and his cronies, a potential military foe. On February 22, 1988, the Joint Chiefs of Staff issued a planning order for Southcom to write an operational contingency plan for the defense of the Panama Canal and American lives and property in Panama, taking into consideration a hostile PDF.

In less than a month, General Frederick Woerner, the Southcom commander, signed the original draft of Operation Blue Spoon and submitted it for review by the JCS. The Command received JCS approval that July, and Blue Spoon was entered into a family of contingency plans known generically as PRAYER BOOK. They included plans covering everything from the mass evacuation of American civilians and military dependents in the event of local terrorism, to the forcible recapture of Canal assets from a PDF backed up by Cuban "advisers," to the active defense of American military bases in Panama, under the terms of the 1977 Panama Canal Treaties.[2]

Later that month U.S. Forces Command at Fort McPherson, Georgia designated the XVIII Airborne Corps as the "war-fighting" organization to execute Blue Spoon, when and if the president so ordered.

As it evolved, Blue Spoon became an altogether different type of OPLAN. It was an invasion of a sovereign nation designed to cripple that country's military in a single thrust of overpowering offensive force, to decapitate its leadership, and in so doing restore a semblance of democratic rule to Panama, an objective that presupposed that the new democratic government would be pro-American. In the twenty years since Noriega's mentor, General Omar Torrijos, had overthrown the last democratic government, the PDF had grown from a small national guard into a substantial military force, with over 15,000 total uniformed members and an effective combat strength of about 6,000. And, in the eighteen months since Noriega's drug indictment—which had seen two failed military coup attempts against him—the PDF had increasingly become Noriega's personal instrument of repressive power.

In June 1989, when it became obvious that Noriega had no intention of accepting a political compromise by which he would abdicate and seek asylum in a third country, Blue Spoon was amended to include his capture and transfer to federal Drug Enforcement Administration officers for arrest. In effect, the Defense Department was planning the assembly of the largest posse in history.

The tragic fiasco of the failed October 3 coup attempt and America's bungled response to it had only stiffened the resolve of General Max Thurman, the new Southcom commander, to cross all the *t*'s and dot every last damned *i* of the Blue Spoon OPLAN. And Jerry Murguia could state from personal experience that Thurman had made it abundantly clear to his staff that Manuel Noriega would not embarrass the United States of America again when Blue Spoon was executed.

To make sure of this, Thurman lobbied to have Lieutenant General Carl Stiner, commander of the XVIII Airborne Corps, named commander of Joint Task Force South, the force that would execute the OPLAN. Stiner was a tough para-troop commander with extensive Special Operations experi-ence. Thurman had full confidence in Carl Stiner's ability to execute the plan with the minimum level of violence necessary to topple the PDF without inflicting massive enemy military casualties or unacceptable "collateral damage" on the civilian population. Panama would need some type of military after Noriega was gone, and the current PDF was the logical place from which to recruit this new force. But crushing Noriega with excessive use of firepower would only alienate a current enemy who had the potential of being tomorrow's ally.

During several visits to Panama, Stiner conferred with Thur-man and his staff and Major General Marc Cisneros, the com-mander of U.S. Army forces in Panama, to "tweak" the operations plan. The objective of overpowering the PDF with-out massive casualties necessitated some of the most de-manding tactics and strictest rules of engagement (ROE) that Murguia and his colleagues had ever seen. Instead of the stan-dard battlefield preparation involving airstrikes and artillery barrages, the OPLAN called for using ultrahigh-technology weapons systems, including the Stealth fighter-bomber, Apache attack helicopters, and AC-130 gunships, to selectively prepare the ground for simultaneous assaults on twenty-seven separate PDF objectives across central Panama at H-hour. Thurman and his staff believed that such an audacious, simul-taneous assault would so stun and demoralize the PDF that resistance would be brief and sporadic. The general stressed the need to employ "violent and overwhelming combat power . . . primarily at night" in order to exploit America's long suit in high-technology weapons and night-vision systems, while forcing the PDF to fight on American terms.

The success of these widespread assaults depended on many unpredictable factors, the most important being tactical sur-prise. But, if the best PDF units received advance warning of the planned American invasion, there could be terrible conse-quences. One worst-case war-game scenario run on Southcom's computers in November forecast the PDF marshaling thou-sands of Dignity Battalion volunteers to conduct sabotage against the Canal and take American civilians hostage. Another such scenario projected the neutralization of America's superiority in helicopters and fixed-wing "slow movers" through the widespread use of Cuban-provided SAM-7 or SAM-14 shoulder-fired antiaircraft missiles.

That same month, yet another dangerous prospect emerged as American economic sanctions and diplomatic pressure forced Noriega into a tighter corner. Southcom J-2 received hard intelligence reports that Noriega had entered into a bizarre partnership with the Colombian drug cartels, an actual military alliance to supplement his long-standing illegal business relationship. The object of this alliance was a terror campaign against Americans in Panama, particularly the military. The J-2 briefed the staff that Colombia cartel saboteurs had constructed several car bombs using Soviet-made Lada station wagons, a cheap vehicle popular with small farmers in both countries. The cars were reportedly loaded with at least 200 kilograms of high explosive, similar to car bombs that had devastated government ministries, courthouses, and police stations in Bogota, Medellin, and Cali. For two weeks in November, normal business at American military bases in Panama was almost shut down. Every vehicle entering every base and housing area had to be stopped and searched; the lines of vehicles—themselves a prime target for a drive-by terrorist attack—sometimes stretched for over a mile. Once more, the United States was subjected to scorn as a fearful, musclebound giant.[3]

But the "mad bomber" campaign had merely inconvenienced Southcom, not rendered it helpless. During the height of the bomb scare, Thurman stepped up the most effective and devious of the Blue Spoon preparation operations. These were the Sand Flea and Purple Storm exercises, during which American military units, in most cases the same ones that would execute the OPLAN, actually rehearsed their portion of the operation in PDF territory, right under the noses of the PDF. Ostensibly, the exercises—Sand Fleas were small units, Purple Storms battalion-size—were the straightforward exertion of America's right to military movement in the old Canal Zone. In reality, the Sand Fleas and Purple Storms, which had begun slowly in August, were detailed walk-throughs that involved the men and machines so meticulously "tasked" in the OPLAN. In this already tense atmosphere, there were many dangerous episodes, when, for example, a company from the 508 Parachute Infantry Regiment, in full combat regalia and with loaded weapons, confronted the 5th PDF Rifle Company in disputed neutral territory at Fort Amador, a joint U.S.–PDF facility under the terms of the Canal treaties. Usually the PDF disputed the Americans' right to enter a PDF-controlled area. Often the two units would face each other in long standoffs, until inevitably the PDF backed down and permitted passage of the American unit.

Major General Marc Cisneros, a Texan Chicano, understood the cultural dynamics at play in these encounters. From the machismo perspective of the Panamanians, the gringos were merely playing the bully, and in so doing further sullying their already bad image among the people. But the PDF never grasped that the Sand Fleas and Purple Storms were carefully controlled rehearsals for an actual combat operation, not merely spontaneous and illogical outbursts of aggression.

Max Thurman, Jerry Murguia knew, rarely exercised his forces in an illogical manner.

Lieutenant Colonel Murguia finished reviewing the Blue Spoon execution checklist. It was after midnight. In less than one hour, 24,000 American soldiers, airmen, sailors and marines, organized into nine major task forces and dozens of smaller teams, would begin the operation. There were over one hundred major items on Murguia's execution checklist, and that just covered the first night, from H-hour at 0100 on 20 December until 0900. Murguia knew from experience those eight hours left ample time for either brilliant success or utter disaster.

## 0026 Hours, 20 December

The lead element of Task Force Bayonet, a contingent of "Humvees" and deuce-and-a-half trucks from the Alpha Company, 5th Battalion, 87th Infantry of the 193d Infantry Brigade, one of Southcom's organic units, had pulled out of Fort

Clayton five minutes earlier and had only traveled a mile down the Gaitan Highway toward Panama City. As the last Alpha Company Humvee passed the sandbagged American guard post at Albrook Field, the MPs spotted a white PDF school bus speeding north from Balboa. After roaring past the first American convoy, the bus slowed when the driver spotted the second truck convoy, carrying the 5th Battalion's Bravo Company, which was just nearing the guard post. The Panamanian soldiers inside the bus thrust their AK-47 and P-65 assault rifles out the open windows at menacing angles. Both sides opened fire simultaneously. The PDF bus took several M-60 machine-gun rounds, but continued wildly down the highway.

There were still over thirty minutes to H-hour, but the precious element of surprise had just been lost.

In the lead convoy's third truck, First Lieutenant Paul Freudenburgh saw the green AK tracers and the red tracer rounds from the MPs' M-60s slash and career in the darkness. One of his soldiers dove for cover under the truckbed and accidentally jammed his M-16 rifle into another man's shin.

"Down!" someone shouted. "Get down. They're shooting at us."

The lunge for cover was like the Keystone Kops circus routine where nine clowns try to crowd into a toy car.

"Keep your positions," Freudenburgh yelled. "Keep those damn weapons pointed out."

Then two of his fire team leaders tried to rally their men. But it took a while for them to free the rifles and squad automatic weapons (SAW) barrels tangled in web equipment, spare bandoliers of M-16 magazines and belts of machine-gun ammunition. If another PDF vehicle appeared now, or worse, if there were ambushes waiting in the tall kuna grass near the Albrook hangars, his men would not be able to return fire. Freudenburgh swore loudly, something he rarely did. They weren't even in real combat yet and already things were fucked up.

He craned his neck to look ahead down the long flat roadway. He could just see their objective, the DNTT Transportation Police headquarters, a sprawling complex of three concrete buildings near the railway warehouses just beneath the hulking dark mound of Ancon Hill. Since the October coup attempt, this complex had become a major PDF staging post, a well-armed strong point where the PDF trained and equipped some of the better Digbat units. The firing back there along the highway would surely have alerted the PDF ahead that the gringos were coming.

"Shit," Freudenburgh swore bitterly. It just wasn't supposed to be like this.

## 0027 Hours, 20 December

Gander One and Two came off the tanker, banked left and flew in loose trail formation toward their holding orbit, sixty miles from the south coast of Panama.[4] This was the fourth midair refueling of the long night for the two F-117A Stealth fighter-bomber pilots of the 37th Tactical Fighter Wing. But it would not be the last. They had been in the air for over six hours since departing their secret desert base at the Tonopah Test Range in Nevada at dusk. Four other F-117s were in an element reserve orbit to the southeast. They were not tasked for the primary mission, but could take over for Gander One and Two should the two lead Stealths have mechanical problems, or in the unlikely event they were shot down.

To the fuel boom operator lying reclined in his comfortable bubble in the tail of the Air Force KC-10, the two departing aircraft appeared bizarre. Framed against the moonlit cloudscape of the tropical Pacific, the Stealths were jumbled wedges of dull black facets utterly devoid of traditional aerodynamic grace. From this perspective, they looked more like the obsidian lance blades you saw in museums than twentieth-century flying machines. He knew that the only thing that wasn't "stealthy" about them was the long GBU-10 laser-guided 2,000-pound bomb each carried hidden within the bomb bay beneath its centerline belly. But even the bombs were smoothly tapered cylinders sporting guidance winglets and polished optical acquisition probes on their snouts. Dropped from above 5,000 feet, the bombs could strike a target the size of a telephone booth.

As the Stealths cleared the tanker's three-mile safety radius, the boom operator saw their strobes and navigation lights wink out. The two aircraft, he knew, were still squawking a secure Identity Friend or Foe (IFF) link, visible on the radar screens of an E-3 Sentry Airborne Warning and Control System (AWACS) aircraft down the coast. But soon they would sever even that link and become completely invisible to human senses, be they natural or enhanced by electronic artifice—including the "God's eye" perspective enjoyed by the AWACS. This was a combat operation, not just another rigorous training exercise.

In less than one hour, the war was about to begin.

"Dogpatch, Gander One," the lead Stealth pilot called, switching from the tanker's radio frequency and back to that of the AWACS orbiting higher and further out to sea. "Topped up and inbound to India Papa."

"Gander, Dogpatch, copy." The voice of the woman controller in the AWACS sounded soft and comfortably feminine. But even on this secure Tactical Satellite UHF channel, she kept the communication to a terse minimum.[5] The exchange was being monitored by an Airborne Command, Control, and Communications (ABCCC) post flying at medium altitude below the radar horizon south of Panama City.

This was the last scheduled radio contact for the two Stealths. From now on, they would be "freebies," unfettered by aircraft traffic control. Their extremely accurate internal navigation equipment, controlled by redundant ring-laser gyroscopes with constant updates from the Global Positioning System Milstar satellite, guided them unerringly to their object: the PDF's Rio Hato military reservation, home of the 6th and 7th Infantry companies. Only if the Stealths strayed out of their preprogrammed route and the flight leader requested assistance, or if their targeting requirements changed, would the ABCCC reassert control. And unless they squawked secure IFF information again, the Stealths would remain invisible to the AWACS; American radar was no more proficient than that of any other nation in detecting the strange airplanes.

The airborne command post—a converted model of the venerable Lockheed C-130D—was jammed with officers in gray flight suits, hunched over radio consoles. Their job was "deconflicting" the movements of 144 American C-141s and C-130s carrying Rangers, heavy weapons and equipment for airdrops, and armed vehicles for air assault landing, which were converging in long streams and small clots of radar data blocks on the Republic of Panama.

This aerial task force was just the small lead element of the largest airborne operation since World War II. The transports were escorted by fighters, which in turn required dozens of KC-135 and KC-10 aerial tankers and Search and Rescue aircraft, strung out for 2,000 miles between the southeast coast of the United States and Panama.

The Blue Spoon operations plan being executed called for over a hundred more heavy transports, carrying a full brigade of the 82d Airborne Division, to reach Panama forty-five minutes behind these lead columns. During that time, the lower airspace over central Panama would become saturated with more than one hundred additional blacked-out American military aircraft: UH-60 Black Hawk, UH-1E Huey, and CH-47 Chinook troop-carrier helicopters, a variety of helicopter gunships, including the new ultrahigh-technology AH-64 Apache gunship, Special Operations AH-6 "Little Birds," and a dozen powerful AC-130 gunships, each mounting the firepower equivalent of an infantry battalion. Air National Guard A-7 Corsairs from units in Ohio and South Dakota and A-37 Dragonflies stationed at Howard Air Force Base in Panama would also soon be airborne to provide additional fixed-wing fire support, should it be needed. And over both the Caribbean and the Pacific, beyond any possible Panamanian radar surveillance, multiple four-plane Combat Air Patrol flights of F-15s loitered near the orbiting tracks of KC-135 tankers. No one expected the Panamanian Air Force to oppose the coming attack, but the men who had planned Blue Spoon had left absolutely nothing to chance.

Should Noriega manage to escape by aircraft, either fixed wing or helicopter, these F-15s would intercept him. His three most probable escape routes were to Cuba, Nicaragua, and Colombia. The air corridors to these three destinations were the primary focus of the Combat Air Patrols.

## 0032 Hours, 20 December

Colonel William "Buck" Kernan, commander of the 75th Ranger Regiment, swung gingerly down the narrow steps from the flight deck of the C-130 and squeezed into the sling seat on the forward bulkhead. Like the other sixty-three Rangers in the dim, gaping cargo compartment of the aircraft, Kernan wore full combat web gear and a T-10 main parachute. But he had not yet clipped on his reserve parachute to the main harness or put on his Kevlar helmet. Instead he grabbed a radio headset and punched up four digits on the secure Satcom keypad. Kernan's C-130 was the third "chalk" (troopcarrier aircraft) in a long air column streaming south toward the Pacific across the lightly populated jungle spine of Panama, fifty miles west of the objective of Task Force Black: Rio Hato.

There were twenty C-130s in Task Force Black. Thirteen carried 837 Rangers for the airdrop, and the rest were assigned to heavy-equipment drops or the eventual airlanding of the Rangers' "armor"—gun jeeps mounting M-60 machine guns and 90 mm recoilless rifles, supported by outriders on stripped down, souped-up 300 cc black Yamaha motocross bikes.

"Gold One, Black One," Buck Kernan called, addressing Lieutenant Colonel Tony Koren, who led Task Force Gold. Colonel Koren's task force was ninety miles east. Aboard that air column were 731 Rangers, commanded by Lieutenant Colonel Robert Wagner of the 1st Battalion, scheduled for airdrop from C-141 Starlifter jet transports, also supported by heavy-drop C-141s and C-130s. The objective of Task Force Gold was another airport, the sprawling Torrijos International Airport–Tocumen Air Base complex, eighteen miles east of Panama City.

"Gold, you just copy JTF South?" Kernan asked Tony Koren.

"Roger that, sir." Unlike other branches of the Army, the Rangers did not indulge themselves in elaborate radio protocol, replete with "say agains," "overs," and "understands." The conditions under which the Rangers normally practiced their profession—the "forced or covert entry of enemy territory"—did not encourage loquacious radio chatter. With secure Satcom UHF, this should not have been a concern, but Kernan and his officers ran the regiment by the strict standards of Ranger discipline. Every man, from rifleman privates on fire teams, to junior NCOs, on up the chain of command to field-grade officers, was expected to understand tactical messages the first time around. The Rangers Kernan was leading into combat had been trained to be as tough mentally as they were physically.

Kernan clicked his Transmit button twice and hung up the headset. The dull orange glow of the bulkhead lamp cast enough light for him to study his objective map, sealed within a clear plastic shield on his knee board. He was not pleased with the message he had just received on the flight deck's secure computer terminal from Joint Task Force South, the war room headquarters of Lieutenant General Carl Stiner at Fort Clayton, the stately tropical Army post near the Miraflores Locks in the old Canal Zone. Stiner had just ordered H-hour advanced from 0100 to 0045 in the area of Panama City, trying to resurrect a semblance of tactical surprise following "premature contact" between the PDF and American forces. And that was not all. The Air Force had also just advised that weather over Rio Hato was worse than predicted during their last en route briefing two hours earlier. A low stratus cloud deck forming over the coast might prevent the two Stealth aircraft from accurately hitting their objectives. Therefore, "target prep," the striking of the PDF's garrison area west of the long Rio Hato runway, might have to be scrubbed.

Great, he thought, fantastic. No tactical surprise and maybe no air prep. For a moment he dwelled on the Intel briefing about the Cuban-supplied ZPU-4 antiaircraft guns at Rio Hato. They would be jumping from only 500 feet, well within the lethal range of those guns.

Kernan stared down the double row of Rangers wedged shoulder to shoulder on their nylon sling benches the length of the cargo hold. They were sharp-looking troops, obviously prepared for combat, physically, at least. Their faces and hands were smeared with tan and green camo paint. Their Kevlar helmets were covered with ripped strips of old BDU camouflage uniforms. Every man's parachute harness, rucksack, general purpose (GP) bag, and weapons pouch was clean and rigged out exactly according to regs, even though these same men had dragged themselves, mud-caked and exhausted, back to their barracks compound after the final demanding training exercise only thirty hours earlier. And he was confident that, had he ripped open the Velcro tabs of their weapons pouches, he would have found their M-16A2 rifles—one-third of the unit's riflemen were equipped with over-and-under 203 grenade launchers on their M-16s—their M-60 machine guns and squad automatic weapons (SAWs), their light anti-tank weapon (LAW) and AT-4 antiarmor missiles, and their sniper rifles spotless, all lightly oiled and ready for battle. He also knew the men's rucksacks were heavy with extra two-liter canteens, grenades, bandoliers of M-16 magazines and Claymore mines. No one carried much in the way of creature comfort, just a dry pair of socks and one MRE ration pouch (Meals, Ready to Eat—"Meals Rejected by Ethiopians," or "Motherfuckin' Re-ject Eats," depending on the man you asked).

In a Ranger outfit, a commander didn't have to sweat details like sharp appearance and clean, well-functioning weapons and equipment, as would his counterpart in a regular Airborne unit, or, God forbid, a "straight-leg" outfit. The battalion sergeants major, company first sergeants, and the buck sergeant fire-team leaders made sure no Ranger climbed aboard the aircraft for an actual operation with weapons or equipment deficiencies.

The Rangers had a tradition, dating back to Major Robert Rogers, commander of the legendary Rogers Rangers of the French and Indian Wars. His fourteen Standing Orders began with the simple but vital requirement for the successful soldier operating deep inside enemy territory: "Don't

Forget Nothing." And Kernan was confident his subordinate officers and NCO leaders had followed that admonition to the letter.

He was more curious about their frame of mind, a good indicator of how they would perform on the objective. Most of the men were now awake, after managing several hours sleep on the unusually smooth flight down from Fort Benning, Georgia. Some stared into the neutral space of the C-130's exposed control cables and hydraulic plumbing, avoiding eye contact with the guys facing them across the bundles of reserve ammunition and equipment. By military doctrine, the planes were all crossloaded, with fire teams from different companies thrown together on each chalk so that no single unit would be crippled should an aircraft go down or be forced to abort its drop. And the flight to a combat drop was not an easy time to make buddies with relative strangers.

Buck Kernan had seen this look before, on Chinooks and Hueys, inbound to a hot landing zone in Vietnam's II Corps. And he had encountered that same expression of thoughtful resignation in the eyes of the paratroopers of the battalion he had commanded during the invasion of Grenada, six years before. It was not overt fear. Instead, these young Rangers projected a sense of aloofness, of individual isolation, as if each one had separately just been forced to consider the prospect of his own death or maiming within the coming hour.

That in itself wasn't necessarily bad, as long as the men kept their minds on business. Once you were in your chute harness, aboard the plane, there simply wasn't much use being morbid. Besides, to paraphrase Winston Churchill, who had once commented during the geopolitical wars of his own challenged empire, there was nothing so exhilarating as being shot at and missed.

Thomas Duke, the stocky Guamian sergeant major of the 2d Battalion, worked his way forward lugging a black, five-gallon plastic water can, which the men were using as an improvised urinal. They had been in their parachute harnesses for over eight hours. Waiting in the freezing rain back at Fort Ben-

41

ning's Lawson Army Airfield to board the C-130s, Kernan had insisted every man drink as much water as he could stomach. In Grenada, he'd seen the disastrous effect of the sudden transition from peacetime training in the temperate north to combat in the sweltering tropics. Dehydration could cripple a heavily laden trooper just as quickly as a round from an AK-47. Now the men's kidneys were working just fine, proof that they were well hydrated. Kernan watched one young soldier with a Mohawk haircut heft the sloshing can, then, using his thick-bladed K-Bar knife, scratch a prominent "X" on both sides of the can.

The kid slipped the knife back into the sheath on his web gear and shouted above the engine noise. "Sergeant Major, I just wanna be real sure I don't drink any water out of *this* sucker tomorrow."

The men around him doubled over with laughter. Buck Kernan joined their belly laughs. They were able to think about tomorrow, past the danger of the night ahead. They were a team of Rangers again, not a collection of scared young men.


Charlo Gonzales snapped off the mircophone of his security net radio and went to the second floor balcony of the Comandancia staff headquarters building. Panamanian soldiers had been fired on by gringo convoys between Albrook and Clayton. During all the provocations of the past months, no American MP had fired on a Defense Forces vehicle. There was definitely something different about tonight. A few minutes before, he'd received a call from the G-2 electronic monitoring station located high on Cerro Tigre, halfway up the Canal to Lake Gaitan. There was an incredible amount of scrambled American radio traffic coming over the G-2 FM and UHF frequency scanners. The radio section naturally could not decipher any of this traffic, but the electronic profile was larger and more dispersed than anything they'd ever tracked before. This was yet another confirmation that the gringo invasion was about to begin.

Fifteen minutes before, Gonzales had heard the G-2 section's preliminary coded warning order go out on the main Defense Forces tactical radio net: "The game is on for 0100," the message simply said. But there had been no confirming message to activate the alert sections of the Dignity Battalions standing by throughout the thirteen provinces. Major Gonzales suspected another yanqui trick. The turd-eating CIA or those Quisling Puerto Ricans in Southcom's 470th Military Intelligence had probably recruited more traitors in G-2, and they had released the alert order as a false alarm. Charlo Gonzales leaned against the cool concrete flanks of the balcony and stared out at the city below.

He loved Panama City deeply. Despite the blighted slums of El Chorrillo and the poor squatter *colonias* along the Trans-Isthmus Highway, Panama was the undisputed jewel of Central America, the prosperously sleek and sophisticated capital of a cosmopolitan nation that was at once both more fortunate and more energetic than its neighbors to the west in Central America and to the east on the festering mainland of South America. Panama was a nation with a natural right to prosperity. The Good Lord had placed this land here as a bridge between oceans and continents. As the *Jefe* always said, their Canal was only the tangible symbol of Panama's natural right to a place at the table of the world's leading powers. Unlimited commerce, banking, and high finance—unfettered by the hypocritical gringo regulations, which, after all, were written by Jews in New York penthouses, then dictated to their lap-dog regulators and Congressmen in Washington—was at the heart of his country's future. When Panama received its total sovereignty and was finally free of the gringo yoke in the year 2000, it would be among the world's richest countries, analogous to the wealthy emirates of the Persian Gulf. And, under Noriega, that wealth would be shared among the patriotic soldiers who defended the nation from the gringos.

Gonzales stared up at the brooding tree-clad hulk of Ancon Hill, which rose as a mocking insult above the squalid roofs of El Chorrillo. From this angle, he could not see the huge Panamanian flag that the gringos had finally deigned to permit after the Carter treaties. In almost exactly ten years, the last gringo officer would drag his flat-chested, fat-assed wife and crack-smoking teenage children off that sacred mountain and Gonzales would install his own family in one of those stately old mahogany villas beneath the arching banyan trees.

But now Thurman, that priest-loving *maricon* of a gringo general and his mulatto boss Powell obviously had other plans. Even if General Noriega was too tired from his long day's travels to grasp the seriousness of the situation, loyal younger officers like Charlo Gonzales would act for him to save the day.

Major Gonzales carefully dialed the number of his counterpart at the Rio Hato base, Captain Tomas Garcia, commander of the 6th Defense Forces Mechanized Rifle Company, the Macho de Monte.

"Tommy," Gonzales said, getting straight to the point. "There's something strange happening here in the city."

"I heard the radio report," Garcia answered. He sounded tired but wide awake.

"Listen now," Charlo Gonzales continued, "I think you'd better put some troops on alert."

"I've already got half the force standing-to in the barracks," Garcia replied. "I'll get the rest up and issue ammunition."

"Okay, *bueno*," Charlo said. "But don't take too long. Get them on line and get the armor out of that motor pool. We should have all the vehicles dispersed."

"I've already issued that order," Garcia said. "The armor is loading ammunition right now."

"Good, good, you've done well." Gonzales stared out the wide office window at Ancon Hill. "Just be careful, Tommy. There's definitely something happening."[6]


## 0043 Hours, 20 December

They were twenty minutes out from the Rio Hato DZ. It was time to raise the seats and clear the aisles before hook up. Buck Kernan watched the jumpmaster, a lanky sergeant first class, stride purposely forward to the center of the cargo bay, where he could be heard by both sticks of jumpers. Kernan was fully rigged out now, in reserve chute, weapons pouch and Kevlar helmet with a painfully tight chin harness.

"Stand up!" the sergeant shouted, stooping to rise with his arms cocked and his palms open, as if he were lifting an invisible bundle before his chest.

The men rose in clumsy unison and reached awkwardly back behind the hunchback bulges of their main chutes to raise and secure the red nylon sling benches against the ribs of the cargo bay. The sergeant nodded respectfully to Colonel Kernan. It was time for Kernan to speak. Before leaving Benning, Buck Kernan had asked his chaplains to conduct a brief Protestant and Catholic service for the troops, a precombat blessing for the men who might die or be maimed. Now it was time for another form of inspiration. Kernan knew from his own combat experience that once those green AK tracers started flying, you forgot about flag and country pretty damned toute de suite. You fought for your buddy and the pride of your outfit. If you did not have that kind of esprit, you did not fight well. And if you did not fight well, you took high casualties.

Kernan squared his shoulders as best he could in the binding embrace of the main harness. In a loud, calm voice, he started to chant the Ranger Creed.

"Recognizing that I volunteered as a Ranger. . . ," he began.

". . . Fully knowing the hazards of my chosen profession," the men echoed from the dimly lit cargo hold. "I will endeavor to uphold the prestige, honor and high esprit de corps of the Rangers."

The chant continued, clear and forceful above the engine roar: "Surrender is not a Ranger word. I will never leave a fallen comrade to fall into the hands of the enemy. . . ."

Finally, the creed was complete, the men promising to "fight on to the Ranger objective and complete the mission, though I be the lone survivor."

Kernan paused and stared into his men's eyes. Then they shouted in bellicose unison, "Rangers lead the way!"

Kernan heard the propeller pitch change from a bass rumble to a whine. They were descending to the run-in and the low jump altitude of 500 feet. It was time for practical matters once again.

"Hook up!" the jumpmaster ordered.

The men snapped their static-line clips to the taut overhead cables on either side of the cargo bay.

"Check your static lines!"

Everyone yanked down hard on the chunky steel clip, the required three sharp jerks. This always reminded Buck Kernan of kids playing some stylized schoolyard game. He licked his dry lips, tasting the sweet, greasy camouflage war paint. It would be nice to drink a glass of cool water. But that would have to wait.

# 2

# 20 December 1989

—

# H-Hour: Paitilla Airport

*0051 Hours, 20 December*

Commander Tom McGrath stared across the greasy-calm water off Punta Paitilla at the glittering high-rise skyline of Panama City. Astern the sixty-five-foot fiberglass patrol boat, fourteen combat rubber raiding craft (CRRCs) were strung out at loose intervals, attached by painters to a floating, two-inch nylon lizard line. Each black rubber raiding craft held eight Navy-Sea-Air-Land personnel—SEALs—from Navy Special Warfare Group Two, based in Norfolk, Virginia. SEAL Team Four was at its rally point, two kilometers off the objective, Paitilla Airport. They had left the beach at Fort Kobbe, adjacent to Howard Air Force Base, just after dark and had approached the city waterfront by a circuitous route, giving a wide berth to the Fort Amador–Flamenco Island causeway and the approaches to the Canal.

As the tide went from high through slack and began to ebb, currents swirled about the taut rubber flanks of the CRRCs, rippling phosphorescent wakes of cold fire in the dark water. The SEALs gazed at the brightly lit city. There was late-night traffic on Avenida Balboa and lights in the high-rise apartments and hotels surrounding Punta Paitilla, a normal night in the handsome tropical capital. It was hard to imagine the war was about to begin.

But Commander Tom McGrath, the captain of SEAL Team

Four, understood combat was imminent, and he was nervous. The command radio linking his patrol boat to the Special Operations Joint Task Force at Howard's Hangar 3 had just informed him that H-hour had been advanced by fifteen minutes from 0100 to 0045, because Panamanian forces had unexpectedly engaged the first American troops en route to their prearranged jump-off points. The war had begun early and the SEALs were still at sea. With the ebbing tide now against them, the boats' outboard motors would have to strain to reach the low bluff at the seaward end of Paitilla Airport.

McGrath went to the rail of the boat and called to the leader of the shore team, Lieutenant Commander Patrick Toohey. "Pat," McGrath yelled, "stand by to cast off. They want us in there early."

"Aye, aye, sir," the commander shouted back.

The SEALs had already uncinched their painters and had their outboard motors in gear. As the rubber boats passed McGrath, he waved to the men squatting in the shallow wells of the raiding craft. They didn't look like traditional SEALs. Rather, they were dressed in regular BDU camouflage and wore standard combat web gear and jungle boots. The image of SEAL frogmen in glistening wetsuits had been replaced by that of regular light infantry. And, like their Army Ranger counterparts, SEAL Team Four wore no Kevlar flak jackets. But unlike the Rangers, the SEALs had also forsaken helmets. However, they did carry a full arsenal of infantry weapons, including M-16 assault rifles, many with under-barrel 203 grenade launchers, M-60 machine guns, and even a 60 mm mortar.

One of the problems with this operation, McGrath recognized, was that the mission itself, although it was within the official limits of SEAL doctrine, could well stretch the combat strength of a single team to the limit.

As the rubber boats passed beside the gunwale, he could see the expression of somber determination on each young man's face. They understood the unit had drawn a rough assignment. But they were too disciplined to allow overt fear or anger about this hazardous mission to show on their faces. Like Colonel Buck Kernan, McGrath had seen such expressions of stoic resolve in Vietnam, where he had served as a young SEAL officer in the green labyrinth of the Mekong Delta. Two decades earlier, McGrath had led raiding parties against Viet Cong positions where the odds at surviving the operation unscathed were just as bad as they were tonight. But he was older now, and a lot more reflective. In fact, McGrath, a multitalented officer who also possessed deep religious faith, had a reputation for being one of the intellectuals in Navy Special Operations. In the rough and tumble SEAL community at the Little Creek, Virginia, Amphibious Base, McGrath was known as a quiet, yet decisive "thinker."[1]

Despite his cool demeanor, however, McGrath cared deeply for his men. And it was a wrenching experience to stand at the rail of this vessel and watch these men turn their boats into the wash of the ebbing tide and head for the low bluff lit by a single red navigation beacon, which marked the south end of the Paitilla runway. McGrath was in his mid-forties, the senior officer on the team's floating command post. He would not be directly commanding his men ashore. He had to trust Pat Toohey and the six platoon officers to lead the SEALs. But most of them were about to experience combat for the first time. A few actually seemed elated at the prospect.

Isaac "Ike" Rodriguez, a stocky, open-faced kid from Texas, grinned up at McGrath as the rubber boat swept past. Rodriguez was a recent replacement in Golf Platoon, a torpedoman's mate second-class who had come to the unit from a West Coast SEAL Delivery Team detachment operating minisubmarines. There had always been a lot of rivalry between the "real" SEALs who wore the coveted gold eagle-and-trident and the guys in delivery teams and special boat units. Like all other replacements, Rodriguez had been on indefinite probation until he had earned the respect and acceptance of his teammates and officers. In fact, it was only aboard the C-130 flying down to Howard from Little Creek that Ike Rodriguez had received his "Budweiser," as the men called the SEAL trident pin, due to its resemblance to the beer-can eagle logo. And Rodriguez had worn his BDU blouse with the prominently displayed gold trident preparing weapons and equipment that first day at

Howard after the rest of the team had stripped down to shorts and T-shirts in the baking heat of Hangar 3.

The boats spread into a loose V-formation with the lead CRRC ten meters ahead of the two flanks. This lead boat carried the security squad, commanded by Lieutenant (j.g.) John Connors, a muscular Boston Irishman with an unquenchable grin. McGrath stared at Connors' boat, reflecting on the unusual circumstances that had brought the young officer to this time and place.

By definition, SEALs were high achievers, required to master several diverse and rigorous military skills before they could join a team. They all had to be Navy-certified scuba divers with underwater demolition expertise, military parachutists qualified for high-altitude–low-opening (HALO) special ops drops, and Ranger-level infantrymen. And beyond these "basic" skills, every SEAL was expected to acquire several individual specialties. So it was difficult to single out truly exceptional young officers among this competitive and hard-charging bunch. But John Connors was obviously exceptional.

Tom McGrath had kept a discrete eye on the young officer since Connors had come to SEAL Team Four the year before from the rough Basic Underwater Demolition/SEAL training at the Coronado Navy Base in California. The Coronado cadre had given Connors the highest marks for leadership potential. Soon after Connors arrived as a probational ensign, the team had been deployed to the Persian Gulf. Iranian Revolutionary Guards had been staging raids on American shipping from offshore oil platforms. Connors' platoon had practiced raiding Iranian positions by "fast-roping" from helicopters onto the U.S. Navy barge *Hercules*. The SEALs dropped fifty feet down thick ropes and braked their descent at the last moment, using only their gloved hands. One stifling windless afternoon, Connors had landed hard and limped away across the hot deck. But he never complained. When it came time to climb the narrow caving ladder back to the hovering helicopter, Connors' leg would not support his weight. Still without complaint, he hauled himself up the ladder hand-over-hand.

Only when they returned to their base later that day was it discovered Connors had suffered a painful stress fracture of his right leg. After wearing a cast for a few weeks, Connors cut it off himself so he could resume training with his platoon.

But that injury had only been a preliminary test of Connors' resolve. When SEAL Team Four had received their Panama deployment orders, Connors had not even been assigned to Little Creek. He was a patient at the Walter Reed Army Medical Center, having just completed half of an experimental twenty-day treatment for leishmaniasis, a dangerous skin disease carried by sand flies, which he had contracted on a jungle warfare course in the Brazilian Amazon. On returning from Brazil in September, he had dismissed the painful, coin-sized lesions on his chest and arms as "annoying," but even a stoic guy like Connors couldn't ignore the fact that the angry red sores would crust around the edges, but simply wouldn't heal.

Each afternoon Connors received an intravenous treatment, followed by an electrocardiogram to check the toxic medication was not damaging his heart. The process required him to lie on a bed while an intravenous drip slowly delivered the healing drugs. This enforced inactivity was irksome. But he had a degree in chemical engineering and had discussed the importance of the treatment with the Walter Reed specialists. Unless arrested by the medication, he'd learned, the leishmaniasis parasite could eventually attack his internal organs. He had every reason in the world to stay at Walter Reed and complete his treatment.

So on the hectic morning of Sunday, December 17, when McGrath was scrambling to get the team ready for immediate deployment to an unknown destination, he had been shocked to look up and see Lieutenant John Connors in the office doorway, grinning widely, his blue eyes warm with excitement. Somebody had tipped him off that the team was on alert. "Good morning, sir," Connors said. "It looks like something's going down."

"John," McGrath said, "we're mounting out." After the shooting of Lieutenant Paz the night before, they both knew the team's deployment could only be to Panama.

"Captain," Connors said, speaking seriously now, "I'd like to get back in the platoon."

McGrath nodded but didn't immediately answer. Connors

was one of the strongest, most resourceful officers in the team. And he was also one of the smartest; the young lieutenant had been a brilliant student who had studied in Spain and Germany and was fluent in three languages, including Spanish. But there was a problem: Connors was still registered as a patient at Walter Reed. His sudden disappearance at this time of obvious crisis would be a serious breach of operational security that could jeopardize the entire mission.

"If you can get yourself cleared from the hospital, John," McGrath said, "I can certainly use you on this operation. If you can't get clearance, I want you back up there before anyone starts asking where you are."

Half an hour later, Connors was back, again smiling broadly. "I'm off medical orders, sir. I told them there was a family funeral and I'd get back as soon as I could."

It would take more than a tropical skin disease to keep Connors away from this operation. "You've got your job back, John," McGrath said. "Go find your men."


Commander McGrath stared into the dark bay, watching the black raiding craft disappear into the clutter of shore lights. The physical and mental toughness of young men like Ike Rodriguez and John Connors was about to be tested in an area a lot harsher than *any* training course.

McGrath raised his binoculars and focused on the objective. Paitilla Airport was a long runway, almost completely devoid of cover or concealment, which stretched from the main seaside boulevard due south over 5,000 feet along a flat tongue of urban seaside. The airport was surrounded by high- and low-rise apartments and embassies on the west, and by a group of private secondary-school compounds on the east. At the southwest extremity of the Paitilla runway stood the posh Club Union, the most exclusive rabiblanco watering hole in all of Panama City.

Paitilla Point was quintessentially the urban terrain emphasized in the military's latest doctrinal buzz phrase: military operations in urban terrain, or MOUT. Giving a War College name to old-fashioned street fighting might be a comfort to flag-rank officers, but the fundamental reality of city combat had not changed since the invention of rapid-fire weapons. Fighting in built-up areas favored the defending force, who had both cover and concealment, while the attackers in the streets usually had neither. Thus the tactic of armed reconnaissance—often in armored vehicles—had evolved. But this option was not available to SEAL Team Four. They had been ordered to secure Paitilla Airport by advancing directly up the coverless runway, avoiding the private homes, embassies, and apartments that formed an almost unbroken phalanx on the city side of the airport. Many of these buildings were known to house PDF officers, some of whom would have armed bodyguards equipped with FM radios.

Nevertheless, neutralizing Paitilla Airport was a vital primary objective of Operation Blue Spoon. General Noriega kept his private Learjet in the open-fronted PDF hangar at the northwest end of the runway, a site that was lightly guarded, according to intelligence reports. Noriega's plane had been gone that morning, but was now reported back in the hangar. Neutralizing the entire airport, however, not simply destroying Noriega's jet, was this operation's goal. But other unsavory characters also kept aircraft at Paitilla Airport, including a number of couriers for the Colombian drug cartels. So it could be anticipated that the SEALs would encounter not only some armed PDF guards at Noriega's hangar, but also armed private "security" officers at the light-aircraft hangars on the right side of the runway.

McGrath and his fellow senior SEAL officers fully acknowledged that Paitilla Airport and Noriega's Learjet had to be put out of action. If the Rangers attacking Rio Hato to the far west and the Special Operations Forces sealing off Fort Cimarron to the east were unsuccessful, and the runway of Paitilla Airport was not neutralized, the airport could become either a rallying point for incoming PDF reinforcements (as had Tocumen Air Base during the failed October coup attempt) or a convenient escape route for Noriega and his high-ranking PDF cronies. So the SEALs had been given the job of "taking down" Paitilla.

Normally, such airport interdiction was an assignment for

the Army Rangers, who trained year-round for airport seizures. Certainly the 75th Ranger Regiment could have spared a reinforced company of 100 men to seize Paitilla by helicopter or seaborne assault, had Special Operations Command given them the mission.[2]

But there had been an informal understanding among senior Special Operations officials, both uniformed officers and Defense Department civilians (some of whom had Navy Special Warfare backgrounds) that the Navy should get its share of the Panama operation. The original operational concept for American military intervention in Panama called for Navy transports and amphibious vessels to land Marine forces along the Canal. But this plan was canceled when Pentagon officials recognized the relatively slow deployment of Marines would give the PDF time to seize American hostages and rally the Dignity Battalions for prolonged resistance.[3] Overall, Blue Spoon was an Army show, with the Air Force concentrated in the Military Airlift Command (MAC) and in the 1st Special Operations Wing from Hurlburt Field in Florida. As the operations plan evolved, it became clear early on that there was not much of a role for the Navy, although the Marines were eventually assured their modest slice of the pie taking on the PDF and Dignity Battalions in the region of Howard Air Force Base and the western approaches to the Bridge of the Americas.

But the only way the Navy was going to publicly contribute to the effort was through a relatively overt use of SEALs. So as early as eighteen months before, Navy Special Warfare had been quietly assured that they would have an important role to play in any eventual military intervention in Panama. The fact that Admiral William Crowe, then chairman of the Joint Chiefs of Staff, could sometimes be a staunch Navy partisan in the internecine armed service struggle for shrinking funds and prestige in the halls of Congress was not lost on members of the Special Operations community who began to question the SEALs' Paitilla mission. Being able to fight in a low-intensity conflict (another War College seminar term), coupled to the rapid deployment of specially trained "light" forces, were attributes viewed with favor in the congressional committees holding the military's purse strings. And "jointness," the ability of a service to function well in a command led by a senior officer from a rival service (i.e., the Navy working well in Army General Max Thurman's Southcom), had long been another positive attribute in congressional eyes.[4]

So, when Chairman Bill Crowe let it be known that the Navy *would* have a decent chunk of the Panama action, ambitious Navy Special Warfare officers gladly seized the opportunity. Obviously, Navy aircraft carriers, submarines, and amphibious units would not be of much use taking down the PDF. But there might be plausible missions for the SEALs beyond their usual covert reconnaissance tasks. And most veteran SEAL officers agreed that these missions did exist. Some, however, pointed out early on that using a SEAL team as light infantry to seize Paitilla Airport was not one of these missions.

But several of McGrath's superiors in Navy Special Warfare had eagerly embraced the assignment. There were many on the Norfolk and Coronado staffs who felt they had been over-eager, trying to not only please the Navy's senior admiral but also to expunge the SEALs' less than sterling record during the botched invasion of Grenada in 1983. (The SEALs had lost four men drowned, had been driven off one objective, and had been held siege at another.)

In any event, McGrath had had no choice but to train his people for the operation plan that his superiors had personally written and had also personally walked through the critical briefing process with Special Operations Command, prior to the formalizing of OPLAN Blue Spoon.

One of the many problems with the SEAL assault on Paitilla Airport concerned hard intelligence as to enemy strength and intentions, normally a key factor in Special Operations involving small units of lightly armed troops. Because the PDF hangar at Paitilla was used extensively by Noriega and his inner circle, it was almost impossible after the October coup attempt to penetrate their security ring to get a firm, usable estimate of enemy strength among the guards at the hangar. It was simply accepted as a given that the airport would remain lightly guarded, regardless of the security situation elsewhere in Panama. On arriving in Panama, however, the SEALs had requested a pre-H-hour tactical reconnaissance of the objective. Specifically, they wanted a close final inspection of the PDF hangar no earlier than mid-morning, December 19. This request went to Major General Wayne Downing, commander of the Special Operations Task Force. Downing was an officer under intense pressure to perform well in a demanding, risky assignment that, if successful, promised little public reward, and if flawed could destroy his career. He consulted Southcom, which had no specific updates on enemy strength at Paitilla. Unofficially, Intel officers urged Downing not to unleash gung-ho "SEALs in frogman outfits" who might blunder attempting daylight reconnaissance of Paitilla and compromise the entire operation. Downing refused to authorize the tactical recon.

But the SEALs would not accept this rebuttal. In a flurry of last minute Southcom and Pentagon lobbying, the Navy managed to have General Downing's decision overridden by Max Thurman. Later that day, a small group of SEALs, dressed in civvies and driving civilian vehicles, conducted a circumscribed reconnaissance of Paitilla Airport.

One group drank a Coke on the second-floor terrace bar of the Pilots' Club cafeteria, just off the Via Israel. The terrace was the unofficial departure gate for colorfully dressed Kuna Indians waiting for the rickety air taxis that flew between the capital and the landing strip on Porvenir Island in the San Blas archipelago off the Atlantic coast. The muscular, short-haired SEALs, wearing an unconvincing mufti of wrinkled Banlon shirts and jeans, could hardly pass muster as tourists. The Indians, suspicious of Europeans at the best of times, shied away from the Americans and did not even try to sell them the pastel Mola embroideries that their brightly kerchiefed women habitually carried.

But the terrace did provide a good view of the runway below, and of the private hangars lining the eastern edge of the airport. The Cessnas and Beechcrafts of legitimate bush pilots and of drug couriers stood in clear view across the runway. These light planes and the service vehicles near the hangars would provide material for the barricades the SEALs planned to establish at 1,000-foot intervals along the runway. Best of all, there was no evidence of any reinforced guard posts around the private hangars.

But this recon team did not have a clear view of the PDF hangar, which stood several hundred meters to the left, completely obscured by the peaked corrugated metal roof of a large maintenance building. After a few uncomfortable minutes on the terrace, the SEALs left the Indians to their plates of fried eggs and plantains and tried to amble nonchalantly down the stairs to the car in the muddy parking lot below.

Twenty minutes later, the second recon team, also in a civilian car, rolled slowly down Calle 68 Este toward the curve of Via Israel, where the wide seaside road crested a slight rise at the northern end of Paitilla Airport. From here the open-mawed PDF hangar was in full view across the northern corner of the runway. But so was the recon team. The driver waited with his left-turn signal blinking as the normal press of late-morning taxis and clanking, gaudily painted private buses streamed around the corner. The traffic provided the waiting vehicle a plausible excuse, but also disrupted close examination and clandestine photography of the objective. However, this team did attain several key pieces of tactical intelligence: As they had been advised, Noriega's Learjet was gone for the day, so they had a relatively clear view into the empty hangar bay. There were no gun jeeps or armored cars guarding the hangar. And there were no obvious new fortifications, such as sandbags or barbed wire, around the structure. But from this distance the SEALs had no way of seeing into the low, white cinder-block office wing along the hangar's left side or the maintenance rooms at the rear. They observed no unusual radio antenna or stacked ammunition crates that would have been obvious indicators the PDF had transformed the hangar into a heavily fortified position.[5]

But this hurried, drive-past scan was hardly the thorough recon job in which the SEALs prided themselves. The foray did confirm certain unpleasant realities, however. To disable Noriega's Learjet—assuming it would be back at the airport on schedule later that afternoon—the SEALs would have to get near the hangar. And the approach to the hangar's open front would have to be across flat grass parking ramps and a concrete apron as wide as a football field. There were five or six single-engine and light twin-engine aircraft parked on the grassy ramp, perhaps fifty meters from the hangar front. But these planes provided little concealment, and certainly scant cover from fire. Worse, the recon team noted that the line of fire from the office and workshop windows led directly across the apron and open runway to the well-lit control tower and DNTT maintenance hangar beside the tower. Unless the airport's power supply was knocked out during the H-hour assault, SEALs approaching the hangar would be silhouetted against the floodlit administrative complex across the runway.

The two recon teams were obliged to take circuitous routes back to Howard, using traditional cutouts to avoid a surveillance tail. It was midafternoon before they had their recon pictures developed, almost time for SEAL Team Four's final briefing. In effect, this superficial reconnaissance only reinforced potentially dangerous intelligence gaps. Without Noriega's Learjet in the hangar, it had been impossible to predict the actual deployment of his personal security guard. And prohibited from using clandestine penetration of the airport perimeter, the recon men had been unable to establish the actual defensive posture of the hangar.

To several men in the team—veterans of the Grenada operation in which murky intelligence spelled disaster—the assault on Paitilla was beginning to seem like another fuck-up.[6] All along, these SEALs had noted that the operation would succeed against a small, lightly armed security detachment. But three, sixteen-man SEAL platoons, no matter how well motivated and trained, were simply not strong enough on the ground to take on a heavily defended and well-fortified position.

In fact, some of these men had agreed with disgruntled Special Warfare staff officers who had opposed the entire "John Wayne" approach to the Paitilla operation. Back at Little Creek these officers, with years of combat in Vietnam behind them, and the experience of Grenada still fresh in their memories, had proposed an alternative plan: the clandestine insertion of small SEAL formations from hidden staging sites in the surrounding neighborhood. One proposal called for using a civilian stake truck with its bed covered by a tarpaulin as a kind of Trojan horse to deposit just before H-hour a reinforced SEAL platoon at the parking lot directly behind the PDF hangar. Another alternative plan would have staged SEALs dressed in civvies through the nearby open-air cafeterias—including the Pilots' Club—with their weapons hidden in sports bags. The logic behind these alternate plans was that a clandestine approach would guarantee tactical surprise, which was the key to overpowering the hangar security guard, no matter what its strength or armament.

Another area of disagreement among the veterans concerned air support. Navy Special Warfare Group Two had submitted a fire-support plan to Special Operations Joint Task Force calling for the SEALs to be covered by a fixed-wing AC-130 Spectre gunship. The veterans recognized that the Spectre had awesome firepower, but they also know the relatively high-flying gunship's automatic cannons and its 105 mm howitzer could not be used in truly tight quarters. They would have preferred a helicopter gunship, perhaps one of the MH-6 AHIPS armed with a multibarrel 7.62 mm minigun, with which they had worked in the Persian Gulf the year before. The AHIPS "buzz saw" was nimble and quiet and could lay down devastating fire safely in a confined area. But these veterans' superiors had written a plan using the Spectre, which required the presence of an Air Force Combat Control Team.[7] In effect, the SEALs were being asked to stage a dwarf amphibious assault, when a paramilitary police-type raid might stand a better chance of success. But it was just this type of clearly *naval* amphibious attack that would highlight their service's effective "jointness."

All these issues preyed on the minds of the SEAL officers as the team's boats ran in against the ebbing tide toward Paitilla Point. They were still hoping for tactical surprise, but the sudden advancement of H-hour meant such surprise was probably impossible. And the operation's strict rules of engagement prevented them from conducting a standard frontal assault, employing the proven method of "reconnaissance by fire," which would have allowed them to pin down *any* enemy while elements of the team went about blocking the airport by dragging vehicles and light aircraft across the concrete runway.

Despite the misgivings of some veterans, the forty-eight members of the reinforced SEAL Team Four (augmented by an Air Force Combat Control Team—CCT—to coordinate air support) who were now motoring toward the low, dark bluff of the southern end of the Paitilla runway, were as well prepared as they would ever be. They had been trained to perfection, assaulting a similar coastal airport in Florida over ten times during training exercises in the past eighteen months. They all knew their jobs intimately. During the last training exercise only four days earlier, they had succeeded in blocking that runway with Cessnas and Beechcrafts, and surrounding the "PDF hangar" in under ten minutes. But that training scenario had included compliant private security guards and a small contingent of "PDF" soldiers easily intimidated. The exercise had also been posited on the factor of complete surprise. And they now had to accept the fact that tactical surprise in this operation had undoubtedly already been lost.

Not only had McGrath received confirmation from the Special Operations Task Force that H-hour had been advanced because of early contact, but the SEALs themselves had been spotted by a Panamanian fishing boat two hours earlier, as the rubber raiding craft swung from the lizard line behind the patrol boat. The Panamanian boat, a rust-flecked trawler, had chugged to within thirty yards of the blacked-out SEAL flotilla. Just as the fishing boat passed abeam of them, the Panamanian skipper had turned on a brilliant floodlight, illuminating the weird and vivid scene: a squat gray U.S. Navy patrol boat trailing a long string of rubber raiding craft, each holding a small group of heavily armed commandos with blackened faces and dark wool watch caps. Although there had been no verbal exchange between McGrath's patrol boat and the fishing trawler, it was obvious that the Panamanian crew had had time to carefully scrutinize the SEALs at their rally point. That unfortunate incident had occurred well before midnight. And McGrath had no idea if or when the trawler crew had passed on this vital intelligence to the PDF. But he was afraid that the operation was already badly compromised before it had even begun.

To compound these problems, the Air Force Combat Control Team had been unable to establish secure FM communication with the Air Papa AC-130 Spectre gunship orbiting over Paitilla Point. The CCT's senior NCO had already changed batteries and antennas on his secure FM sets. But he had not yet made contact with the Spectre. McGrath could only hope they wouldn't need that gunship until the Air Force sergeant straightened out this communications glitch.[8]

SEAL Lieutenant (j.g.) Mike Phillips was the deputy commander of Golf Platoon. He watched John Connors' boat slip through the reflected glare of the shore lights and into the shadows of the low bluff. Phillips had considerable respect for Connors. The two young officers had become close during the tough months of jungle training in Brazil. He was glad Connors was back on the team. Before leaving the beach at Kobbe, Phillips had noted the size of Connors' rucksack, which was jammed with extra belts of M-60 machine-gun ammunition, radio batteries, and medical supplies. Typically, Connors had volunteered to carry the heaviest load. He'd also taken his squad's combined M-16 rifle and 203 under-barrel grenade launcher. This meant John Connors was obliged to wear a heavy pouched vest with extra 40 mm grenade rounds.

"How much does all that stuff weigh, John?" Phillips had asked.

Connors had looked up from his load on the dark sand. "About a hundred pounds I guess," he'd answered.

"You planning to *run* with that load?" Phillips had teased.

Connors flashed his famous grin. "Try and catch me."

Both young officers had laughed loudly, an incongruous burst of humor among the quietly waiting SEALs on the beach.

But that lighthearted exchange had been before the team departed at sunset. Since then Phillips and his teammates had had little to laugh about. Being spotted by that fishing trawler had spooked everyone. And advancing H-hour at the last minute had put the cap on it. People were edgy, strung tight.

As he watched Connors' squad drag their boat ashore and move quickly up the grassy bluff, the city shoreline beyond the high-rise buildings to the left suddenly exploded with a rumbling orange glare. The distinctive crack of heavy machine guns was punctuated by the rattle of small arms. From his position a hundred meters off the point, Phillips watched a gaudy fountain of tracers wobbling up from the city center. He saw return tracers slashing down from helicopter and Spectre gunships, which lit up the scattered low clouds, giving the distant buildings the appearance of hulking volcanoes. That had to be the attack on the Comandancia. And it was loud enough to wake the dead. Unfortunately, any PDF guards on the runway were not dead yet. The operation that had begun so inauspiciously seemed to be careening toward disaster.

(Despite later press accounts, the SEALs' boats were never stranded by low tide in the mud flats off the point.[9])

Connors' squad fanned out in the grass at the end of the runway. They heard the crackling of automatic weapons and the hollow thump of cannons echoing from beyond the high-rise buildings to their left. The SEALs sprawled in the low grass, their weapons ready, searching for PDF guards at this end of the airport. The concrete runway stretched north, empty and featureless, toward the dome of yellow light around the stubby control tower and hangars. They saw people moving up there, but the south end of the airport was deserted. So far, so good. Just to their left the terraced grounds and orange-tiled roofs of the Club Union were floodlit, an incongruous bit of civilian luxury. In their final briefing, the SEALs had been warned to watch out for late-night drunks from the Club Union who might wander onto the airport once the assault had begun. These people were to be quickly ordered out of harm's way. As for other civilians encountered on the airport, including private security guards, the SEALs were ordered to use "diplomacy," not brute force. The squads formed up, the men humped beneath their packs and weapons. The order came from Commander Toohey to move out.

Toohey's shore team command post, including the medics' triage point and the Air Force control team, set up here at the dim southern end of the runway. The other SEALs advanced up the runway toward the floodlit hangars with precise maneuvers, just as they had during their long training. One squad crouched to provide cover while another squad dashed ahead, their cleated rubber boots pounding on the concrete. This leapfrog movement flowed quickly. Three hundred meters to the north, one squad peeled off to search for material for the first runway block. They found an abandoned vehicle and debris at the side of the taxi ramp. So far, the SEALs had not been discovered. The firing from the Comandancia and Fort Amador had reached a steady crescendo now, punctuated by the crack of heavy weapons on a Spectre gunship. Streams of glowing tracers wobbled above the city skyline.

The SEALs' own fire-support Spectre whined through the night overhead, unlighted, an unseen, reassuring presence. Unfortunately, the CCT was still unable to establish secure FM communications with the Air Papa Spectre gunship.

Halfway up the runway, the team encountered the first aircraft hangars—gaping, doorless buildings with corrugated metal roofs. There were dozens of small planes lined up on the parking ramps, good raw material for runway blocks. But as the SEALs began dragging these aircraft onto the runway, Panamanian night watchmen appeared, shouting protests.

Some were obviously legitimate security guards, wearing faded khaki uniforms and armed with nightsticks. Others were clearly more sinister, watchmen for the drug runners' aircraft. Each squad had a Spanish speaker, and the SEALs brusquely ordered the watchmen away. But the men guarding the drug dealers' planes protested, despite the presence of the heavily armed American forces.

Several of these Panamanians were husky black Creoles who were far from intimidated by the well-armed SEALs. The textbook special ops squad advance up the runway suddenly degenerated into an angry shoving match, more like a bar fight than a military maneuver.[10]

"Stay de fuck back, mon!" one Creole watchman shouted.

A man in the shadows suddenly brandished a sawed-off

shotgun and the SEALs began clubbing guards with their rifle butts. The Americans finally prevailed, however, but only after they had been forced to subdue and bind several shouting watchmen with flex cuffs.[11] This unexpected incident had delayed the advance by several minutes. Had there been a full-strength American infantry force on the airport, a platoon could have encircled and disarmed the protesting guards while the main force continued the leapfrog advance. But the thin number of SEALs, restricted by the stringent rules of engagement, was crippled in the element of "shock" essential to the combat effectiveness of small-unit assaults.

The noisy confrontation also destroyed what little remained of tactical surprise, which had degenerated to nothing more than confusion among the Panamanians as to the Americans' exact intentions on the airport. As Golf Platoon resumed its advance up the runway, the SEALs saw uniformed PDF soldiers with binoculars and hand-held radios on the balconies of nearby high-rise buildings. The PDF watchmen were shouting into their radios, pointing toward the advancing squads of SEALs, who had now entered the humid dome of floodlight near the administrative buildings.

In a more conventional combat situation, the two SEALs carrying sniper rifles equipped with night sights would have simply shot these enemy sentries. But because the PDF had not initiated fire, the Americans were constrained by the strict Blue Spoon Rules of Engagement from firing first.

While John Connors' platoon was still delayed by the civilian watchmen, Phillips' Golf Platoon, led by Lieutenant Tom Casey, dashed toward the aircraft parked around the hangars on the left side of the field. Noriega's Learjet stood inside the brightly lit PDF hangar. Phillips saw enemy soldiers, some just roused from sleep and still in their underwear, scurrying for cover inside the cinder-block workshops and the adjacent office wing. They were all armed, some clutching their AK-47s and swinging ammunition pouches in one hand and their pants and boots in the other. Apparently they had left a bunkroom and were taking shelter in prepared positions inside the hangar. There were other PDF running north among the corporate jets and twin-engine turboprops of Aero Perlas parked to the right.

Golf Platoon used the small planes for concealment as best they could as its two squads maneuvered closer. Mike Phillips' squad was covering Casey's while the platoon leader and his men ran abreast of the PDF hangar, only thirty meters away.

Once again, an unexpected standoff ensued, this time with the two armed groups separated by the floodlit concrete apron. The SEALs had ducked behind the Cessnas and Pipers parked on the grassy ramp, while the PDF were visible at the open windows of the maintenance rooms and office wing. Of the two opposing forces, the Panamanians had the only decent cover from small-arms fire; the SEALs' feet and legs were protected only by the landing gear of the light planes, and the thin aluminum skins of the aircraft fuselages would never stop heavy AK rounds.

"Drop your weapons," one of the PDF yelled in Spanish from inside the hangar. "Drop them or we will shoot."

"No!" Petty Officer Carlos Moleda shouted back in Spanish. "You drop *your* weapons."

Casey hand-signaled his squad to deploy right, to gain better cover among the twin-engined Aero Perlas turboprops parked in the shadows.

As the men began to make their move, Phillips heard another voice in the open hangar shout in Spanish, *"Ponganse en posicion . . . Preparense para disparar"* (Take positions . . . Prepare to fire).

Just as Mike Phillips yelled a warning to Casey, the PDF opened fire from concealed positions. The first bursts of PDF fire were aimed low, at the SEALs' exposed legs. The Panamanians skipped their fire off the concrete hangar apron, hitting Casey's men as they began to sprint for better cover. All the PDF troops inside cut loose, blasting with assault rifles on full automatic fire, raking the SEALs on the open grass only thirty yards away. Seven of the eight-man squad fell. Only Casey himself was able to return fire.

Phillips rushed his squad forward, firing at the PDF muzzle flashes in the windows. As he approached he saw the full devastation of the enemy attack. There were men down all around, some lying still, others thrashing to shuck their ruck-sacks and return fire. Luckily Casey's M-60 machine gunner, Scott Norton, was able to hammer back with his automatic weapon, pounding the open windows of the workshops and slashing down the hangar's hanging lights. But Phillips saw Norton was seriously wounded, an awful chunk of flesh ripped from the calf of his right leg. Bright arterial blood spouted onto the grass, gleaming like spilled jewels in the muzzle flashes.

"Heavy wounded," Phillips shouted into his radio. "Bravo, get up here."

"Where's the Spectre?" one of Phillips' men shouted. "Where the fuck is that gunship?"

As the SEALs took to the dubious shelter of the light planes and fired into the PDF positions, no one in Phillips' squad had time to call a fire-support request back to the Air Force combat control team at the end of the runway.

But, even if they had made the request, the CCT was still unable to make contact with the Spectre on secure FM. As Lieutenant Commander Toohey dashed up the runway, leading his small headquarters unit to reinforce the hard-pressed SEALs at the hangar, the senior CCT sergeant finally made contact with the Spectre on 243 MHz, the open Guard Channel.

"Hey," he yelled after the running SEALs, "tell the commander I've got Air Papa."

But it was too late.

In the Spectre, holding its assigned station in a tight orbit 3,000 feet above Paitilla, the fire-control officer watched the terrible scene below. He wondered why no one had called for fire support. Then he saw that the wounded SEALs lay far too close to the enemy hangar. Even with their sophisticated night-vision sights, the gunners on the Spectre probably couldn't fire without endangering the wounded.[12]

Phillips kept his squad moving in the poor cover of parked airplanes, as they lay down fire on the PDF positions. But still the Panamanians raked the fallen SEALs on the parking ramp. Now the SEALs saw they were also being fired on by PDF hidden in the tan cinder-block offices of the civilian hangar to the left and by snipers in the second-floor windows of the airline hangar to the right. To compound their problems, the men of Golf Platoon spotted the muzzle flashes of snipers firing from the northern end of the airport and from nearby apartment buildings. There had to be at least twenty assault PDF rifles laying down a curtain of fire. None of the intelligence briefings had predicted such resistance.

In the surrounding neighborhood, civilians rushed to their roof terraces and porches to witness the fighting at Paitilla Airport. Señor Ricuarte Goti, the airport's operation manager, lived in a pleasant villa two blocks from the north end of the runway. He stared with shock as he recognized what was happening. The tiny dark figures of American troops were sprinting among the light planes parked near the Defense Forces' hangar, firing tracers into nearby workshops. But the blasting volume of fire from the Panamanian positions did not diminish. Americans dropped and tumbled in the shadows, like the little terra-cotta figures at a festival shooting gallery. Goti knew the Defense Forces had constructed virtual bunkers in the workshops and offices surrounding General Noriega's Learjet hangar. These positions were reinforced with concrete-filled barrels and were invulnerable to small-arms fire.

He heard the distinctive rumbling whine of a heavy turbo-prop aircraft circling overhead in the darkness.

*My God,* Goti thought, *the soldiers will kill all the Americans. And then the gringos will bomb the entire neighborhood.*

One street away on Calle 69, retired U.S. Navy Petty Officer Jack Kerr rushed to his front porch when he heard the staccato blast of the firefight. His view across the seaside avenue was unobstructed. He saw men firing and falling, then a light aircraft catch fire. In the distance toward Quarry Heights, the skyline was lit by orange flashes and cascades of glowing tracers. The noise of battle was painfully loud, even this far away. It was as if the entire grand finale of a fireworks display had exploded on the ground.

Then the firing at the Paitilla PDF hangar swelled again. Jack Kerr knew Noriega kept his plane there.

*I hope they catch the bastard,* he thought. *I hope they kill him.*

*   *   *

Only moments after calling for reinforcements, Phillips heard John Connors' squad pounding up behind him. Connors did not hesitate. Using hand signals he spread his men to a line formation and led them forward, directly toward the PDF positions. He planned to shield the wounded SEALs so they could be dragged back to safety. Connors was hunched beneath his heavy rucksack, winded from the long run. Phillips could see his friend's face. His eyes were focused with absolute determination. He showed controlled intensity, but no fear.

But as Connors sprang from the cover, he faltered a moment, jerking to the left. "I'm hit," he shouted. The bullets had struck his web gear and grenade pouches, pounding him with sledgehammer force, but not inflicting serious wounds.

Phillips rushed forward. But amazingly, Connors regained his stride and ran ahead, directly toward the enemy, firing as he advanced.

With Connors' squad in position, Mike Phillips sent a senior petty officer, Chris Tilghman, and his medical corpsman, Alfredo Morino, forward to retrieve the wounded. But the volume of fire from the PDF positions was too heavy to suppress with rifles alone. The SEALs now realized that the cinderblock walls of the hangar shops must have been heavily reinforced on the inside. And the Panamanians had plenty of ammunition. Their automatic fire pounded the parking apron, throwing up clods of dirt and chunks of asphalt.

Among the wounded in Lieutenant Casey's squad, Carlos Moleda had been hit in the back. He dragged himself on his elbows toward the shelter of a light plane because he had lost all feeling in his legs. But the disciplined young SEAL had enough presence of mind to pull along with him the bulky AT-4 antitank rocket that he had carried into the battle. Moleda knew the weapon would be needed. To his horror, he saw an enemy round rip into his limp right leg, shredding the BDU cloth and his living flesh. But he felt no pain. It was then he realized with a terrible flash of sorrow and anger that his spinal cord had probably been severed by the first rounds that hit him. One of his squadmates, Petty Officer Tony Ducci, had been hit in both legs, but still managed to fire his M-16 into the enemy hangar. And Scott Norton continued to chop at the PDF positions with his M-60, even though he was rapidly losing blood from the massive wound in his leg.

A SEAL from Phillips' squad dashed forward to grab Norton by the back of his web gear and drag him toward the shelter of the parked aircraft. As he was being pulled away like a heavy sack, Norton swung his machine gun across his legs to keep up the suppressing fire. Corpsman Al Morino had already retrieved one wounded man and had low-crawled back into the worst of the kill zone to grab another. He was pulling this man to safety, when an enemy round clipped him in the head, ripping loose a gaping flap of flesh and skull, his pulsing white brain horribly visible in the glare of the firefight. Chris Tilghman was blasted headlong across the grass by a burst of enemy fire as he carried a gravely wounded comrade.

The courageous attempt to rescue the wounded from the PDF's concentrated aiming zone had degenerated into a disaster. If there had been a strong enough SEAL force at Paitilla, they could have followed better light-infantry procedure, with one group establishing overwhelming fire superiority while another went forward to rescue the casualties. Instead, the hard-pressed young men were expected to do both simultaneously, an impossible task.

John Connors was clearly gripped by enraged frustration as he saw his friends cut down around him. He was shooting his M-16 from a prone position on the dark grass. Suddenly, he rose to one knee in order to better aim his 203 grenade launcher. "Fuck diplomacy," he shouted, cursing the rules of engagement that had restricted the SEALs' options and resulted in this shambles. He leveled the weapon toward the nearest shop window. At that moment, a heavy-caliber automatic rifle blasted. John Connors flew backwards in the darkness, hit squarely in the abdomen.

Phillips was beside his friend in a moment. Disregarding his own safety, he dragged Connors out of the line of fire. Other SEALs joined Phillips, each taking one of Connors' limbs to bundle him down the runway to the medical corpsman's triage point. They cut away his bullet-torn pack and web gear and ripped open his shirt, searching for wounds. But, in the faint glow of the corpsman's chemical light, bullet holes were hard to find among Connors' parasite sores.

As Phillips watched helplessly, John Connors' face lost its color and his eyes flashed with desperation. "Jesus . . . oh, Jesus, help me," he mumbled. Then his eyes closed. As the corpsman tried vainly to resuscitate Connors, the nearby firing rose and fell in echoing waves. Phillips was needed back there. Reluctantly he turned from Connors' body and dashed back toward the firefight.

As he approached the PDF hangar, other SEAL squads maneuvered beside Phillips. The enemy positions were pounded by accurate fire from the SEALs' M-60 machine guns. Grenades exploded inside the hangar. An airplane on the grassy ramp caught fire, and bright orange flames spurted among the crossing tracers.

All the hangar lights had been shot out and the enemy positions were now lit only by the occasional muzzle flashes of their weapons and the white-hot blast of exploding grenades. At fractured intervals the SEALs could hear the screams and panicked shouts of the wounded PDF, trapped now inside their fortified posts as the Americans' superior fire pounded them. Phillips snatched up a PVS-4 night-vision scope and scanned the hangar for Noriega's white Learjet. He ordered one of his men to fire an AT-4 rocket, aiming just behind the plane's cockpit. The antitank weapon cracked with an echoing blast, and the missile ripped into the sleek white plane, hitting just above the two-tone blue decorative stripe on the forward fuselage. The plane's interior glowed a molten orange as the fireball raced through it.

More antitank missiles cracked from the surrounding darkness, streaking through the windows of the PDF positions. Several M-60 machine guns blasted steady streams of tracers through the workshop windows. Two enemy soldiers tried to dash for shelter in the rear of the hangar and were practically torn apart by the SEALs' massed fire. There was now no further resistance from the PDF hangar and the surrounding positions.

A flaming tongue of spilled aviation gas had spread across

the grass parking ramp. A second, then a third light plane caught fire, forcing the SEALs to pull back. But their concentrated fire was no longer needed. The PDF inside the hangar were either dead, wounded, or had abandoned resistance.

Sirens warbled unexpectedly at the northern end of the airport as a small convoy of civilian fire trucks and ambulances cautiously approached, their red Mars lights casting a weird glare over the scene of devastation. The SEALs were emotionally and physically spent by the brutal encounter. One young officer stood and languidly waved the terrified firemen forward to extinguish the flaming planes. Another officer shucked out an empty magazine and reloaded his M-16, then nodded brusquely for the Panamanian ambulance crew to enter the shattered PDF positions.

Several SEALs accompanied the civilians into the blasted hangar workshops. There was absolutely no resistance, and no movement other than the thrashing of wounded PDF soldiers, sprawled among the chunks of masonry and shards of glass. There was blood everywhere. The SEALs came back out into the open air and let the Panamanian medics carry on their grim work. As the Americans watched, one ambulance was loaded with dead and another with wounded. One SEAL NCO had the presence of mind to begin collecting wallets and ID cards from the PDF dead.

But then the airport came under sniper fire again, and SEALs scattered to regroup in the dark and return the fire. By the time they had suppressed that sniper, the civilian emergency vehicles had retreated to the relative safety of the nearby streets.

After the airport perimeter had finally been secured, Mike Phillips rushed back to the triage point. The surviving corpsmen worked with silent precision on the wounded. Three dead SEALs—John Connors, Chris Tilghman, and Chief Don McFall—lay side by side on the grass. Ike Rodriguez, the proud new SEAL who had worn his trident for only two days, was bundled in a poncho, hovering near death among the wounded. Corpsman Al Morino lay silently on a stretcher, his entire head swathed in green field dressings already soaked dark with blood. An officer crouched in the darkness nearby, swearing into a radio microphone, demanding an explanation why the promised medevac helicopter had not yet arrived.

The power was out now in this entire section of the city. A parachute flare from the team's mortar popped overhead with a chalky magnesium glare. Phillips stared down at his dead friends. In this bizarre light, the young men's faces were smooth, freed of pain. As if they were sleeping.

# 3

# 20 December 1989

---

# H-Hour: Rio Hato

*0057 Hours, 20 December*

The pilot in Gander One adjusted the contrast of his forward-looking infrared (FLIR) screen, which was the dominant feature, high and in the center, of the relatively austere instrument panel. What the F-117A Stealth cockpit lacked in reassuring old-fashioned "steam gauge" dials, it more than compensated for with the most fully integrated navigation and attack-system avionics in the world. Engineers at Lockheed's Advanced Development Projects—the company's famous "Skunk Works"—had taken the best technology from several operational aircraft systems and combined them in the Stealth fighter's cockpit. In many ways the plane was a pilot-tended computer, with precise navigation data, laser target designation, and pinpoint weapons guidance melded into a single instrument "suite."

Now Gander Lead took full advantage of this system's potential, as he verified the final weapons release coordinates from his programmed mission-plan memory and eased the fly-by-wire side stick slightly forward, adjusting his heading so that his amber aircraft symbol overlapped the computer's flight path among the flickering data blocks on the screen and his airspeed matched the computer's recommendation. Automated systems helped maintain a proper heading for each leg of the mission, but the Stealth pilot manually controlled the engine throttles and trimmed for the required airspeed. And correct speed was an important factor tonight.

Gander Lead was a field grade officer for whom this technology was still spectacular. He often told the younger captains who had just chalked up their qualifying 1,000 hours in fighters and signed on to fly Stealths in the 37th Tactical Fighter Wing (TFW) that their misspent youth in video arcades stood them in good stead. But it was he, not one of the young guys, who was leading the Stealth aircraft into its first combat.[1]

The image on his FLIR screen had the diffuse black-and-white quality of an old TV kinescope recording. The approaching coastline, however, was an actual target, not a late-night rerun of "The Honeymooners." The FLIR used the infrared spectrum instead of visible light. Relatively warm objects, such as masonry and the long concrete Rio Hato runway—radiating solar energy absorbed during daylight—appeared in shades of white and gray. Cooler ditches, fields, and vegetation were grainy black. The blocks of flight data superimposed on the screen were lime green.

The sooty dark Pacific rolled to the bottom of the screen and the mottled grays and blacks of the Rio Hato Military Reservation crept toward the center of his targeting grid. Although still a secret weapon unfamiliar to the public, the F-117A Stealth, the "Nighthawk" to the pilots of the 37th TFW, had been fully operational for six years. Gander Lead and his wingman had practiced hundreds of such nighttime strikes. And with the aid of this reliable technology, putting a 2,000-pound GBU-10 laser-guided bomb into a five-foot target circle was relatively easy. Bombing with a Nighthawk was certainly a lot less challenging than flying the same mission in an F-16 or F-15. Pilots of those aircraft had to hug the earth to avoid detection, then pop up in a high-G maneuver and "toss" their bombs. Invisible to radar, the F-117A could fly straight and level, release its single bomb, then slip into a slow, flat turn, keeping the laser-designator pipper on the target until the bomb rode the beam down to impact.

This was the plan tonight. Gander One and Two would con-

tinue in trail formation, descending to cross the coast above
the eastern edge of the fishing village of El Farallón del Chirú
on a heading of 015 degrees and an altitude of 4,000 feet.
Their orders were to guide two GBU-10s into open ground in
the PDF company areas, near but not on the barracks buildings, a complex of one- and two-story cinder-block buildings
set among a distinctive grove of sea pines. Lead's original target circle—the spot he planned to place his laser designator—was on a parade ground to the left of their flight path.
Gander Two's target was in a field to the right. The purpose
of the strike was to stun and disorient the sleeping PDF just
before the Rangers jumped onto their drop zone along the
runway. The fire-support request from Colonel Kernan, the
commander of the 75th Ranger Regiment, had called for a
strike that would leave the enemy "dizzy and shaken up." But
Gander flight had been ordered to keep their two bombs seaward of the barracks, well clear of the PDF dispensary.

During their final briefing, the commander of the 37th
TFW, Colonel Anthony J. Tolin, had cautioned the pilots to
avoid damage to the dispensary. "It's okay to drop short,"
Tolin had emphasized. "Just make sure you don't drop long."[2]

Dropping the bombs long might needlessly kill young PDF
soldiers, or, worse, possible civilian patients in the dispensary.
Although the pilots were not informed, there was another reason to drop their bombs short: Southcom J-2 had learned
there might be up to 250 teenage cadets training over the
Christmas holidays at the Herrera-Ruiz Military Institute,
which lay a kilometer inland. Dropping a bomb in *that* corner
of the PDF reservation would have been a disaster.

But identifying exact ("zero-meter") aiming coordinates in a
naked stretch of parade ground or field of kuna grass by infrared signature alone was not possible. Instead of an exact target, the pilots would choose spots on the cool, dark
ground—as seen in their infrared instruments—that were the
correct distance short of the barracks, but close enough to produce the desired effect. Unlike any mission the pilots had
trained for, this raid had no specific aiming point; the critical
factor was distance from inhabited buildings.

Fortunately for their peace of mind, they were not aware

this "offset" distance had been the subject of intense debate at the highest levels of the Pentagon. Chairman of the Joint Chiefs of Staff General Colin Powell, himself, had ordered that the offset seaward from the barracks be increased from the originally planned 55 yards to approximately 200 yards. But the pilots obviously *were* aware a key factor in the night's operation was to minimize Panamanian casualties.[3]

The other critical factor was timing. The bombs had to strike only one minute before the Rangers' C-130s swept in from the coast, and only 30 seconds before the AC-130 Spectre gunship engaged the antiaircraft guns dug in beside the runway.

As if these stringent requirements were not enough, there had been an unexpected final adjustment to the targeting as the pilots were preparing to launch from Tonopah. A shift in the forecast wind—from the west, not the northeast—made it preferable for the pilots to swap targets, with Lead hitting the field on the right and Two taking the parade ground to the left. It was possible that smoke from the first bomb might disrupt Two's laser target designator's beam unless this swap was made.

The pilots took all this in stride. They had a quiet discussion on the Tonopah tarmac, agreeing to "pickle" on the other's original target. This was no big deal; they were not overly concerned about the lateral positions of their impact points. The offset seaward was the critical element.[4]

Gander Lead advanced his throttles and trimmed the aircraft to a precise 400 knots. The pilot watched the sparkling infrared constellation of the village's corrugated metal kitchen roofs, still radiating the heat of late suppers, slide past the left corner of his screen. A green thirty-second warning clock appeared at the lower right and began a silent countdown. The white-and-gray infrared images of the PDF military reservation rolled down from the top of the screen. He easily identified the black parade ground near the cool gray mess hall and locked on his pulsing laser designator.

FLIR visibility was good. Gander Lead slid over the ghostly black-and-white sprawl of the PDF barracks area. He had a rock-solid laser lock on the original target in the parade ground and decided not to reverse bomb "pickling" sequence. Now he punched up the correct weapons-release sequence on his keypad and felt the familiar shuttering thump as the bomb-bay doors behind him swung open. The FLIR screen automatically winked to the downward-looking infrared (DLIR) port on the underside of the aircraft's flat lancetip nose. This effortless transition from looking forward to down always pleased Nighthawk pilots, reminding them of their plane's reliable advanced attack system. A blinking hexagon appeared around the laser crosshairs, signaling that the sensor in the bomb's nose had positive acquisition. At the top of the screen the flashing "A" (Acquisition) went to a solid "L" (Lock-on). The bomb's sensor had locked onto the laser beam. Gander Lead clicked the weapons release button on his side stick and immediately forced the plane's nose back to level flight as the aircraft pitched up, freed of its one-ton payload.

He kept his gloved right hand lightly on the stick, easing the plane into a yawing right turn, well clear of the trailing plane, but shallow enough to keep a positive laser lock on the target. The pilot watched the DLIR intently, acutely aware that the first bomb dropped in anger by a Stealth aircraft was about to strike its target.

The GBU-10 was a warm gray dart on the screen. It slashed into the target-lock hexagon and the screen blossomed with white heat. That had been a perfect strike, with the bomb hitting exactly on the laser-designated spot. He had been so intent on achieving the proper seaward offset from the barracks, that he now realized he had bombed well to the left of the flight path and had not, after all, swapped target zones with Two, as they had agreed back at the base. But he saw there wasn't enough wind for smoke to obstruct Two's aiming.

Lead watched his wingman's bomb impact among the pine trees and outbuildings of the 6th Company barracks sector, another silent white blossom on the DLIR. Two's offset distance was also excellent. He was pleased with their performance.

But he and Two couldn't stick around to watch the rest of the fireworks. The blinking clock on his DLIR screen read 0101:34 Local. An AC-130 Spectre gunship followed by an

AH-64 Apache attack helicopter and a couple of AH-6 Little Bird gunships were scheduled to make their runs on the airport. If the PDF actually had any SAM-7 missiles down there, as Southcom J-2 feared, now was when they would light them off. And he sure had no intention of blundering into a stray missile.[5]

## 0102 Hours, 20 December

The four attack helicopters swept down the coast in two flights, only fifteen feet above the line of gentle white surf. Two were dark, rakish AH-64 Apache gunships from Task Force Wolf, a composite unit of the 82d Aviation Brigade. Compared to the fifty-foot-long, ten-ton Apaches, the two AH-6 Little Birds appeared like bumblebees keeping company with giant dragonflies. And as the Apaches cranked open the throttles of their twin engines and went to higher rotor pitch, the slower but more nimble Little Birds banked out to sea and began a slow turn back toward the fishing village west of the Rio Hato military complex.

The Apaches were operating on a demanding schedule and, as with the Stealth pilots, the Army aviators were painfully aware that their expensive, high-technology weapons were about to receive their first combat test. If the previous three weeks were any indicator, that test was not going to go well. Since November, eleven of the task force's Apaches had been transported to Panama from Fort Bragg aboard giant Air Force C-5 Galaxies and hidden in Hangar 1 at Howard Air Force Base. The Apaches flew training missions only at night and were rolled off the tarmac and back into the hangar before dawn each day, so that PDF spies on the base wouldn't learn that the U.S. Army had imported its most powerful helicopter gunship—a considerable upping of the ante in the tense standoff between the Americans and Noriega.

The Apache had been designed as an all-weather, day/night antiarmor gunship, principally for use against the massed tank armadas of the Soviet army in Europe. The gunship was flown by a pilot and a pilot/gunner seated in reinforced "aircrew capsules" in a tandem cockpit. It carried a 30 mm chain gun automatic cannon, slung beneath its protruding "chin," which housed the bulbous sensors and laser of its advanced target acquisition and designation system (TADS). The tips of the Apache's stubby wings mounted cylindrical canisters, each carrying thirty-six 70 mm rockets. Inboard from these canisters hung the gunship's true heavy firepower: two clusters of eight Hellfire laser-guided missiles, capable of destroying the heaviest Soviet tank at ranges of up to two miles.

The Apache had been given self-sealing fuel tanks, protective armor around the tandem cockpit, and a variety of other unique design features (including redundant gear boxes that could run dry for thirty minutes). It was meant to survive in the world's toughest combat environment. But the tropical heat and humidity of Panama soon played havoc with the Apache's computerized avionics. And there was an unexpected rash of engine and control subsystem failures, which put a punishing workload on maintenance personnel. During the weeks of Sand Flea and Purple Storm exercises, the number of inoperable aircraft often equaled the "up birds." The hardpressed maintenance crews developed ingenious and unorthodox remedies to the persistent equipment failures. They eventually resorted to the expedient of heating the Apaches' optical and infrared sensor electronics in ovens.[6]

Many Army aviators quietly worried that the state-of-the-art Apache simply would not pass muster in a small-scale tropical war.

The night of D-day that apprehension seemed well founded. As the pair of Task Force Wolf Apaches assigned to Rio Hato warmed up on the blacked-out ramp at Howard Air Force Base, the number two bird suffered a hydraulic-pump failure and was grounded. A replacement aircraft was quickly assigned to the flight, but the pilots in the two helicopters knew the important first combat mission was off to a shaky start.

And they also knew that a complete mission failure would be disastrous. Their task was to "prep" the Rio Hato drop zone, sweeping across the airfield below treetop level thirty seconds before the first Ranger airdrop C-130 roared in from the sea at 500 feet. The Apaches were ordered to attack the three ZPU-4 14.5 mm antiaircraft gun sites dug in along the runway, then continue inland to the PDF's 6th Mechanized Rifle Company's motor pool to attack the V-300 and V-150 armored cars. If the gunships failed, the Rangers' aircraft might easily be blasted from the sky. The four-barreled ZPU antiaircraft guns put out a high volume of fire and had an effective vertical range of 1,400 meters. They could lace the air space above the runway with a devastating barrage of fire, shooting down the lumbering C-130s and killing scores of Rangers in their parachute harnesses. The 6th Company's armored vehicles were just as dangerous. If they broke free to race down the runway after the airdrop, the machine guns on the smaller V-150s and the 90 mm cannon on the larger V-300 would massacre the Rangers on the drop zone.

The PDF troops concentrated at Rio Hato were part of Noriega's best-trained and most loyal forces, which also included Battalion 2000, stationed at Fort Cimarron, east of Panama City. Task Force South commander, Lieutenant General Carl W. Stiner, definitely had these assets in mind when he asked that the F-117A Stealth fighters and the Apaches be given part of the fire-support mission at Rio Hato. Stiner was a longtime Airborne Ranger and he didn't want to see these elite forces slaughtered by their elite, better armed PDF counterparts during the crucial minutes of the airdrop when they were most vulnerable. And there was another dangerous uncertainty at Rio Hato and at other key PDF objectives across the country. General Schneider's Southcom J-2 shop had had persistent but unconfirmed reports that Noriega had received a shipment of advanced Soviet-built SAM-7 Grail Mod 2 or SAM-16 shoulder-fired antiaircraft missiles from either the Cubans or the Nicaraguan Sandinistas. If Rio Hato were defended with numbers of these advanced missiles, the Rangers' air column would be in serious trouble.

To increase the chances of success, Stiner had assigned an AC-130 Spectre gunship from the 1st Special Operations Wing (SOW) to back up the Apaches and Little Birds. The Apaches' first priority was to destroy the ZPUs. And the Little Birds were to take out any PDF missile troops who showed themselves. But none of these fire-support aircraft could be safely used if the PDF managed to break free of their barracks compounds and mix it up on the drop zone with the Rangers.

The two Apaches clattered over the palm-thatch beach cabanas and the cantina at Santa Clara, their rotor wash blowing down a newly planted shade palm and scattering a pile of rickety tables under the cantina's corrugated roof. Each pilot wore ANVIS-6 night-vision goggles mounted on his aviator's helmet. In the forward cockpits, the pilot/gunners hunched intently over their rectangular TADS screens watching the ghostly green landscape rushing toward them at 140 knots. The gunships popped over the low bluff at Punta La Peña, cleared a stand of acacia trees by inches, and flew up the long runway, searching for targets.

Tiny PDF soldiers, some still pulling on their shirts and web gear, trotted across the grassy margins of the runway from the barracks area. A few were already in sandbagged trench positions near the control tower. They cut loose with AK-47 assault rifles, sending bursts of green tracers wildly toward the sound of the approaching helicopters. The Apache gunners ignored them, scanning instead for the heavy antiaircraft machine guns. The three mobile ZPU-4 antiaircraft guns were reasonably well hidden to the left of the runway. Each of the four-wheeled gun carts was set in a low sand-bagged position. The lead Apache banked right to engage the gun at the far end of the runway, while the second Apache slid left to take on the first gun. With stabbing tongues of flame, the Apaches' 30 mm chain guns erupted. A PDF soldier was frantically traversing the first ZPU when he was caught by the second Apache's initial burst. The man was blown into several bleeding chunks, which were thrown completely out of the gun position by the blast of cannon fire.[7]

But as the Apache flared to a slow hover to engage the second ZPU, 200 meters down the runway, the pilot/gunner's TADS imagery screen flickered and went dead. The multimillion dollar attack helicopter was suddenly defenseless. Luckily, no one was manning the second ZPU. The gunship banked sharp right and broke for safer ground, while the pilot/gunner in the forward cockpit worked desperately to bring his weapons system back to life.

The lead airdrop C-130 was due across the drop zone threshold in less than thirty seconds, and there was still an undamaged ZPU along the runway. But the first Apache was already at the airport's northern perimeter, having been unable to locate any PDF armored vehicles out in the open. The pilot's orders were to stay clear of the drop zone until the almost 850 Rangers had jumped. As the lead Apache sped north above the scrub brush to rendezvous with the other chopper gunship, the crew looked back to see the airport sparkling with streams of red and green tracers. PDF troops were rushing from the barracks area now, firing out to sea at the rumbling noise of the approaching aircraft column.

The crew of Air Papa 03, the AC-130 Spectre flying a tight oval holding pattern east of Rio Hato, watched the two Apaches swing right and clear the runway. The upper fuselages of both helicopters were marked with a recognition pattern in silvery glint tape that showed up well in the Spectre's FLIR target-acquisition sensors and in the aircraft's low-light television sights. Every American helicopter flying that night had similar markings. Southcom feared Noriega might attempt an escape aboard a PDF UH-1 Huey or a smaller military helicopter. So the 1st SOW's Spectres had orders to shoot down any chopper not wearing the correct recognition stripes.

Air Papa 03's fire-control officer sat at a console beside a senior NCO in a darkened cubicle forward in the Spectre's wide cargo compartment. Using a computerized target designator, he moved the cursor controlling the Spectre's long 105 mm howitzer across the image of the Rio Hato runway.

"We've got a live one on that first ZPU, skipper," he said into his headset, informing the aircraft commander on the flight deck that the miniature figure of a PDF soldier had just dashed from cover to mount the firing saddle of the first gun position. The officer bracketed the enemy soldier with the crosshairs of his laser rangefinder that was superimposed on the low-light television screen. The man must have heard the

Apaches clear the airport perimeter as well as the drone of the approaching drop aircraft. He was a brave but foolish soldier.

At this range, Air Papa's fire-control officer could have employed either the twin 20 mm Vulcan Gatling guns mounted forward in the left fuselage, the 40 mm Bofors further aft, or the big long-barreled howitzer. He chose the number six gun, the 105 mm howitzer. The NCO beside him at the fire-control console flipped switches to lock the weapon's laser target designator onto the ZPU. Acutely aware of the approaching airdrop, the fire-control officer forced himself to verify his sight and make sure the master computer approved the fire request.

"Okay," he finally said, releasing his thumb from the safety button on his console. The big cannon cracked with its distinctive hollow roar. Two seconds later, the open sandbagged firing position and the jutting angles of the four-barreled ZPU disappeared in a silent flash. When the officer's screen cleared again, there was only a smoking hole where the gun position had stood.[8]

The Spectre banked gently right to take up its holding station. Air Papa 03 had done all it could to prep the drop zone. Neither the Spectre nor the Apaches could approach the airport perimeter again until the Rangers were on the ground and their Air Force combat control "Colt" team issued formal fire requests.

## 0103 Hours, 20 December

Colonel Buck Kernan stood halfway down the long line of the port stick of jumpers. He heard the C-130's engine pitch soften once again. Out an oval porthole he saw a dull green flash that marked the partially obscured lighthouse on Isla Farallo. They were a thousand meters from the end of the runway, cruising along quietly at 110 knots, just 500 feet above the dark water. This was one of the smoothest rides Kernan had ever had in an airplane, certainly the gentlest lift to a drop zone.

Before leaving Lawson Army Airfield at Fort Benning, Kernan had issued specific instructions to the Air Force colonel commanding the troop carrier planes. "I don't care if you give us a late green light on the drop zone," he'd said. "Just don't give us an early one." He'd pointed at the heavily laden Rangers trudging through the freezing rain up the ramps of the C-130s. "We can walk a lot easier than we can swim."

Wedged in among the jumpers, his left arm cocked with his fist around his static line, Kernan caught another glimpse of green. But these flashes were not the dull loom of a coastal navigation beacon. They were tracers. He stooped to look ahead through the porthole. The sky was cut with ribbons of red and green tracers. The lead chalks were over the DZ, the drop zone, right in the middle of all that enemy fire. For a moment he felt a pang of compassion for the young soldiers and airmen four planes ahead of him in the column, who were catching the worst of the PDF fire.

Then the quiet, whistling ride through the darkness was broken by the metallic clang of small arms striking the wings and fuselage around him. The lighter rounds sounded like hail on the roof of a car in a bad Georgia thunderstorm. The heavier stuff was like somebody banging on your roof with a crowbar.

Six years earlier at Point Salines on Grenada, Air Force C-130 pilots had broken off their approach to the drop zone when the planes carrying Rangers had encountered similar groundfire. But none of the C-130s in this air column were breaking.

"Move up to the door!" the jumpmaster shouted. The stick shuffled aft.


Staff Sergeant Louis Olivera was the jumpmaster on the first chalk. He gripped the sides of the gaping door, his boots together, his knees flexed and touching, his chin tucked low so that his Kevlar helmet protected his forehead and neck. The grassy expanse of Rio Hato airport rolled past the open door. The prop blast roared as it always did, even with the engines throttled back and the door spoiler correctly deployed. Orange and green tracers floated through the night, lazy near the ground but slashing crazily past the aircraft. He saw three small-arm rounds hit the trailing edge of the starboard wing, a dozen more flew past his face. The plane's tail was hammered.

"Hot DZ," Olivera yelled. "They know we're coming."

The red light beside him flashed twice, then went green. He was out the door. Burdened with a rucksack full of munitions slung beneath his reserve chute, his M-16 in a weapons pouch clipped to the left side of his harness, and the cold tube of an AT-4 rocket clipped on the right, Olivera knew that his exit position was not perfect. But there was nothing he could do to correct it. Jumping at 500 feet, he had perhaps a quarter of a second to pull his reserve if his main canopy did not deploy properly.

Good Airborne Ranger that he was, Olivera silently counted his One Thousand-One, One Thousand-Two . . . waiting for the familiar jolt of his main opening. He felt the risers twanging and heard the distant elastic boom of the canopy. He had a good chute. The ground suddenly tilted below him. Hot tracers flew at wild angles in the dark. Then he went through the treetops and bounced hard against a power line. His helmet protected his head. But his neck felt wrenched. And the AT-4 had banged hard against his right leg, painfully injuring his knee. He hung in his harness between two girdered power-line towers. Jumpers were dropping through the darkness nearby, crashing through the trees and into the ground. Olivera swung in his harness, his canopy firmly anchored in the wires overhead.

His ears cleared and he heard the snap and dry tapping of small arms, then the heavier rattle of automatic weapons. Despite the burning pain in his right knee, Olivera reached up and hit his canopy releases, and dropped ten feet to the muddy ground below. He tore open his weapons pouch and shucked off the harness. Working with desperate speed, he unclipped his rucksack, slung it on and dragged out his radio. With this injured leg he was going to need help. He knew from these power lines and trees that he had landed left of the trailing edge of the drop zone. He suspected he was on the enemy side of the runway, close to the 2d Battalion's first objective, the 6th and 7th PDF companies' barracks. As the first man out the door, he had been the first to land, which meant the rest of the chalk was probably further east.

As Olivera tried to raise someone from C Company on the radio, he heard a helicopter whine low overhead. Then the trees around him snapped and sparkled with incoming machine-gun fire. He definitely was in an enemy sector, and that chopper was coming back for a second firing pass.

Sergeant Olivera jammed his radio back into the pouch on his web gear, shouldered his pack, and hobbled as fast as he could through the trees, in the direction he hoped led toward the main body of the regiment.

His knee was badly dislocated, burning with pain. But he used the AT-4 tube as a makeshift cane as he thrashed through the branches. The sound of firing, both AK assault rifles and the sharper crack of M-16s, echoed all around him. When he was about 300 meters into the trees, Olivera could no longer hear the helicopter gunship overhead. He planned to stop in another minute and try to raise someone on the radio.

The brush ahead flamed with muzzle flashes. Some kind of sledgehammer pounded his left shoulder, flipping him backward. Olivera heard the breath blow out of his lungs. The darkness went white. He shook his head to clear his vision. He had been hit twice by an AK assault rifle. Sprawled on the ground, Olivera looked up at the legs of Panamanian soldiers trotting toward him across the dead leaves and twigs. Hands flipped him over. His rucksack was gone. They were speaking Spanish, but it was hard to understand. Someone had his rifle. He looked up and saw the muzzle of a stubby AK-74 moving toward his face. There was another flash. And that was all he saw.

The two sticks on chalk Number Five were almost out the doors. Sergeant Tom Whelling was third from the last in the port stick. The belly of the plane and the wings were snapping with small-arms hits. Whelling kept his right hand cocked on his static line and shuffled doggedly ahead, humping his heavy rucksack across his knees. Then Plexiglas snapped beside him and he was on his knees.

"I'm hit!" he tried to shout, but his voice emerged in a fluid wheeze. The round had broken ribs and collapsed one lung. He tried to move, but his legs were far away. The two men behind him did not hesitate. They unsnapped their static lines, stumbled across Whelling's sprawled body, and hooked up again to the swaying anchor cable overhead. They didn't have time to verify their static-line clips before they were out the door. If the clips were not fully locked, they were dead men.

Colonel Buck Kernan was out the door and in the dark prop blast. His canopy opened fast and he swung beneath it, watching the bright strings of tracers gliding through the night. He had maybe ten seconds to view the drop zone. As he had hoped, the "shot pattern" of jumpers was grouped tightly along the right edge of the runway, with only a few chutes drifting toward the trees to the left. No matter what happened in the minutes and hours ahead, he knew that his decision to drop the regiment with plain-canopy, unsteerable T-10 main parachutes instead of the newer MC1-1Bs had been correct. The Dash-1 was a good chute, probably safer than the old T-10, but the newer chute had two toggle lines that allowed the jumper to steer the canopy. With this amount of fire coming up, the younger kids would have probably been steering into each other. And there was no way to recover from a collapsed canopy at this low altitude.

There was certainly plenty of enemy fire coming up, but he saw no long, distinctive muzzle flames from four-barreled ZPUs. And he was able to note several bursts of candy-red tracer fire from the right forward edge of the drop zone. That would be the Rangers' M-60 machine guns, already returning fire.

Kernan was so intent on observing his battlefield that he didn't see the curved steel lamp post beneath him. His canopy snagged and he jerked like a yo-yo on a string, his boots dangling in the darkness.

In the smoky, flashing night, he knew immediately where he was: near a PDF training and recreation complex replete with a stylized thatch-roofed campesino village and a circular, low-walled equestrian arena the Intel people had dubbed the "Bullring." Kernan stared down at the ground. It was difficult to judge exactly how high he was, so instead of popping the Capewell riser releases and dropping free, he carefully un-slung his weapons pouch and reserve and slipped free of his entire harness. He was prepared to tuck into a proper para-chute landing fall, but his boot toes had already touched the wet grass. Kernan had been hanging only inches above the ground.

He flipped off the safety of his M-16 and began searching for his headquarters unit. It was time to go to work.

Command Sergeant Major Thomas Duke crashed through the peaked thatch roof of one of the PDF training village's *ranchitos*. The hardwood twigs and dried palm thatch broke his fall, but it also slashed his exposed hands and face.

"Shit," he swore, trying to free himself of the jumble of shroud lines and thatch.

The small circular enclosure was dark and cloudy with musty dust from the shattered roof. As Duke struggled with his gear, a chubby figure in white T-shirt and boxer shorts rolled from the far side of a cot and bolted clumsily for the open door. Duke was grappling to free his pistol when the man disappeared into the darkness. The bastard had taken refuge here when the fighting started and obviously had not expected an American paratrooper to come crashing through the roof.

Just as Sergeant Major Duke broke free of his harness and the roofing, a Ranger lunged into the hut, his M-16 leveled into the darkness.

"Don't shoot, for Christ sake," Duke bellowed. "It's me in here."

The young soldier stuttered an apology and lowered his weapon. If faced with the choice of encountering an armed enemy or an angry command sergeant major, the Ranger would have definitely preferred the former.

Some men in the later chalks hit hard on the asphalt parking ramps on the right side of the runway. Still shaking out their risers to check their canopies, the Rangers crashed into the pavement, completely unprepared for impact, their ammo-heavy rucksacks smashing down into their legs. Several men had broken ankles. One Ranger had two broken ankles and a smashed knee. The injured men shucked off their rucksacks, discarded their extraneous equipment, and crawled toward their assembly areas. No one in the regiment would have expected or requested a medic or a stretcher bearer. They could still guard the perimeter, even though they couldn't walk or run. And they certainly did not want to slow down the rest of the unit.

Sergeant Dan Brown smashed into the ground so hard that he was certain he'd been hit. (This is not his real name. "Brown" is now training for Special Operations and prefers to remain anonymous.) He lay on his side, pulsing green spots dancing before his eyes. When he tried to breathe, no air came. After what seemed a long time, his vision cleared and the dancing spots were replaced by real tracers snapping overhead. He could breathe again. He unclipped his harness and checked his limbs for fractures. Everything seemed intact. Around him, men were shouting and automatic fire rattled. He pulled himself to his knees and struggled with his rucksack. This was the heaviest load he had ever carried, fully 140 pounds. Brown had eight thirty-round magazines for his M-16, several blocks of C-4 plastic explosive, two belts of M-60 ammunition, a LAW antitank rocket, and assorted grenades, radio batteries, and canteens.

He knelt over his pack, shaking his head to better clear his vision. His Kevlar helmet had protected him from a skull fracture, although he knew he probably had a light concussion. But that could not slow him down. Brown bent deeply to pull on his rucksack and jerked to his feet. Men were running through the night, shouting softly and pointing down the runway. He turned to follow them.

Parachutes lay everywhere, long shiny green blankets. It would have been nice to curl up and sleep for a while. But the men were shouting louder. Far down the runway, he saw dark objects moving with a smooth mechanical flow.

"Fucking PCs," a man yelled beside him.

Now Brown's brain was fully alert. Three enemy V-150 armored personnel carriers were moving past a low cluster of concrete buildings and turning toward them. Although it seemed completely improbable, the vehicles seemed to be flashing directional signal lights. Brown heard the distinctive roar of diesel engines.

"Where's the air?" another man yelled.

But Brown saw the enemy armored was too close for the air support to safely engage. A platoon sergeant trotted by, passing out squat AT-4 rockets, like a coach on a playground distributing sports equipment. The men needed no further orders. Each Ranger squatted to strip back the safety tabs of his missile, then rose to one knee to aim the weapons.

As the three enemy vehicles roared toward them, the improvised Ranger antitank squad cut loose with their weapons. There was only one miss in the volley. Two V-150s flashed with impacts. A flaming tire, blasted free of its vehicle, careened across the grass. Smoke roiled around the column. The surviving APC jerked and darted away from the runway. A pursuing helicopter roared overhead.

Brown stumbled beneath his load and turned back toward the assembly point for his original objective, the fenced compounds of the 7th PDF Company.


One young Ranger dropped onto the lanes of the Inter-American Highway, which crossed the Rio Hato runway between two traffic gates. As his canopy collapsed around him, a green pickup truck with three fleeing PDF soldiers raced past. The truck's rear bumper caught the man's parachute canopy and dragged him bumping and screaming along the rough pavement.

Just as he managed to pop his Capewell riser releases, he saw a Ranger stride free of the tall kuna grass and stand in the truck's headlights, leveling a LAW at the vehicle. The rocket blasted into the cab to explode with a doomsday blast.

The Ranger on the pavement low-crawled away from the flaming truck. It wasn't until much later that he noticed that the skin and flesh on the backs of his knuckles had been scraped down to the white, bleeding bone.


Private First Class John Mark Price jumped with his fire team from A Company, 2d Battalion. As the men cleared the door, the aircraft was struck by interlocking streams of groundfire. Several rounds cut into Price's taut static line, severing the yellow band. He plunged feet first through the slipstream. At 500 feet, he didn't have time to complete his main canopy count before the dark ground swallowed him.

# 4

# 20 December 1989

—

# H-Hour: Task Force Pacific

*0046 Hours, 20 December*

Telephones and stuttering teleprinters were the loudest sounds in the stuffy Southcom operations center deep inside the tunnel. The officers seated around Lieutenant Colonel Jerry Murguia *felt,* rather than actually heard, the thump and rumble of heavy weapons below Quarry Heights. Overall, the atmosphere in the command post was amazingly calm. They had all lived in crisis mode for so many months that the execution of the actual operation seemed almost routine. But Murguia knew that the military dependents from Quarry Heights who were crowded into the outer tunnel had to be scared and uncomfortable. Sleepy little kids and their nervous mothers were jammed three- and four-deep on the rubber tile floor along the southern wall, leaving a narrow path for messengers. The hot exhaust of the air conditioners in the crypto room vented directly onto this unlikely group of refugees.

At least the Quarry Heights dependents were safer than the families—including his own—who were about to come under fire at Fort Amador. Murguia knew this was going to be a night of unique and dangerous events. Almost unnoticed, one of the most singular episodes of D-day had already taken place at Fort Clayton. The command post had received confirmation that the new government of the Republic of Panama had just been sworn in by the country's chief justice in a windowless

92

basement room at Clayton's Building 95. President Guillermo Endara and First Vice Presidents Ricardo Arias Calderón and Billy "Pico Gallo" Ford were taking the oath of office seven months late and on soil that was technically not yet even part of Panama. Instead of an honor guard of brightly uniformed Panamanian soldiers, the ceremony was protected by heavily armed, nervous young American MPs in camouflage flak jackets. But the occasion was more than ceremonial. By sponsoring and endorsing the installation of Noriega's opposition, who had been duly elected in May but brutally prevented from taking office, the United States had officially cast its lot with the new nominal government of Panama.

This meant there could be no compromise in Operation Blue Spoon short of total victory. Everyone at Southcom certainly hoped that the operation would unfold smoothly, and that the massive use of American force would quickly subdue the PDF without heavy casualties on either side. But even if resistance was stronger than expected, or if Noriega managed to rally his supporters for prolonged guerrilla warfare in the hills, the die was now cast. There was no going halfway on this one. There would be no more back-room negotiations with Noriega, and certainly no cease-fire with the PDF still intact. This was to be a decisive military action, not the muddled gradualism of Vietnam or the clumsy use of an understrength token force as with the ill-fated Marine deployment to Lebanon. Nor would the Panama invasion suffer from the botched and hasty preparation that had plagued Urgent Fury, the "hip pocket" operation in Grenada. Indeed, the collective memory of Vietnam, Desert One (the failed Iranian hostage rescue), Lebanon, and the embarrassing Pyrrhic victory in Grenada was prominent in the minds of the officers who planned Blue Spoon. Those familiar with the OPLAN were confident that it would succeed. The only question remaining was the ultimate cost of the victory.

Jerry Murguia was forced to forget about these political considerations. He became preoccupied with the movement of multiple strike task forces from their staging areas to lines of departure all across the former Canal Zone and at other key objectives around Panama City and Colon. There were twenty-seven of these combat task forces, most of which combined conventional ground forces with transport and attack helicopters; several of the key offensive units had dedicated Spectre gunships flying air support. Six Special Operations teams, supported by helicopters from the Army's 160th Special Operations Aviation Group, were also striking at H-hour.

The combat task forces in Colon and Panama City followed a basic operational concept. Their mission was to first fix the enemy forces in place by surrounding key PDF installations such as the Comandancia, Departamento Nacional de Investigacion (DENI) stations, and fortified barracks. Then the American troops—many assisted by Psychological Operations teams—would offer the PDF the opportunity to surrender. If the enemy did not respond, unit commanders had the authority to unleash "firepower demonstrations," escalating up to the use of howitzers, if necessary. If the enemy still resisted, the American forces would assault and clear their objectives, following standard artillery or air-support "preparation" of the enemy facility. Naturally, American forces were free at all times to return fire to defend themselves. And, in the event the PDF did shoot first, heavy American firepower would be employed to devastating effect, not simply as a demonstration.[1]

In principle, this approach would fulfill Blue Spoon's goals of decapitating and neutralizing the PDF with minimal casualties and damage to military installations and civilian neighborhoods.

The Operation Blue Spoon Rules of Engagement were the strictest ever imposed. General Thurman had insisted that fire support be used judiciously. Only a field grade officer, preferably a battalion commander, could authorize indirect fire from howitzers or mortars. General Stiner himself had the sole authority of authorizing air strikes from the Air Force A-7 and A-37 fixed-wing attack jets now orbiting in strike packages high above the Canal.

Murguia studied the wide computer printout of his Execution Checklist, logging the times of the "lift up" calls from the helicopter units carrying troops from Fort Kobbe across the Canal, Fort Sherman on the Atlantic side, and from the Special

Operations Task Force at Hangar 3 on Howard Air Force Base. He also logged the latest position reports from the Rangers' airdrop columns converging on Rio Hato and Tocumen-Torrijos Airfield.

The Rangers were right on schedule. But a full brigade of the 82d Airborne Division—the combat muscle of Task Force Pacific—was hopelessly delayed. One of the worst ice storms in recent years was sweeping across the southern United States, and had struck with disastrous effect at Pope Air Force Base, adjacent to Fort Bragg, North Carolina. Almost 3,000 82d Airborne troops were rigged out, ready to board their C-141 Starlifters. But the airlift was stalled on the ground due to limited deicing equipment; only a few planes at a time could be deiced for takeoff. Major General James H. Johnson, the division commander, had requested a one-hour delay in departure, which would have meant the brigade's airdrop at Tocumen-Torrijos Airfield also being delayed by an hour. General Stiner had denied the request, so Johnson had been forced to compromise. At 2230 hours, he had reported to Stiner that, "Eight (8) pax A/C are up (chalks 1–6, 9, 10); all heavy equipment A/C are up. All Bn and Bde Cdrs are airborne. The lift of eight will make the original TOT of 0145. . . ." Only eight of Johnson's twenty Starlifters (plus heavy equipment drop planes) would unload on the Torrijos drop zone forty-five minutes after H-hour, their original time on target (TOT). The eight "chalks" would contain all the battalion and brigade command groups, but the bulk of the division's combat force would come straggling in as the aircraft were deiced at Pope and formed up into serials.[2]

Whatever happened, the Rangers were going to seize Tocumen-Torrijos before the 82d dropped. The airport was only a staging area for the division's air assaults on three important PDF/Dignity Battalion strongholds, Panama Viejo, Tinajitas, and Fort Cimarron. Once the paratroopers assembled on the runways, they'd be picked up by helicopters from Task Force Aviation. The assault plan Johnson and Stiner had so carefully devised called for the 82d's paratroopers to hit their landing zones at these objectives well before dawn. Obviously, they weren't going to keep that schedule. This meant troop-carrier helicopters escorted by Apache gunships and covered by AC-130 Spectres were going to hit hot LZs in daylight. The potential for American and Panamanian casualties was high.

At least the first helicopter lifts of the operation were under way on schedule. By Murguia's count, there were almost 120 blacked-out helicopters, flown by pilots wearing night-vision goggles, now moving through the darkness along carefully selected air corridors on both sides of the canal. They were restricted to altitudes below 1,000 feet. The air space above them was reserved for fixed-wing aircraft. In theory, all this movement would flow smoothly.

But Southcom had never been able to rehearse this massive airlift under combat conditions. There was a serious potential for disastrous midair collisions, especially around objectives where helicopter gunships were prepping targets just ahead of converging troop carrier helicopters. No one had ever attempted such a coordinated night air assault before, although darkness was essential to the success. Noriega's PDF was well equipped with modern Soviet bloc antiaircraft artillery (AAA), including multibarrel ZPU 14.5 mm and, reportedly, 23 mm guns. The American military's experience in Grenada against similar weapons had made it amply clear that daytime helicopter air assaults or airdrops on objectives defended by such weapons meant disaster.

The PDF, however, had no night-vision equipment and had not trained extensively for night air defense. So, theoretically, the huge airlift now under way was protected by the overcast tropical night. But there remained the nagging uncertainty about surface-to-air-missiles, SAMs. After the first failed coup in February 1988, Noriega had opened the door to Cuban military advisers. Beyond their shopworn revolutionary fervor, the Cubans had brought with them plane- and shiploads of hardware. And Southcom's J-2 shop had so far been unable to determine whether this arms buildup included sophisticated, Soviet-made missiles. Acting on Soviet orders, the Cubans were known to have distributed large quantities of shoulder-fired SAM-14s to the Nicaragua Sandinistas, who in turn peddled the SAMs to leftist FMLN querrillas in El Salvador. And during the guerrilla offensive there in November, the FMLN had shot down several Salvadoran planes and helicopters.[3]

Army Intelligence and the CIA station in Panama had confirmed that the PDF had received several planeloads of suspicious Cuban hardware since the last failed coup attempt in October. Agent reports stated some of the long crates unloaded at Tocumen and Rio Hato had been prominently stenciled in English: "Drilling Equipment" or "Surveying Instruments," a recognized Soviet deception technique, which had been used to mask shipments of SAMs elsewhere in the Third World. These missiles were a great equalizer for Third World troops. Armed with either modified SAM-7s or the newer SAM-14s, soldiers on the ground did not need sophisticated night-vision devices to spot blacked-out enemy aircraft. The heat-seeking infrared sensor in the modernized SAM easily acquired low-flying helicopters, and gave the missile man a simple audio warning of approaching aircraft. Once fired, these modified missiles could discriminate between the heat sources of turbine engines and the spurious infrared decoys of flares. If the PDF had been secretly equipped with SAMs, American helicopters might start exploding at any moment.

Southcom's low casualty estimate would not survive the first missile. And the only way to suppress modern air defenses would be through massive air and artillery strikes, which in turn would provoke unacceptable "collateral damage" among Panamanian civilians. SAMs were the principal worry among the senior officers seated at tables in the crowded command post.[4]

In fact, some Southcom officers had considered the PDF's potential SAM threat a valid reason to execute Blue Spoon sooner rather than later. If America had waited after Lieutenant Paz's killing, Noriega's Cuban advisers might have distributed SAMs and quickly trained PDF and Digbat troops to use them. Although no one was comfortable discussing the matter, if the Macho de Monte hadn't provided an acceptable pretext for intervention by killing Lieutenant Paz, Southcom might have had to force the issue.

At the surrounding tables in the command post, officers spoke with quiet precision into red scrambler phones and the heavy green handsets of the tactical net. Status reports from the disparate units were flowing in steadily now. But General Thurman's carefully structured communications pyramid filtered out distracting, irrelevant messages. Joint Task Force South at Fort Clayton was not required to request authority from Thurman or General Bill Hartzog for every minor adjustment in the OPLAN. General Stiner's command post simply kept Southcom informed that progress on the Execution Checklist was proceeding.

Had any SAMs been fired, Stiner would have informed Thurman at once. The lack of such a report was the best news so far that evening. And Max Thurman believed in passing on good news. His isolated single line to the Pentagon's National Command Center was kept open. Thurman's philosophy was to keep his superiors constantly informed of the operation's progress, so that they didn't have to pull information from the lower command. Once the Joint Chiefs started along that path, Thurman had told his staff, the command would be quickly inundated with irrelevant, mundane questions and would be bogged down chasing minute details. Colonel George Compton or Colonel George Monroe took turns passing on status reports from the Blue Spoon checklist to Lieutenant General Tom Kelly, the Operations Officer for the Joint Chiefs of Staff. During the first Southcom status reports, Murguia only heard Kelly's voice on the speaker phone tersely acknowledging the information. But as the operation progressed, he heard Secretary of Defense Dick Cheney's carefully phrased questions and General Colin Powell's occasional brief clarifications. At no point did he hear the voice of President George Bush or National Security Adviser Brent Scowcroft.

The word in the Southcom command post was that President Bush was at home in bed. Unlike other recent commanders in chief, George Bush had faith in his generals and their professional staff who had written a workable war plan. So he was letting them fight their own war.

The only unexpected Washington intervention had come earlier, when the staff assembled in the command post was shuffling their schedules to accommodate the advanced H-hour. An officer passed a sheet of yellow paper down the operations table that noted the Pentagon had just decided to rename Blue Spoon "Operation Just Cause."

To the officers sweating over their checklists, Tac phones, and maps, however, the name change meant little. Washington politics were a remote distraction. Here on the ground there were desperate battles being fought, and whether or not the American cause was just, was irrelevant to their outcome.

## 0055 Hours, 20 December

The parallel columns of blacked-out aircraft descended over the dark mud flats and banked left across the Panama Bay. There were twelve C-141 Starlifters and four C-130s in the two serials. On board the eleven airdrop planes were 731 jumpers. They included a small headquarters group of the 75th Rangers, as well as the regiment's 1st Battalion, reinforced by Charlie Company of the 3d Battalion. Men from the 4th Psychological Operations Group, the 96th Civil Affairs Battalion, a medical augmentation "package," and an Air Force Combat Control Team were jumping with the Rangers.

The other five aircraft carried heavy drop equipment. Most of this was standard military communications vans and ambulances. But the five Starlifters also carried the Rangers' gun jeeps mounted with laser-sighted 90 mm recoilless rifles and the combat motorcycles of the jeeps' outriders. This heavy equipment would be parachuted from 800 feet into the southern drop zone at the objective, Torrijos-Tocumen Airfield, eighteen miles east of Panama City.

The Rangers and their augmentation teams had been carefully crossloaded aboard the planes at Hunter Army Airfield near Fort Stewart, Georgia. They would jump at 500 feet in a precisely timed pattern. The northern drop zone straddled the long runway of Tocumen Air Base. The other drop zone ran between the parallel runways of Omar Torrijos International Airport, just to the south of Tocumen on the sprawling airfield complex. Like the Rangers at Rio Hato, the reinforced 1st Battalion's mission was to seize the enemy airfield, eliminate PDF resistance, and defend it against counterattack. But unlike the

Rio Hato task force, the Rangers jumping on this objective were under an extremely tight operation schedule.

They had only forty-three minutes to neutralize the estimated 200 men of the 2d PDF Rifle Company, the 150 Panamanian Air Force personnel, and the reported thirty armed security guards at the Torrijos civilian terminal. Above all, the Rangers had to be certain to eliminate PDF air defense weapons and to secure the airfield's perimeter against enemy reinforcements. A brigade of the 82d Airborne was scheduled to drop inside the Torrijos perimeter, beginning at H+45 minutes. Considering the fact that there were an estimated 380 armed enemy troops on the big objective and less than 750 Rangers, the normal doctrine of a two-to-one numerical advantage for the attacking troops would not apply.

But it rarely did with Rangers. What we lack in numbers, Lieutenant Colonel Bob Wagner, commander of the 1st Battalion, always told his men, Rangers make up in skill, discipline, and fighting spirit. The element of surprise was usually on their side as well. However, as Wagner stood in the open left-hand door of the lead chalk, staring across the dark water at the distant skyline of Panama City, he knew surprise was no longer an option. The unmistakable orange flash of exploding ordnance and roiling columns of flame were visible around the dark base of Quarry Heights. Like so many officers in this operation, Wagner had served in Panama before, as commander of the 1st Battalion, 508th Infantry, stationed at Fort Kobbe across the Canal. He knew his old outfit was part of the task force attacking the Comandancia. And from what he could see, the fighting there had already started.

The slipstream keened through the perforated spoilers on the forward edge of the door. He felt the aircraft bank again and settle onto its final heading for the run in. Out in front of them, the sparkling yellow webs of village and shantytown lights ringed the open airport compound. He recognized the amber necklace of runway lights and the floodlit parking lots and ramps of the civilian terminal. It looked as if they were on final approach to a modern Stateside airport in peacetime. But he knew their AC-130 Spectre and AH-6 Little Bird fire support gunships were sweeping the airport, two minutes ahead of the lead chalk. Then the runway and terminal lights went black. The Spectre had done its job. The dark ground ahead was laced with stabbing red muzzle flashes. Tracers rose in silent spirals. The PDF was waiting for them.

As the C-141 Starlifters of the 437th Military Airlift Wing (MAW) descended onto the base leg of their approach to the Tocumen-Torrijos drop zones, an officer on an orbiting Airborne Command, Control, and Communications plane (ABCCC) requested that the parallel serials "squawk" Identification Friend or Foe on a secure frequency. This was a vital safety requirement to make sure the airdrop planes were not inadvertently entering a sector already occupied by combat helicopters.

The secure IFF squawk was standard procedure. But, as often happens in modern war, a minor technical detail almost provoked disaster. The IFF frequency the Starlifters were told to squawk was *not* secure. The second they transmitted, the civilian air traffic control radar at the Torrijos International Airport terminal blossomed with sixteen pulsing data blocks in two unmistakably military parallel formations.

*"Madre de Dios,"* the air traffic controller was heard to shout. He transmitted a panicked message that American nuclear bombers were about to strike the airport, then dived under his table.[5]

Lieutenant Colonel Wagner hunched in his harness, just behind the jumpmaster. Each of the Starlifters in the serial was lightly loaded with only sixty-eight men. They had planned the jump in great detail, and rehearsed the operation several times on an alternate runway at Eglin Air Force Base in the Florida panhandle. At a jump altitude of 500 feet and 135 knots airspeed, the Tocumen drop zone was exactly thirty-three seconds long. The drop on the Torrijos runway at the same altitude had to be completed in forty-four seconds. And they only had one drop pass. Two sticks of thirty-four men would jump simultaneously from the left and right doors at an exit rate of just over two heavily laden men per second. On this kind of drop, you didn't shuffle up to the door as an individual; you were part of a thrashing human snake. Anyone not getting out would have to stay with the planes.

The bulk of the forces were jumping on Tocumen Airfield, the home base of the PDF's 2d Rifle Company, which also housed the main Panamanian Air Force security detachment. The five drop aircraft running in to Torrijos carried Charlie Company of the 3d Battalion. Their objectives was to secure the civilian terminal and neutralize the security guards. The gun-jeep and cycle crews were also jumping on Torrijos and would link up with their equipment in the southeast corner of that drop zone. These men had a vital mission: guarding the perimeter against PDF armored reinforcements from nearby Fort Cimarron.

The red light blinked. They had their green. Wagner was out the door, acutely conscious of the man just behind him. Jumping from a Starlifter throttled back to almost stall speed was less violent than jumping from a C-130. He had time to note several reassuring details. True to their word, the brave crews of the 437th MAW were flying straight and level down the center of the Tocumen runway. Their commander had told Wagner that his planes would deliver the Rangers exactly "as advertised," with no jinking to avoid groundfire, and no break in the formation, even if SAMs were fired. That took guts. At least the Rangers were rigged to jump, and some of the men probably could have gotten out of a crippled aircraft. But the crew on the flight deck would be doomed by a SAM hit.

Another reassuring observation Wagner noted waiting for his opening shock, was that there were no orange ZPU tracers lashing through the serial. The fire below was mainly small arms from the low, metal-roofed PDF and FAP barracks strung between the control tower and the big hangar. There was only one obvious automatic weapon working from some high ground over to the west. And the entire airport complex was blacked out. The Spectre and Little Birds had done their job. As his main canopy burst opened, Wagner caught a splintered glimpse of the entire air column, vaguely silhouetted against the broken moonlit overcast. The sky was full of parachutes. It was too late for the PDF to use any SAMs they might have kept in reserve.

## *0104 Hours, 20 December*

Manuel Noriega's suite at the Ceremi guest quarters encompassed several renovated rooms of the old bungalow hotel off a shady traffic circle adjacent to Tocumen Airfield. During the years before the new international airport had been built on reclaimed marshland just to the south, the La Siesta Hotel had been a pleasant and prosperous establishment. Now the fieldstone walls and mildewed tile roof projected an ambiance of luxurious melancholy. The old-fashioned wrought-iron garden furniture and the narrow tile swimming pool bore witness to better times in years past. But the garden of mature exotic shrubbery and handsome old shade palms was still attractive.

Because Tocumen no longer drew civilian passengers, the PDF had bought the establishment and transformed it into the Centro Recreativo Militar, in principle a guest house for Panamanian soldiers and their families transiting the capital on military flights. In reality, Ceremi had become a suitably remote rendezvous for discrete assignations for Noriega's inner clique and their paramours of both sexes.

As with his other personal quarters, Noriega's suite at Ceremi was furnished with an eclectic mix of Scandinavian modern and replica antique furniture, pseudomilitary accoutrements, and garish original paintings. The bedroom ran to lavender velour and Art Deco lamps with colored bulbs. There were ceiling mirrors and a video system to play sex tapes. And, of course, Noriega maintained a small Santeria shrine, which was periodically purified by one of his Brazilian spiritual advisers, whom he kept in comfort at Quarters No. 152 at Fort Amador, the building the Americans called the "witch house."

One of the reasons Noriega enjoyed Ceremi was the quiet. The new bypass road off the Inter-American Highway leading to Torrijos Airport had isolated Tocumen. There was none of the city's ubiquitous traffic noise. And, if his tastes of the moment ran toward the unusual, Noriega could decree absolute privacy here at Ceremi.

Captain Ivan Castillo noted that was what the General had in mind tonight. He had slept in the back seat of the white Hyundai all the way out from Fort Amador, oblivious to the increased military traffic on the streets. And he had slept again, waiting for Gloria to arrive. Ten minutes after Sublieutenant Pinto, a member of the security detail, brought the woman to Noriega's suite, the general appeared at the door still fully clothed. As often happened after a brief sleep, Noriega seemed sober again, despite the long day's drinking.

"Ivan," he called Captain Castillo. "This simply will not do." He pointed to the squad of uniformed security guards lounging close by among the birds of paradise and hibiscus. "They're too obvious."

Castillo ordered the men to fall back to the garden entrance and take positions in the shadows of the fieldstone wall. He wasn't sure whether Noriega was worried about attracting the attention of any lurking gringo Delta Force commandos, or if the general simply wanted to be left alone with his woman.

A few seconds after 1:00 A.M., Castillo was shaken out of his doze by several loud explosions and the rattling sound of strange automatic weapons to the west. A soldier ran into the garden from the parking lot.

"Captain!" he yelled. "There are airplanes all over and *paracaidistas.*"

Castillo fastened his pistol belt, grabbed his Uzi submachine gun and dashed after the soldier. The Tocumen-Torrijos airport complex was dark, but in the reflected glow from the village Castillo witnessed a terrible sight. Huge camouflaged jet airplanes roared low overhead, immune to the widely scattered groundfire from the base. Hundreds of paratroopers streamed from the transports, their green canopies barely opening before they disappeared behind the blacked-out buildings. This was no gringo bluff. This was the invasion Noriega had refused to believe would ever happen.

Back in the garden, Lieutenant Pinto already had the general and the woman out of the suite. The men of the security guard crouched at the garden wall gazing at the sky with expressions of abject terror. Castillo saw at once that Noriega's apparent sobriety earlier had been a sham. The general was glassy-eyed again, staggering. His open shirt was soaked with sweat.

Captain Castillo took charge, bundling Lieutenant Pinto behind the wheel of the Hyundai and Noriega and the woman into the car's back seat. The security squad clambered into their escorting Land Cruiser, and Castillo directed Pinto from the front seat of the Hyundai. The two vehicles sped down the rutted side road along the perimeter cyclone fence of the Tocumen base.

"Where are we going?" Noriega asked, staring behind him at the spectacle of the airdrop.

Before he could answer, Castillo saw another terrible apparition: American soldiers, their helmets floppy with camouflage strips, trotting down the service road separating the Tocumen and Torrijos runways. For a fleeting moment, the car's headlights fell on the soldiers' green-and-brown face paint. Ivan Castillo brusquely ordered Pinto to speed into an alley behind a shuttered bodega and the car bounced across muddy ruts before rejoining the paved road, past the Tocumen fence.[6]

Castillo had always assumed the general, the architect of the PDF's byzantine G-2 intelligence apparatus, must have had a secret escape route including a network of safe houses. Now Castillo realized the man in the back seat had no rational plan whatsoever. Instead, Noriega was incoherently stammering that they had to turn back to the Ceremi recreation center. In their hasty flight, he had forgotten one of his most important Santeria charms, a necklace talisman of great potency that would protect him from the pursuing gringos. Lieutenant Pinto finally managed to persuade the General that it was too dangerous.

"We will send a guard for your possessions," Pinto said. "Now we must think of your safety."

Noriega was twisted in the narrow seat, gazing back at the dark airport. Sporadic flashes and tracer fire broke the darkness behind them.

"What are we going to do?" he mumbled drunkenly.

## 0105 Hours, 20 December

Private First Class James Markwell had just shucked off his harness, dragged his canopy free of the runway, and slung his rucksack when the Rangers around him began firing at a vehicle. A blacked-out pickup truck roared down the Tocumen taxi ramp, its windows lit by muzzle flashes. There was more fire coming from around the tower to the right, where Panamanians from the 2d Rifle Company were making a disorganized stand in their low cinder-block barracks. Markwell was one of the 1st Battalion's medics. He quickly assessed the situation and identified where he would be most likely needed: with the fire teams maneuvering toward the enemy barracks. If there were wounded, that's where he would find them.

He got to his feet and sprinted east, toward the rattling noise of the firefight. He had only run a hundred yards when he was cut down. Although all the Rangers on the drop zone were trained in first aid, there was no other medic nearby to give the young soldier the treatment he needed. Markwell bled to death on the coarse grass, the battalion's first casualty.[7]


Within five minutes of the drop, Lt. Colonel Bob Wagner knew they were going to secure Tocumen on schedule and with minimum casualties. The men were maneuvering perfectly across the dark air base, firing only when fired on, and then with discipline and devastating precision. On his tactical radio net Wagner heard squad and platoon leaders position their men to assault the specific objectives in the 2d Rifle Company barracks and the Panamanian Air Force (FAP) buildings along the eastern edge of Tocumen. The officers and NCOs were referring to landmarks and positions on the base "like that water tank at Eglin," or "same as in the FTX," the last extensive field training exercise. During that exhausting ten-day dress rehearsal in Florida, the fire teams and squads had repeatedly maneuvered across a carefully structured mock-up of Tocumen on which plywood replicas of the objective buildings had been installed in exactly the same positions as they were on this base. Although most of the Rangers had never been in Panama, they knew exactly where they were and where they would find and destroy the enemy.

Two fire teams had quickly mousetrapped the FAP pickup truck on the open high ground to the west that had been firing the heavy machine gun during the drop. When the Rangers destroyed the vehicle with LAW antitank rockets, the crew had already fled. And that pattern prevailed all over Tocumen. Apparently, the PDF troops had no effective leadership, no coherent defense plan. They were fighting as individual soldiers, simply shooting up all the ammunition on hand, then turning tail to run. When Alpha Company cleared the 2d Rifle Company's barracks, the Rangers found boots and uniforms scattered on the floor among the litter of expended brass shell casings. The Panamanian soldiers were out there in the smoky night, barefoot, dressed in their underwear, running for their lives.

As Wagner listened to his people call in their "Objective Secured" reports, he knew they were going to pull this one off.[8]

Three platoons of Charlie Company of the 3d Battalion landed well within their drop zone along Runway 03 Right of Torrijos International Airport. They suffered only a few jump injuries. But the fourth platoon was scattered on the kuna grass margin west of the concrete runway. So it took several minutes for the company to assemble. The initial heavy fire from the Tocumen runway to the north had died away to a strange, dark silence, then flared again in sporadic waves. Once the teams were on their start lines, the men moved out toward Objective Bear, the main terminal of the civilian airport.

It was a weird place to attack. The terminal was a wide concrete-and-glass block, built on the functionally efficient design of all modern airports. The baggage carousels, Customs area, and arrival hall were on ground level; the departure gates on either end of the second floor led along raised, glass-enclosed walkways to satellite piers, each with three jetways. A balcony waiting area on an upper level overhung the departure hall. With the acres of plate glass, polished steel settees, and glittering duty-free boutiques, the Torrijos Airport terminal represented MOUT—military operations in urban terrain—in the extreme.

The 1st Platoon peeled off and moved to Battle Position Two, the satellite loading pier at the southern end of the terminal. So far the operation had proceeded exactly as planned, an eerie replication of the long training exercises the Rangers had completed only three days earlier. When they unexpectedly spotted an Eastern Airlines Boeing 727 parked at the terminal's central jetway, however, the men of the 1st Platoon realized the night would not continue so smoothly. No one had warned them there would be a civilian airliner unloading this late.

The platoon broke into squads and began clearing the shops and outbuildings flanking the main terminal. In the employees' cafeteria they found a handful of mechanics and cleaning women huddled under tables. There was at least one Hispanic Ranger in each squad to act as a translator. They quickly reassured the workers they would not be hurt.

The twelve men of the second squad cut through a double chain-link fence and leapfrogged fire team by fire team through the darkness to the elevated roadway connecting the parking lot and the terminal's main entrance. Just as they had been briefed, the Rangers found that the sandbagged PDF guard shack had been blasted by the Spectre gunship growling through the clouds overhead. The young men had never seen what a direct hit from a 105 mm howitzer round did to human beings. Now they realized combat was something much different than a training exercise.

While one squad set up a roadblock and positioned Claymore mines along the entrance highway, the other squads continued to clear the workshops on the terminal's northeast corner. Charlie Company was securing its objectives right on schedule. Up to this point no one had been shot at. The 1st Platoon did a squad rush and entered the main terminal, swept past the ticket counters and up the stationary escalator to establish a prisoner collection point on the upper level balcony, overlooking the long, dark departure hall. The blacked-out terminal echoed with their pounding boots and the clatter of their weapons. From this balcony, the Rangers had a good view of the empty duty-free shopping arcade. There was nobody there, just shuttered jewelry and electronics shops. The soldiers dragged furniture and the heavy concrete tubs of decorative plants into a loose defensive position, well back from the plate-glass windows. Within minutes another squad arrived with a frightened column of airport maintenance workers and the staff from the rental car counters on the main floor. Some of the civilians chattered excitedly. Others complained sullenly. They all fell silent when they heard the pounding blast of small arms and automatic weapons from the north end of the terminal.

Charlie Company's 3d Platoon had surrounded the airport fire station and managed to coax the firemen and their three PDF guards into surrendering. As they were leading these prisoners back to the terminal, however, two PDF soldiers hiding beneath the elevated walkway of the northern departure pier opened up with AK-47s, wounding several detainees and two Rangers. The platoon leader sent a squad after the fleeing PDF, who were seen sprinting into the main terminal and down a flight of stairs to the lower arrivals hall. The Rangers pursued the PDF soldiers into the men's restroom near the baggage carousel.

A Spanish-speaking sergeant and a backup NCO with a shotgun cautiously pushed open the door of the restroom and ordered the PDF inside to surrender. They were met by a blast from an assault rifle. The man with the shotgun was down, hit in both legs. The gunfire was deafening in the confined darkness. Three more Rangers burst through the door, grabbed the wounded man and backed out into the arrivals hall. As the door swung shut, they tossed in two grenades. Even with the door closed, the blast rattled the wide windows of the hall.

Chests pounding under their heavy web gear, the fire team kicked open the door and entered the cloud of smoke and plaster dust. Both PDF were still alive. In the confused melee that followed, one was cut down as he swung his weapon from behind a toilet stall. The other managed to burst out of the restroom and stagger through the door to the tarmac. He was hit by fire from three Rangers when he ignored the order to surrender and instead tugged at his pistol.

A Ranger squad cautiously climbing the blacked-out stairs to the third floor was fired on by three enemy soldiers. The Rangers returned fire and chased the PDF down the darkened corridor to the airport security office. Using benches and waiting-room seats as best they could for cover, the Rangers followed the tight discipline of MOUT training to advance on the office. When they got there, the men saw the PDF inside burning a pile of documents. The room filled with choking smoke, but the enemy soldiers seemed intent on their task. Even a concussion grenade could not convince them to surrender.

The squad leader juggled the smooth round ball of a fragmentation grenade, his finger on the pin.

Once more the squad's Spanish speaker shouted, *"Rendirse!"* But the PDF inside did not reply.

"I'm gonna frag the bastards," the squad leader shouted to warn his men.

But before he could throw his grenade, the burning documents ignited drapes and furniture, and the office puffed with flames. The enemy soldiers finally stumbled outside, choking, their hands in the air. As several Rangers knocked them to the ground and frisked them, the squad leader and two men dashed into the room, swinging their rifle butts to knock down the burning drapes. No sooner had they entered than the overhead sprinkler system finally burst, drenching them in a harsh spray of tepid water. They stood there a moment in the steam and smoke. The water felt good.

Down in the far corner of the ground-floor arrivals hall, the two fire teams of the 2d Squad encountered four well-armed PDF hiding in the baggage claims office. The enemy soldiers dashed ahead of the shouting Rangers and swept around the crowd of terrified passengers cowering among the Customs booths. These hapless travelers had been caught in this dark limbo when the battle began.

Now the PDF planned to use them as hostages. While the Rangers took cover behind the stalled baggage carousel, the

PDF dragged several obvious Americans, including two women with small children, from the crouching civilians and herded them toward the swinging doors of the arrivals hall. But the enemy soldiers froze when they realized the main terminal entrance was already guarded by well-armed Rangers. Retreating into the Customs stalls, the PDF shoved their hostages to the floor and crouched beside them, their assault rifles swinging wildly in the dark.

The leader of the 2d Squad grabbed his radio to tell his platoon leader that they definitely had a bad deal on their hands down here.

## 0020 Hours, 20 December

The night had not gone well so far for Major Kevin M. Higgins, commander of Alpha Company, 3d Battalion, 7th Special Forces Group. His mission had been originally planned as a four-man reconnaissance post at the Pacora River bridge, ten kilometers east of Tocumen-Torrijos Airport. Such a small recon team would have been just a footnote to the large combined operation by Army Special Forces and the Delta Force in and around Panama City. The Blue Spoon OPLAN had originally called for twelve small recon teams to shadow PDF garrisons and lines of communications at H-hour. In the final planning for the actual operation, however, the reconnaissance requirements had been scaled down, and this mission had grown into a sixteen-man assault and blocking operation at the nondescript concrete bridge spanning the wide gully of the deep, fast-moving Pacora River, a natural choke point on the Inter-American Highway. Any reinforcements from the PDF's Battalion 2000 at Fort Cimarron, twelve kilometers further east, would have to cross this bridge. And those reinforcements might include the battalion's V-300 armored cars, mounting 90 mm cannon. They would be a deadly threat to the lightly armed Rangers securing the airport complex.

During Higgins' final briefing that afternoon, the Green Beret troops were told to definitely expect PDF armor along that road once the Ranger airdrop at Tocumen-Torrijos came down. Therefore it was vital for the Special Forces to time their helicopter insertion at the bridge precisely. If the two MH-60 Pave Hawks from the 160th Aviation Group brought them in too early, the noise of the choppers might alert villagers along the river's northeast bank, or night watchmen at the gravel quarry near the bridge on the southeast bank. Once alerted, the PDF might move inland to bypass the bridge, or simply overwhelm Higgins' forces with a flanking infantry attack. But Higgins couldn't delay the insertion too long, either. He had to get his small party down and properly dispersed along the steep embankment of the bridge's western approach so that they had time to cover the straight concrete highway leading from Fort Cimarron with their AT-4 and LAW antitank rockets and machine guns.

That evening as the team went through their final weapons and radio checks at the isolated Special Forces hangar on Albrook Air Force Station, Higgins learned that a third helicopter, a UH-60 Black Hawk from the 228th Aviation, was available. He quickly added eight more men to his force, but still planned to use the postage-stamp-size landing zone of a small pasture 200 meters northeast of the bridge.

Higgins' force now totaled twenty-five and included Air Force Staff Sergeant John Ecklof, who made up a one-man Combat Control Team (CCT) to work with the Air Papa AC-130 Spectre gunship. The Spectre's accurate firepower, especially the big 105 mm Number Six gun, would tilt the odds in the Americans' favor, even if the PDF sent all of their V-300s against the bridge.

At 0020 hours, Higgins was loading his people on the Albrook apron when the hangar came under fire from the tall kuna grass near the chain-link fence along Gaillard Highway. The tracers twanged harmlessly off the hangar's corrugated metal roof, but no one was very comfortable about that fire with all the fuel and ordnance on the ramp. As the loading proceeded, Higgins received word that this premature enemy fire around Albrook had caused the JTF South commander to advance H-hour by fifteen minutes. More alarming, the Joint Special Operations Task Force Intelligence reported a large PDF convoy moving west from Fort Cimarron along the Inter-

American Highway. There was no confirmation that enemy armored cars were in the convoy, but Higgins had to assume the worst. He scrambled on board the lead chopper and the three chalks were airborne.

The troop bay of the MH-60 Pave Hawk Special Operations helicopter was smaller than its standard Black Hawk counterpart because of the large fuel bladder just aft of the flight deck. Higgins wedged himself forward of this bladder to kneel behind the two pilots. Both airmen wore night-vision goggles, and were experienced in high-speed, low-altitude team insertions. Higgins had chosen not to wear night-vision goggles on the lift because they could be "maxed out" by bright ground lights or the muzzle flashes of nearby enemy weapons. In this type of operation, he trusted his own eyes more than electronics.

Higgins grabbed a headset to talk to the aircraft commander. "I've got news for you," he said into the mike. "They advanced H-hour by fifteen minutes, and there's a PDF convoy highballing for that bridge."

"I've got news for *you*, Major," the pilot answered. "We're not going to fit all three aircraft into the LZ we briefed on." The pilot held up a folded air navigation chart in the dim glow of the instrument panel. "We're going to have to put you down in that field just west of the bridge."

"Whatever," Higgins replied anxiously. "Just get us there as quick as you can."

The Special Ops pilots had originally planned their route carefully to avoid PDF installations, as well as the fire zones of gunships working in the city center. But there were also airborne hazards to avoid. Four separate Delta Force snatch teams comprised of MH-60 Pave Hawk and MH-6 AHIPS helicopters were prowling low over Panama City's affluent eastern suburbs, hunting for General Manuel Noriega. The choppers had staked out the approaches to Noriega's luxurious villa in the Alto del Golf neighborhood and the homes of several of his closest associates, where he might take refuge after the attack.

Another blacked-out Special Operations helicopter was also maneuvering out there in the darkness, carrying a team of saboteurs to disable the powerful transmitter of Channel 2, Panama's national television station, which the PDF had used so effectively to rally support during the unsuccessful coup attempts. Originally, the special operators had planned simply to destroy the transmitter and tower with a rocket barrage from an Apache or Cobra gunship. But Colonel Jorge Torres-Cartagena, commander of the 1109th Signal Brigade, had proposed an interesting alternative. He lent the Special Ops task force two volunteer technicians who knew everything required about electronics, but nothing about commando raids. In a compressed training course, the Special Ops men taught the technicians how to fast-rope from a blacked-out hovering helicopter into the narrow, fenced transmitter compound. That team was on its way now, somewhere out there above the sprawling city. They would insert just before H-hour. The Special Ops men would take down any PDF guards, while the technicians would disable the television transmitter by simply removing two circuit cards.[9]

To avoid these aircraft, Higgins' pilots had carefully laid out a "deconflicted" dogleg route around these danger zones and also given Tocumen-Torrijos a wide berth. Now they had to readjust their flight plan en route as they headed almost due east, 200 feet above the city rooftops. The lead chopper's copilot was on the secure FM, frantically advising the task force commander of their new route. Air traffic control down in these crowded chopper altitudes was a critical matter.

The three helicopters flew in a tight trail formation, Two and Three following Lead's infrared strobe with their NVGs. For Blue Spoon, all the American helicopters had been equipped with a deep-spectrum IR strobe beacon visible only through the ANVIS-6 goggles. All the American combat troops wore "glint strips" on their left arms reflective in the same spectrum. Even if the PDF had Soviet night goggles supplied by the Cubans, enemy gunners wouldn't be able to pick up these strobes or uniform markers.

A straight course from Albrook to the Pacora River bridge was just over eighteen nautical miles, about thirteen minutes flying time at 140 knots. As Higgins sweated with tense frustration on the windy, vibrating aluminum deck of the chopper's troop bay, he mentally rehearsed the critical initial deployment of his men around the bridge. It was vital that their antiarmor weapons be immediately positioned effectively. This was combat, not another tedious exercise; results, not a fancy, well-charted defensive plan, were the only thing that mattered.

They were past the airport now, only 100 feet above the highway. Higgins tugged off the headset, pulled on his cap and leaned out past the right door gunner's shoulder, scanning the dark landscape ahead. The highway ran like a pale ribbon, due east through a broken geometry of scrub jungle and rectangular pastures. Security lights around the gravel quarry buildings beyond the bridge gave him a good reference point. The Pacora River was a wide, black band. But he could not yet see the bridge itself.

Leaning back into the troop bay, Higgins knelt behind the two pilots again, braced against their seats. He stared past their helmets, through the dark windscreen. Suddenly there were dim lights ahead, an evenly spaced procession of vehicle head-lights moving relentlessly toward them from the east.

"There's your convoy," the pilot said.

"Okay," Higgins answered. "I've got it. Where's the bridge?"

The pilot nodded grimly, his head bug-eyed with helmet and goggles. "The lead vehicle is just about *on* the bridge, Major."

"On final," the copilot said calmly into his microphone, alerting the trailing choppers. They were coming down.

The three helicopters pitched nose-high, and flared over the highway and the mildewed flanks of the bridge's concrete guardrails. For a moment, they were actually above the enemy convoy, in a tight buttonhook turn back west to the LZ on the Panama City side of the bridge. Lead was still five feet off the ground, with Two and Three strung behind, when the Special Forces soldiers unclipped the safety straps across the open doors and leapt into the coarse grass along the road shoulder. The choppers pulled rotor pitch and banked off sharply right.

Higgins did not have to give any unnecessary orders. The men all knew their missions. They broke into three elements along the steep southern road bank. The first vehicle in the enemy convoy, a two-and-a-half-ton military truck, had already rumbled onto the eastern end of the bridge. There certainly was no time for digging in or to fill the bundles of empty green plastic sandbags. There was no time to set the Claymores. There was hardly time to strip the safety tabs from their AT-4s and LAWs.

Due to the change in landing zones, the lead helicopter had set down furthest from the approaching enemy. In effect, Higgins was separated from the PDF convoy by the two chalks that he had originally planned to have land behind him. But Special Forces troops were trained to be resourceful, to act independently when required. This hard training now paid off.

Staff Sergeant Daniel McDonald, Higgins' communications specialist, did not hesitate, waiting for orders. He had been beside Higgins during the flight from Albrook and had heard all the innercom exchanges between the major and the pilots. No one had to tell him where the enemy was. He scrambled up the embankment, threw down his rucksack and dragged free the narrow tube of a LAW. Standing directly in the middle of the road at the western end of the bridge, McDonald shouldered the weapon and fired in one smooth motion. The rocket smacked into the undercarriage of the approaching truck with a loud orange explosion. The truck stopped, five meters onto the bridge span.

Higgins' men could hear the roar of heavy diesel engines behind the stopped truck. They feared armored cars were jockeying to push past the crippled vehicle and onto the bridge. Now two men rushed up to fire AT-4s across the bridge. They were followed by three more. Soldiers armed with 203 grenade launchers dashed onto the bridge and fired. The vehicles in the convoy sparkled and flickered as the rockets and grenades struck.

If there were any V-300s in that column, Higgins realized, they were now either damaged or their crews weren't very anxious to come forward. In the flash of the exploding munitions, he got his first clear view of the convoy: big square military trucks with open troop bays. PDF soldiers were dropping to the ground, scrambling for cover. They were from the Battalion 2000, some of the troops who'd saved Noriega's ass in October. The lead vehicles mounted machine guns above the cabs. But there was no armor in sight.

Higgins was aware of Staff Sergeant Ecklof, his one-man CCT, in the shadows beside him, speaking intensely into the black lump of his secure FM, establishing hasty contact with the Air Papa Spectre somewhere up there in the scudding clouds.

"Sir," Ecklof shouted above the crack of small-arms fire from the American troops along the edge of the road, "Spectre says he can work that convoy, but we're way inside his safety margin."

Higgins could see the enemy soldiers jumping down both road embankments across the bridge and fanning out along the brushy river bank. If they managed to get well dispersed, the Spectre would be less effective.

"Let's do it," he told Sergeant Ecklof. "Get some 20 mike-mike on them."

The sergeant snapped off a hasty "Yes, sir," and crawled down the roadside to get a better view of the enemy column. As Higgins watched, the trucks suddenly began to chatter, their furled tarpaulins fluttering in some strange wind. Then he heard the rippling crackle of the Spectre's twin 20 mm Vulcan guns. PDF soldiers were thrown in odd directions. A truck caught fire. The Spectre rumbled by above.

To the troops with night-vision goggles, the entire road warmed with a milky chartreuse glow. The Spectre was shining its powerful infrared searchlight onto the enemy convoy. Higgins' team was firing with short bursts now, aiming on individual targets. The enemy no longer moved in disciplined groups. They were down there in the brush off the road, hiding from the unseen monster in the sky.[10]

# 5

## 20 December 1989

---

## H-Hour: Task Force Bayonet

*0025 Hours, 20 December*

Captain John H. Hort, Jr. stood in the humid darkness studying his map in the dim red glow of his flashlight. The Tactical Operations Center of Headquarters and Headquarters Company, 1st Battalion, 508th Infantry (Airborne), consisted of one truck and one Humvee parked behind an officer's quarters beside the Fort Amador golf course. His three combat platoons and the attached unit of M-113 armored personnel carriers (APCs) were clustered in the shadows of the driveways and porches in this line of pleasant, tile-roofed houses. A light breeze rustled the tall palm trees along the road. The houses were lit with strings of Christmas lights.

In the driveways on either side of this house, the lieutenants commanding Hort's two SCAT (Combined Scout and Anti-tank) platoons were still supervising the loading of TOW missiles into their hardshell Humvees. The late arrival of this ordnance was just one more screw-up of the long night. Hort's war was scheduled to begin in thirty-five minutes, and his troops were not ready. But his company had one of the most difficult and sensitive missions of the whole operation.

Fort Amador was a stately old post on a breezy peninsula flanking the Canal, shared jointly by U.S. forces and the PDF. Under the terms of the 1977 treaties, the Panamanian military was given the barracks and office buildings along the Canal

side, and the Americans retained the comfortable field-grade
married officers' housing across the wide golf-course fairways.
Over the past two years, this once amicable arrangement had
deteriorated to the point where Fort Amador was a pressure
chamber of harassment and animosity. Building 4, halfway
down the line of barracks, was the command post of Noriega's
military police, where American servicemen were often harshly
interrogated after arrest on some pretext. Since the October
coup attempt, the PDF had constructed a line of bunkers on
the edge of the fairway. The sandbagged slits of the machine-
gun positions pointed across the golf course at the backyards
of the American families where kids played on swings and
overworked fathers occasionally had time to grill hamburgers.
Equally ominous, the Macho de Monte had moved one V-300
and one V-150 armored vehicle and a ZPU-4 antiaircraft gun
onto Fort Amador, and positioned this hardware on the water-
side road to protect Building 8, Noriega's personal headquarters.

Hort's mission was to seal off Fort Amador at H-hour, preventing the resident PDF's 5th Rifle Company from reinforcing Panamanian forces in the city. His soldiers were also
ordered to seal the causeway road at the fort's seaside entrance
to prevent UESAT Special Forces troops from transiting the
base en route to the Comandancia. The small American unit
was expected to keep the fort and causeway blocked until the
battalion's Alpha and Bravo Companies arrived in a helicopter
air assault from their home base at Fort Kobbe across the Canal at H-hour, 0100. Had it not been for the presence of almost 200 American family dependents on Fort Amador,
Captain Hort's mission might have been relatively straightforward. But there were dozens of American families in these
houses, and his troops were their only protection, should the
PDF break loose from their fortified barracks and storm across
the open golf course.

John Hort was a serious young man who planned a career
in the Army, and he knew he faced his most challenging professional test. Unfortunately, things were not going well. Not
only was the SCAT Platoons' allotment of TOW (tube-
launched, optically tracked, wire-guided) missiles—their main

defense against the PDF armor—hours late, but the officer in charge of the MP guards at the main gate had never been briefed on the operation. For all that lieutenant knew, the carefully orchestrated staggered arrival of Hort's trucks and Humvees had just been another routine Sand Flea exercise. And the man seemed stunned when Hort told him that his MPs had the vital task of neutralizing the PDF guards, with whom they shared the main-gate guard post. The officer had just departed to brief his soldiers, when Hort's radiotelephone operator (RTO) handed him the headset.

"It's the commander, sir," the kid said.

"Headhunter Six," Lieutenant Colonel Billy Ray Fitzgerald said, using Hort's formal call sign, "this is Devil Six. Things are starting early, I'm afraid. Be prepared to execute the op order."

"Roger, sir," Hort said nervously.

He called his two SCAT Platoon commanders and told them to saddle up and get ready to move. Then Hort walked down the line of dark vehicles and spoke to the men of Lieutenant Bill West's Mortar Platoon, who had the initial mission of waking the sleeping dependent families to warn them to keep down until they could be evacuated. Hort was still talking to West when the colonel called again from Fort Kobbe.

"Headhunter Six," Fitzgerald said, "execute op order now."

"Roger, Devil Six," Hort replied formally, "understand execute now." He looked at his watch. It was 0027 hours.

"That's affirmative, Headhunter Six. *Now.*"[1]

Hort had always known that combat would be far different than the most realistic training exercises. But he had never expected things to be this screwed up.

He yelled across the hibiscus hedge for the two platoons to move out. First Lieutenant Paul Vinyard's unit, eighteen soldiers loaded on a truck and two hard-shelled Humvees, sped off to block the causeway entrance to the base. First Lieutenant Joe Manauis' eighteen troops raced toward the front gate, their hardshell Humvee mounting a M-60 machine gun. As soon as the units had departed, the Panama City waterfront a kilometer across the bay exploded with small arms and automatic weapons fire. Hort and his small headquarters staff watched the area below Quarry Heights light up with tracers. They saw a lumbering dark gunship up there in the clouds, hosing down automatic-cannon fire on the jumbled roofline of the Comandancia. Antiaircraft machine guns on the apartment roofs of El Chorrillo cut loose wildly. Some of the big red ZPU tracers were aimed low. They ricocheted at crazy angles off the mud flats and whipped through the palm trees of Fort Amador.

When the SCAT Platoon vehicles screeched up to the front gate, the soldiers were confronted with a bizarre scene. Two American MPs in Kevlar helmets and flak vests seemed to be waltzing drunkenly with their PDF counterparts: bearded Macho de Monte soldiers in tight black T-shirts. As instructed, the MPs had ordered the PDF guards to surrender, but then hadn't had the stomach to shoot them when they refused. A clumsy wrestling match ensued.

But the Machos panicked when they saw the SCAT Platoon arrive, and retreated into their sandbagged position. The platoon interpreter shouted at them to come out. Staff Sergeant Dick Meadows took his squad forward to disarm the two guards. Lieutenant Manauis was waiting for the prisoners to be searched, flex-cuffed, and taken away before unloading the concertina wire and tire-piercing road jacks for the front-gate barricade. His platoon sergeant, José Corvino, was 500 meters back inside the fort, setting up a security position where the main road split around the golf course, its two branches leading to the Panamanian and American sides of the base.

"Bus full of PDF," Corvino shouted on the platoon's tactical radio. "No lights, headed your way fast."

Manauis and his men froze for a moment, then dashed for cover behind their Humvees. A big white school bus roared out of the darkness, narrowly missing the parked vehicles. As the bus sped past, the PDF soldiers crouching inside thrust AK-47 and P-65 assault rifles out the windows and opened fire with ragged, unaimed bursts. The American troops did not hesitate; they returned fire with their M-16s. Staff Sergeant Dave Estes jumped from the cover of his Humvee, leveled his weapon, and fired three short bursts through the windshield of the bus, killing the driver. The bus rolled to the right and climbed the curb. The PDF inside were still firing out when the bus smashed into a huge coconut palm, 200 yards down the road. The SCAT Platoon soldiers continued to fire. After a minute or so, there were no more muzzle flashes from the shattered bus windows.

One of the unarmed PDF guards who had just surrendered was sprawled in the dark inside the guard post. His beard was matted with blood and there were terrible chunks of flesh ripped from his torso. Standing helplessly in the center of the entrance, the man had been hit squarely across the neck and chest by a blast of automatic fire from the bus window. The American soldiers stood above him, trembling with shock. None of them had ever seen so much blood. The night crackled and smacked with distant explosions. Finally, two of the sergeants dragged the dead man away by his boots, and Lieutenant Manauis got his men to lay down the roadblock across the gate.

No sooner had they positioned their vehicles and scattered the sharp-pointed road jacks than they heard another speeding vehicle approach from the line of dark PDF barracks inside the fort. A big tan Chevy sedan with six Panamanian soldiers inside was zigzagging toward them, flat-out. Soldiers in the front and back seats fired assault rifles. This time one of the young soldiers, PFC Don Mountain, took the decisive action. He stood up behind the Humvee and fired a three-round burst, right into the driver's face. The man never had a chance to turn the wheel. The speeding sedan crashed squarely into the back of the first Humvee. A PDF soldier in the front seat flew into the window, spidering the Plexiglas. But the soldiers in the back seat continued to fire, blowing strips of metal off the American vehicles. Now all the Americans concentrated their fire on the back seat. The PDF stopped shooting.

One of the platoon's Spanish speakers screamed for the PDF to surrender. A weak voice replied indistinctly. Then the sedan's right back door opened and a man thrust out the barrel of an AK-47 and tumbled after it. The Americans fired again.

The man lay still on the road. As the men of the first squad approached, they saw that the dead soldier had already been severely wounded. His left leg was gone, his fatigue trousers shredded and bloody. He had probably fallen by accident.

Once more the soldiers of the SCAT Platoon crept out from cover to stare down at the dark pavement, reluctantly comprehending the carnage they saw.

## 0047 Hours, 20 December

Kurt Muse was sleeping in his stifling, airless cell when the first clatter of machine-gun fire shook the La Cárcel Modelo, Panama City's central prison. Muse, a strapping, thirty-nine-year-old American, grown gaunt from eight months' captivity, realized the invasion had finally begun. But he feared his jailers would kill him before the American troops breached the high walls of the old fortresslike prison that stood directly across the street from the Comandancia.[2]

Kurt Muse was an improbable inmate of one of Noriega's most notorious prisons. He had grown up in the family of an American businessman in Panama during the halcyon years of the Zone. After college and military service in the States, Muse had returned and prospered in the family's diverse printing and retailing businesses. His wife, Anne Castoro, was a Zonian. The couple had two children, Kimberly, a teenager, and Erik, ten. Muse worked hard to provide the family a pleasant, if not grand life. He was active in community organizations, especially the Rotary Club. To all appearances, he was an unremarkable family man, equally comfortable in both expatriate gringo and middle-class rabiblanco society.

But in 1987, when Noriega began to simultaneously brutally suppress all opposition to him and to reward the growing body of his sycophants through widespread corruption and graft, Muse realized his adopted home was endangered. Noriega's PDF was steadily usurping the police and regulatory functions of the civil government. In effect, the Defense Forces were growing like a tumor within the healthy body of Panama. To meet his own curiosity about the malignant growth of the PDF,

Muse began to eavesdrop on their radio communications. Using simple Radio Shack police scanners, Kurt Muse and a small group of Rotary Club friends monitored confidential PDF cellular-phone and car-radio channels. Although technically illegal, their activity was hardly espionage. But the eavesdropping gave them some sense of superiority over the increasingly oppressive PDF.

Muse and his friends also realized that the information they now began to keep in detailed logs might be helpful to American or honest Panamanian military officials intending to overthrow Noriega and his cronies. The amateur Rotarian cryptographers next discovered a bit of fascinating electronic trivia: They could monitor the frequency linking the studio of Radio Nacional with its transmitter tower on the hills above the Trans-Isthmus Highway. It would not require sophisticated equipment, they realized, to overpower this carrier beam and broadcast their own signal on the station's powerful transmitter.

By this time Noriega had manipulated social animosities and was rallying the dispossessed urban classes and poor campesinos to the pseudopopulism of his Torrijist banner. All the while, of course, Noriega was bleeding the national treasury and growing rich through drug and arms trafficking. The outraged Rotarians joined the middle-class's political revolt against Noriega, which soon engendered massive anti-Noriega street demonstrations. Predictably, Noriega responded by well-orchestrated populist rallies and the creation of the Dignity Battalions. He also unleashed a murderous wave of oppression against his political enemies.

The Rotarians struck back with a campaign of radio sabotage, interrupting Noriega's speeches with tape-recorded messages "from free and democratic Panamanians." Within weeks, their clandestine signals interrupted Radio Nacional music and talk-show programs throughout the day. And Noriega's secret police—assisted by skilled Cuban advisers—were unable to track the clandestine broadcasts with sophisticated radio-direction-finding equipment. The CIA finally recognized the potential of these amateurs and provided them better equipment than the jury-rigged over-the-counter gear they had smuggled in from Miami shopping malls. By now, the Rotarians' hobby had become *Radio Constitucional,* the recognized voice of the democratic opposition. Every time the Rotarians broadcast, Noriega went into paroxysms of rage.

Although the middle-class conspirators knew the danger they faced, they felt confident they could continue to evade Noriega's secret police. They were wrong. Early in April, Kurt Muse was arrested at airport customs, returning from a business trip to Miami. He held out through an initial period of harsh, but not brutal, interrogation, which gave his coconspirators enough time to seek asylum in the Zone.

Muse's treatment deteriorated, but he was never subjected to the torture typically inflicted on Noriega's prisoners, because he was an American citizen and a representative of the U.S. Embassy insisted on visiting him regularly.

However, Muse did witness acts of unspeakable brutality against fellow prisoners at the various DENI stations, and especially at La Modelo Prison. This overcrowded jail had multitiered galleries of barred cages crammed with hundreds of inmates. Most were common criminals, but many were political prisoners. The sanitation facilities of the "model" prison were overwhelmed by the influx of new prisoners after the anti-Noriega street demonstrations following the annulled May election and the failed October coup attempt.

Muse, who lived in relative comfort in a private cell on the top floor, saw scores of these prisoners savagely beaten by guards wielding rubber truncheons. Some opposition leaders among the prisoners were singled out for special treatment. Two men were strung up from an outdoor basketball hoop and flogged; one was draped in an American flag during his torment. But such beatings were humane compared to the prolonged electric-shock torture some men were subjected to in special punishment rooms near the guard commander's office.[3]

Kurt Muse had been raised in Panama City when the country was still an unofficial American colony. Panama then was an oasis of civil liberties and democratic values in the crueler Third World wilderness of Latin America. But Noriega had introduced terror and cruelty. Now abduction, "disappearance," and torture were almost as widespread as in any totalitarian Latin dictatorship controlled by the extreme Left or Right.

And these same cruel guards had assured Muse that his embassy protectors could not save him if the Americans attacked Panama. He would be the first gringo to die, they said. From what he had seen at La Modelo, he had no reason to doubt them.

The machine-gun fire clattered off a nearby building, sounding like a jackhammer on pavement. Muse threw himself to the floor of his cell. Panicked guards dashed down the gallery walkway shouting indistinct warnings. Suddenly the machine-gun fire was overpowered by an absolute bedlam of heavy explosions and the odd, mechanical tattoo of Gatling-gun cannons firing overhead. Muse realized a huge American gunship was pounding the Comandancia headquarters across the street. The gunship's heavy caliber howitzer was cracking now, one round after another blasting into the PDF compound. Smoke and pulverized masonry dust filled the air, and the billowing clouds flared with the strange lightning of red and green tracers. To Muse, it sounded like World War III had begun.

The dim bulb hanging high overhead went out. The entire prison was now in darkness. An incandescent explosive shockwave pounded the cellblocks. Prisoners who had been howling derisive curses at their guards now went silent. Muse crouched in the concrete angle of his cellblock corner, as far from the door and the barred window as he could crawl. There were more explosions now, obviously inside the prison itself, followed by the chatter of light automatic weapons. Somebody was fighting the guards.

The darkness was ripped by loud flashes. Men were running and shouting. He heard English. A grenade exploded and the corridor roiled with smoke. Then he saw the bizarre, geometrically straight beams of a laser probing the smoky darkness, like something out of a science-fiction movie. The soldier who suddenly appeared at his cell door seemed right in character. He was dressed all in black, his hood pulled back to expose some kind of high-tech communications helmet. The man's face was half-hidden by the bug-eyes of electronic goggles. His weapon was also something out of *Star Wars,* an oddly scooped fiberglass stock with the prominent cylinder of a laser sight. He was obviously a member of the Army's Delta Force, the elite commandos trained in counterterrorism and hostage rescue, whom Muse had prayed he might one day see.[4]

The Delta operator warned "Moose" to stay down while he blew the door with C-4 explosive.

Struggling to put on the Kevlar helmet and vest the Delta man had provided, Muse trotted down the dark corridor behind his rescuer. They were headed for a Delta Force helicopter on the roof. In the glare of the nearby explosions, Muse saw dead PDF guards along the corridor and in the stairwell to the roof. Whoever had planned this operation had known the shortest route to Muse's cell. Only those steel-barred doors needed for access had been blown. This was the rescue of one man, not a general prison liberation.

The scene on the flat prison roof was surreal. A bulbous MH-6 Special Operations helicopter squatted in the noisy darkness, its main rotor thumping. Overhead, Little Bird gunships swooped and whined in the billowing smoke, firing into Comandancia windows. Tracers ricocheted off nearby buildings. High above the smoke, a big Spectre gunship pounded the Comandancia courtyard with cannon fire.

As Muse was pushed toward the helicopter, other black-clad Delta soldiers fell back from their defensive perimeter on the roof. Muse was thrust into the narrow rear seat as Delta men clambered precariously onto the sides of the chopper, their knees hooked around the landing skids and their elbows braced on the rocket pods. The pilot cranked open the throttle and rolled the control stick back, then hard right. As the helicopter cleared a blasted guard turret, the aircraft was hit at least five times in the whining engine compartment above Muse's head. He saw the instrument panel blaze with warning lights. They were going down into the dark canyon between the prison's high concrete walls and the lower fieldstone walls enclosing the rear of the Comandancia across the street.

The pilot hauled back hard on the control stick, so that the main rotor windmilled, providing enough autorotation lift to prevent a disastrous crash. They somehow avoided burning vehicles and a heap of blasted masonry to land intact. Giving the engine full throttle again, the pilot got enough rotor lift to ground-taxi along the pavement and turn into the open prison parking lot. His hand danced across the instrument panel, flipping switches as he fought to resurrect engine power.

The turbine howled and they were climbing again into the smoky sky. The Delta men perched outside fired back now at the muzzle flashes in the Comandancia windows. But the chopper was hit again, this time by heavier caliber fire. There wasn't altitude for autorotation. The tough AHIPS smashed back to the pavement, landing on its left skid and rocket pod, crushing the three Delta men clinging to that side.

Bullets ricocheted overhead. The wounded moaned in the darkness. Kurt Muse was shaken but not badly injured. As the tracers bounced and wobbled through the narrow street, he helped drag the bleeding men to precarious shelter behind some parked PDF vehicles. All around them, the night sparkled with tracers and flashed with cannon blasts. Muse knew it would not be long before the PDF machine gunners found them.[5]

## 0050 Hours, 20 December

Stevin Helin and his wife Kandi sped down the Gaillard Highway past the blacked-out flats of Albrook Air Force Station. Gunfire and explosions echoed from behind them. Helin was an employee of the Panama Canal Commission and his wife was a teacher in the Defense Department school system. They were less than a mile from their home in the PCC housing site at Los Rios.

In a few more blocks they would be within the zone of protection provided by the MPs and Air Force security men fanning out from the main gate of Albrook. Their speeding sedan did not make it that far. PDF troops hidden in the tall grass near the station fence opened up on the couple as their car rolled past. Kandi Helin was hit by a burst of fire that shattered the passenger-side window and chewed up the door. Her husband managed to keep control of the car and drove on to a first-aid station at Corozal. But the doctors there could not save her. She was pronounced dead a few minutes before H-hour.

Richard Paul was also speeding through the dangerous night. The young man was the son of another Defense Department teacher. He and his friend Mark Mirrop were returning from a party to Paul's home in La Boca, near the Canal entrance beneath the Bridge of the Americas. They had already been accosted by armed troops along the roads of the old Canal Zone. There had been plenty to drink at the party. Neither frightened young man was certain if the soldiers on the dark streets were American or PDF.

When Richard Paul saw the roadblock ahead, he made the decision to burst through. They were only blocks from his house.

The American soldiers at the roadblock watched the car speed toward them, careening wildly along the palm-lined road. When the vehicle showed no sign of slowing, the officer in charge gave the order to fire.

Richard Paul was killed instantly. His friend, Mark, was hit by several M-16 rounds, but was successfully treated for his wounds at Gorgas Army Hospital on Ancon Hill.

H-hour had not yet come, but already two unarmed Americans were dead. And the long, dangerous night had just begun.


## 0055 Hours, 20 December

The lead vehicles of Task Force Gator rumbled down the lower slope of Calle Balboa and roared across the exposed width of the four-lane road running below Quarry Heights which the Americans called Fourth of July Avenue and the Panamanians knew as Avenida de los Mártires. The "martyrs" were student demonstrators who died in clashes with American troops in 1964. This highway had symbolic value beyond its rival names, however. It was the demarcation line between the spacious, flowery affluence of the Canal Zone's Balboa neighborhood and the congested squalor of El Chorrillo.

Task Force Gator was a detachment of Task Force Bayonet, and included M-113 armored personnel carriers (APCs) from the 4th Battalion, 6th Infantry Regiment assigned to the 5th Infantry Division (Mechanized) in Fort Polk, Louisiana. Its H-hour mission was to seal off the roads around the Comandancia, which lay in the warren of wooden tenements and taller apartment buildings of El Chorrillo. Once the APCs had cleared the roadblocks and suppressed sniper fire, Gator's principal assault unit, Charlie Company, 1st Battalion, 508th Infantry (Airborne), would take up positions to breach the PDF compound's side wall.

Before the operation, no one had believed that firepower demonstrations would lead to an easy surrender here. Not only had Noriega traditionally stationed his most loyal troops at the Comandancia—including the 7th Company's Macho de Monte since the October coup attempt—but the surrounding slum was a Dignity Battalion stronghold.

As Captain Joe Goss, the tall West Pointer commanding the mechanized infantry's Bravo Company, watched from the crossroads of Fourth of July and Avenida A, the lead tracks came under interlocking small-arms and machine-gun fire from a roadblock just ahead. A Spectre gunship was pumping heavy cannon rounds into the Comandancia buildings. Small, fleeting helicopter gunships bobbed through the clouds and smoke, engaging antiaircraft machine guns on the roofs of two apartment buildings that towered above the low wooden tenements.

Although the 6th Infantry's 4th Battalion had been deployed to Panama since September, Captain Goss's soldiers had been unable to rehearse their D-day assault in Sand Flea or Purple Storm exercises. It had been considered simply too provocative to roll the squat, boxy tracked vehicles armed with .50-caliber machine guns through the center of Panama City and past Noriega's headquarters. And since the shooting of Lieutenant Paz in these crowded streets Saturday night, Southcom had not authorized any final ground reconnaissance.

But Goss's fellow officers and NCOs knew the PDF and the Digbats would be dug in behind roadblocks and in fortified machine-gun positions in the apartments, ready and waiting for the gringos to attack. And they also knew Noriega's troops would defend their headquarters with savage determination. The walled compound was almost sacred to the PDF. But no one anticipated that the PDF's defensive perimeter would extend a full three blocks from the Comandancia.

As the first platoon of tracks entered the narrow shadows of Avenida A, the vehicles maintained a good interval. But Specialist Darren Marcinkevicius saw the lead track was stopped by the roadblock: two rusty orange municipal dump trucks jammed across the road. The APCs billowed thick diesel exhaust as their drivers fought to maneuver the clumsy vehicles in the crossfire. The young track driver watched two APCs collide in the darkness. He heard on the tactical radio net that soldiers inside were injured by the force of the collision. Multicolored tracers bounced and tumbled down the dark gully between the buildings. A rocket-propelled grenade (RPG) exploded among the APCs, and Marcinkevicius raced his engine, the tracks ripping up chunks of asphalt as the steel-shod vehicle dodged for cover.

But there wasn't much cover to be had, and there certainly wasn't much room to maneuver. The five tracks in the lead platoon fought back as best they could. Each track commander stood precariously in his open hatch behind his .50-caliber machine gun. The fifties from the lead tracks quickly silenced enemy small-arms and automatic weapons fire from behind the roadblock, but PDF and Digbats were pouring down small-arms fire and RPGs from the tenement roofs and balconies. The column had to get past the roadblock before the company could split into platoons and fan out to surround the Comandancia.

The track commanded by Corporal Ivan D. Perez careened onto the sidewalk and leapt ahead into the mouth of an alley. This position gave him a good firing angle to sweep the nearby rooftops and balconies. Under the cover of Perez's .50-caliber machine gun, two tracks rumbled ahead to slam the roadblock vehicles aside.

Perez was still laying down cover fire from his open hatch when he was shot by a sniper. Mortally wounded in the head, he plunged across the track's flat roof. Specialist Charles E. Berry dragged the wounded Perez inside the troop bay, then replaced him at the machine gun as the track roared after the lead vehicles.

One of the tracks was hit by an RPG, which slammed through the armored shell and exploded when it struck the inner skin of the opposite hull side. The crew bailed out into the shellfire and tracers of the street. Several were wounded and had to be dragged through the flaming rubble, back toward Fourth of July. The track burnt with sooty flames. Then the .50-caliber and small-arms ammunition on board began cooking off. The burning track, smacking and rattling with exploding munitions, became a more effective obstacle than any PDF roadblock.

Despite the roadblock and casualties, the soldiers of the 5th Mech were on schedule as they punched their way through El Chorrillo toward the Comandancia. But to the men sweating inside the APCs, time seemed to have frozen in an endless blast of confused noise.[6]

### 0100 Hours, 20 December

Captain George Kunkel flew the AH-6 Little Bird gunship while his copilot, Chief Warrant Officer Fred Horsley, scanned the buildings below for targets and worked the radio. They saw the column of tracks blast through the roadblock on the narrow side street off Avenida A and rumble ahead toward the Comandancia. The Spectre was making cannon runs on the PDF compound itself, and Horsley peered beneath the lenses of his ANVIS-6 night-vision goggles to scan the schematic street plan on his knee board.

The plan outlined the Spectre's kill zone and other no-fly sectors where tank guns up on Quarry Heights would use presurveyed fields of fire. The streets surrounding La Modelo Prison building were crosshatched on the map and marked with the prohibition "NFA JSOTF H-HOUR" (No Fire Area, Joint Special Operations Task Force H-Hour). Their own helicopter could work this sector, but the AH-1 Cobras from Task

Force Wolf swinging in from the bay were restricted to a single approach lane to the Comandancia. The courtyard and red tile roof of the prison's main cellblock was boldly marked with the same warning, this one cited for Task Force Gracia, the Delta Force special operators who had snatched the American prisoner from La Modelo. They had heard the Delta pilot's Mayday call, but hadn't seen the helicopter crash. There was nothing Kunkel and Horsley could do, however, to help the downed crew until this antiaircraft fire was suppressed.

Their knee-board maps identified known PDF gun positions on the rooftops of the multiwing, sixteen-story high-rise apartment dominating El Chorrillo. Banking a thousand feet above the dark neighborhood, the two Special Operations pilots watched the tenements twinkle with muzzle flashes. Lazy green tracers rose toward them, but the PDF were shooting blind. Nearer the Comandancia there were a couple of fires burning in wooden buildings. Captain Kunkel spiraled lower and set up for a minigun run on the apartment roof. His night-vision goggles flared with ragged green flashes as two PDF ZPU machine-gun positions on the roof cut loose at the Spectre and at the sound of the Little Birds trailing Kunkel and Horsley's aircraft. Kunkel lined up the first gun position, a sandbagged heap on the flat tar roof, and waited until he could distinguish the heads of the enemy gunners. The electrically driven minigun spun with its distinctive rough burr. The sandbags disintegrated in a dusty cloud. Kunkel flared back and dodged left to escape fire from the second gun. When he had a clear line of fire, he opened up again. The second ZPU was silenced.

They swept across the corner of the apartment rooftop and banked to engage the Comandancia itself. The air was choppy here from the convection thermals of the scattered tenement fires below. Neither pilot heard the groundfire that hit them, but Horsley saw that George Kunkel was having trouble leveling off. The cyclic control stick was flailing in Kunkel's gloved left hand as he fought to manage engine RPM with his right.

"Cross control," Horsley said into his headset mike. "Let me help."

He grabbed the stick and closed his two hands over Kunkel's fist. They had lost hydraulic power and the rotor was running away from them. Handling the helicopter was suddenly like fighting the tiller of a small sailboat in rough seas. It took the strength of both men to steer the Little Bird toward an asphalt driveway between the buildings to their right.

Just before they hit, they yanked back hard on the control stick to level the nose. But the helicopter hardly slowed. They slammed into the pavement so hard both pilots smashed their helmets into the instrument panel. The aircraft slid down the driveway, across a courtyard, and careened into a concrete pillar. The rotor snapped into several pieces and clattered through the darkness.

When Horsley tried to unbuckle his H-harness, he felt a sudden hot numbness across his hips. The force of the impact had crushed some vertebrae down there. He had to get out before his legs froze up on him. But his Plexiglas door was jammed against the pillar. The narrow cockpit was partially crushed and cluttered with charts and logbooks tossed about. And one section of the instrument panel jutted at a strange angle. Horsley's survival vest was tangled on something in the darkness, and snagged as he fought to scramble out the right-hand door after Kunkel. As he struggled to free himself, choking orange flames puffed behind the Plexiglas canopy. The chopper was about to explode and he was stuck inside.

Then he was falling out the door and onto the broken plaster and concrete littering the courtyard from their crash. He saw Kunkel in the shadows and hobbled to him. The Spectre was up there, close by, banking steeply left to pound a nearby building with its 105 mm howitzer. Horsley peered nervously across the dark courtyard and down the smoky lane, trying to match their ground position with the schematic street plan on his knee board. He then realized that the Spectre was shooting into the Comandancia compound, which lay just beyond the wall of the courtyard where they had crashed.

Kunkel was on his PRC-90 survival radio, speaking as calmly as he could, warning the Spectre that they were down near the Comandancia's southern wall.

Horsley crouched in the darkness, his chest heaving. They were alive, but definitely *not* in a good position. They both had read Task Force Gator's battle book and knew the APCs of the 4/6 Mech would be approaching this sector soon. And the commanders on those tracks had orders to lay down covering fire for the paratroopers from the 508th who would be following them. Horsley wondered who would shoot them first, the PDF in the surrounding buildings or their own troops.[7]

## 0100 Hours, 20 December

Lieutenant Paul Freudenburgh's platoon reached their jump-off point on Roosevelt Avenue a few minutes late. They were above the grass-choked railway embankment that separated the pleasant Diablo Heights neighborhood on the north slope of Ancon Hill from the sprawling National Department of Traffic and Transportation (DNTT) compound and the black expanse of Albrook Field. The night was noisy with gunfire. On the other side of the Heights, the broken overcast flashed with tracers and the cannon fire of orbiting gunships. The trunks of the graceful old coconut palms above the embankment flashed chalky gray in the flickering light of the battlefield. The troops heard mortars and heavy machine guns in the distance.

All the men were squared away in the trucks now, crouching, weapons out. The tailgates were down. The platoon had been given a good position, down behind the overgrown berm of the railway embankment, plenty of cover and concealment from the beige concrete DNTT buildings across Gaillard Highway. But just as the men began to dismount, fire erupted from the sandbagged PDF position guarding the corner of the DNTT compound. Green tracers sailed past overhead, ricocheting off the stucco and fieldstone houses up the slope.

The men froze, some still on the open truckbeds, others hidden behind the big tires. This was the second time in thirty minutes they'd been shot at. But this time, Freudenburgh did not have to shout. The fire-team and squad leaders were on their feet, pushing and shoving the faltering troops from behind the cover of the trucks. Freudenburgh saw one shouting sergeant drag two reluctant soldiers by their web gear and almost toss them back into their fire team.

Once the troops saw the welcome shelter of the embankment ditch, they immediately calmed down. Young kids who'd been scared senseless only a minute before were professional soldiers again, purposefully clearing kuna grass for fire lanes and laying out their spare ammunition and 203 grenades in proper sequence. The enemy tracers snapped by, lower now. But no one broke fire discipline to shoot back, because there was another platoon in the way to their left.

An M-60 down the line cut loose, followed by three well-aimed 203 grenades. The sandbagged post across the highway went silent. Freudenburgh crawled and hopped behind his men, telling them to hold their fire until ordered to shoot.

"When you do fire," he called to each team, "mark your targets. Aim at the windows."

Off to the right, a team from the Bravo Company command group began calling the PDF over a bullhorn, telling the men inside the compound they were surrounded, that they had no choice but to surrender.

The PDF replied with a ragged volley of small-arms fire.

"Get ready," Freudenburgh yelled to his NCOs.

The company commander gave the order, and Freudenburgh relayed it. The M-60s started the firepower demonstration, looping hot red tracers under the limbs of the hardwood trees and into the sandbagged windows of the DNTT buildings. Next came the 203 grenades. A few were low, but most smacked through the windows to detonate with orange flashes inside the buildings.

The bullhorn scratched again. "That was a small demonstration. We ask you to surrender. If you do not," the amplified voice echoed, pausing for effect, "we are prepared to level each and every building." When the bullhorn fell silent, a sniper on the flat roof of the right-hand building began firing blindly. An M-60 from the 2d Platoon raked the roof. They saw the man fall like a sack into the dark parking lot. Now several men in civilian clothes, waving white T-shirts zigzagged up the entrance road toward the gate in the chain-link fence. The troops let them advance, then someone ordered them up the embankment. A car careened down Gaillard Highway from the left and entered the platoon's field of fire just past the Christian Serviceman's Club. Freudenburgh's troops were about to fire when he saw they were civilians. The car swept past unharmed.

But another vehicle, a light green Mustang, sped from the other direction. It was trying to escape from the far corner of the DNTT parking lot. The three men inside were not civilians. Machine guns began firing down the line, and Freudenburgh's troops opened up with their M-16s. The Mustang seemed to wobble, then bounced over the far curb and plowed up the grass at the roadside, coming to rest against the chain-link fence. Radiator steam rose, but the car did not burn. No one moved inside.

Again, the bullhorn echoed. But no more PDF surrendered. An armored personnel carrier from the 4th Battalion, 6th Infantry, rolled along Roosevelt Avenue behind Freudenburgh's troops and took a dominant firing position on the high ground. The track's .50-caliber machine gun laid down a deafening fusillade of armor-piercing fire that knocked big, dusty chunks from the buildings across the way.

Once more the bullhorn called for surrender. Again, the PDF replied with green tracers from their AKs.

As Freudenburgh's men provided cover fire, the squads from the 3d Platoon stood up, humped beneath their ammo loads, and moved down the slope, toward the enemy compound. Another APC rolled ahead to crush the corner of the fence, providing a breach. The men of the 3d Platoon would enter there. It was their job to clear the buildings.

Freudenburgh watched them weave through the darkness. He noted their skilled movement, one squad covering the other, and was proud of their resolute discipline under fire.


## 0105 Hours, 20 December

Captain Timothy Flynn shouted above the blast and shock of the heavy weapons, trying to regain control of the confused melee around him. His troops jumped and scrambled from the deuce-and-a-half trucks more like refugees than well-trained Airborne soldiers. Charlie Company, 1st of the 508th, was at its line of departure and they looked like a bunch of amateurs.

They had had a shaky start to their first combat engagement. Crossing through Balboa, some idiot MP or a straight-leg jerk from the 87th Infantry had cut loose on their trucks with an automatic weapon.

But a gutsy young NCO in the trailing vehicle had stood up and shouted the password. "Bulldog, you asshole," the man yelled. "Cease fire."

The unseen gunner had missed them by a country mile, but the fire had put everybody on edge. And when they'd gotten the order to move ahead to the jump-off point, the carefully arranged vehicle sequence was screwed up. The 2d Platoon's trucks were supposed to have been in the lead with the 1st and 3d bringing up the rear. But the order got reversed.

They were on Calle Balboa beneath the eastern flank of Quarry Heights. Mortar rounds smacked the steep hillside above the hulking concrete Canal Commission buildings ahead of them. Their view of the objective was blocked by tall palm trees and the flank of the Heights, but they could certainly hear the fighting. And the thick orange tracers of heavy machine guns streamed through the night sky.

Flynn jumped down from the truck cab, searching for his executive officer, First Lieutenant Mike Mellor. The troops were bunched up near the trucks, some still struggling with their belts of M-60 ammunition and clumsy 90 mm recoilless rifles. Now the fire-team leaders and platoon sergeants quietly took charge, and order suddenly swept through the ranks, a small miracle that always impressed Flynn, no matter how often he saw it. What had been a mob of scared young troops was now a company assault column in proper formation. Each fire team was at its assigned position in the column, crouching at proper intervals along the curb, machine guns and SAWs correctly sequenced, each platoon leader with his RTO radio man.

"Okay," Flynn shouted to his platoon leaders, "get 'em moving."

The young officers stood in the darkness, pumping their fists in the air, "Move out."

Despite their loads, the troops marched with quiet speed along the curved flank of the hillside, straight toward the intersection of Balboa and Fourth of July. With Quarry Heights behind them, the company now had a good view of the objective ahead. And nobody liked what they saw. The entire city center was blacked out. Several wooden buildings near the Comandancia were burning, with flames leaping a hundred feet in the air. A poorly aimed PDF mortar barrage chopped along Fourth of July and was swallowed by the scrub jungle slope of Quarry Heights. There seemed to be an amazing number of machine guns firing in both directions. While the troops watched, another PDF mortar barrage smacked into the wide road, this one landing short right, with the last several rounds clipping the tenement roofs down the hill in El Chorrillo. Smoke puffed from the wooden buildings, then a ribbon of flame.

The last tracks of the 4/6 Mech were rolling into the chaos across the highway, firing at snipers in the taller buildings. Flynn gave the order for the 3d Platoon to follow them, and Mellor brought up the rest of the company. As they sprinted across the road and entered the narrow streets of El Chorrillo, snipers cut loose from balconies. They passed a shattered roadblock. A dump truck had been pushed halfway through a storefront. There was a red Toyota crushed flat, as if by a junkyard compactor. A shattered and bleeding arm thrust out one window. The street was carpeted with broken glass. Every time a sniper fired and the men hit the pavement, they came up bleeding.

The company passed another ruined roadblock, this one a jumble of scorched sandbags. A fire hydrant had been clipped off by the tracks, and water fountained ten feet in the air. The surrounding buildings had sandbagged positions on the wrought-iron balconies. Obviously the PDF had been expecting them. The 3d Platoon's senior NCO, a calm, laconic sergeant first class named Robert L. Smith, kept his people in the relative shelter of the sidewalk and doorways on the south side of the street. The men were moving well now, after the initial confusion. Ahead, the tracks were still engaging machine-gun positions, grinding and rumbling through the narrow streets, billowing dense clouds of exhaust smoke as the drivers struggled to maneuver among obstacles. Overhead the Spectres growled through the smoke, relentlessly pounding the Comandancia. Whining little helicopters swept just above the rooftops, their miniguns buzzing like runaway power saws.

Sergeant First Class Smith saw movement on the balcony of a stucco building across the street. A man jumped up clutching a weapon. Smith crouched on the pavement, raised his M-16 and dropped the sniper with a well-aimed burst. Suddenly the entire block erupted with small-arms fire.

Green tracers ricocheted and sailed wildly down the street. But this time Charlie Company's troops exhibited well-honed discipline. The men took proper cover and held their fire, waiting for the hidden PDF and Digbat gunners to get sloppy and expose their positions. Charlie Company had been selected for this operation because the outfit had gone through the mechanized MOUT training program at Fort Chaffee, Arkansas, the previous August. And those long weeks of hard training now paid off. A platoon leader ordered the trailing tracks to hold position, so that their .50 calibers could engage the heavier PDF guns in the upper windows of the nearby high-rise. The Mech officers called for Little Bird fire support. Now every time the enemy tried to use those guns, the positions were raked by heavy machine guns from below and the devastating fire from the helicopters' miniguns.

The troops in the street had already pinpointed the PDF snipers. When an AK assault rifle cut loose, the balcony or window was plastered with M-16 fire, pinning down the enemy soldier. Then a Charlie Company man would carefully sight his 203 grenade launcher and lob 40 mm grenades into the enemy position. The grenades hit with a distinctive orange flash and an echoing crack among the tight-packed buildings. One by one the snipers were eliminated.

Engineers from the Mech were moving up to prepare a forty-pound cratering charge to breach the back wall of the Comandancia, just around the corner from the high-rise. As the men worked around their track, two of them were hit. Again, Charlie Company effectively eliminated the sniper. Captain Tim Flynn was impressed by his troops' fire discipline. Some wooden buildings had burnt out now, and there were crowds of civilian refugees scurrying down the street whenever the gunfire slackened. Many were barefoot on the broken glass. Most were half-dressed, struggling with sacks and suitcases. The women carried or led screaming children. Every time refugees appeared, an American soldier jumped from cover to shout, "Cease fire!" and help them on their way. The company had four 90 mm recoilless rifles, which would have been devastating against the snipers on the tenement balconies. But the men knew there were still hundreds of civilians up in those buildings, and no one fired the heavy weapons for fear of blasting through the flimsy rooms.

When the firing along the road finally slackened, Flynn had his company properly positioned by squads, inside the cover of doorways and stairwells. The 2d Platoon faced the side wall of the Comandancia, just opposite the compound's long, tile-roofed cafeteria. A track swung around and backed up against the PDF compound. Engineers hurriedly positioned their cratering charge on its tripod legs against the wall. They were conscious of the wounded men they'd left back on the corner of Avenida A and called Flynn, requesting permission to fire the charge. But the young captain ordered them to wait for authority from the task force commander. In theory, the PDF inside the compound were still to be given the chance to surrender before the American troops broke down the walls and came in to clear the buildings.

But the engineers obviously saw this process was ridiculous. The Spectres' fire had been augmented by four Marine light armored vehicles (LAVs), armed with 25 mm chain guns, positioned along Fourth of July Avenue. As the engineers crouched in the shadows of the wall, the compound inside was being pounded by 105 mm and 40 mm cannons from the gunships and raked with 25 mm fire from the LAVs. If that wasn't an inducement to surrender, nothing was.

"Fire in the hole!" an engineer shouted on the PRC-77 radio, signifying the crater charge's fuse had been lit. Seconds later, the street erupted with a volcanic blast. When the choking smoke thinned, a wide section of the wall was down, the street littered with a heap of shattered fieldstone and concrete.

The men of Charlie Company lay in their cover, waiting for the order to move inside.[8]

# 6

# 20 December 1989

---

# H-Hour: The Canal

*0045 Hours, 20 December*

A Liberian tanker, a Japanese automobile transporter, and a cruise ship were approaching the Pacific entrance of the Canal off Flamenco Island at the end of the Amador causeway, when the vessels were hailed by the Balboa Harbor pilots' office on VHF radio. Their watch officers were advised there would be delays entering the Miraflores Locks. When one bridge officer requested an anchorage berth on the city side of the causeway, the pilots' office directed the ship to join other merchant vessels in an alternate anchorage off the mud flats of Punta Guinea to the west. The instructions were unusual. But the ships' officers were confident the delay would not seriously affect their schedules. After all, the Canal had never been closed in seventy-five years of operation.

Further north where the headlands merged, the tall, girdered arch of the Bridge of the Americas spanned the narrows called La Boca. The manmade waterway around the bridge retained the appearance of a tropical river. On the western banks of the Canal entrance, hills of scrub jungle flanked the marshy mouth of the Rio Farfan, masking the Howard Air Force Base–Fort Kobbe complex. The opposite bank was unbroken civilization: the tile-roofed barracks and housing blocks of Fort Amador, the yacht club with its gaggle of moored sailboats and power cruisers, and the industrial sprawl of the tank farm, melding into the docks and warehouses of Balboa Harbor. The dark mound of Ancon Hill with the huge, floodlit flag of Panama dominated this bank.

The only buildings visible near the western approaches to the bridge were the sheds and barracks on the U.S. Navy Panama Canal Station, the base known as Rodman. Three old wooden docks jutted into the harbor. When the first gunfire and grenade explosions echoed across the water from Balboa, the street lamps on the base and the floodlights over the piers blinked out. Marines in full combat gear took positions on the cantilevered tidal bridge connecting the docks to shore. A small unit of Navy SEALs lay in an open, sandbagged machine-gun emplacement near the end of the center pier. The men were surrounded by radios and weapons. They stared across the Canal through magnifying PVS-4 night sights, studying the narrow boat basin inside Balboa Harbor. A dull gray PDF patrol boat was moored alongside two white power yachts, one with an arrogantly high flying bridge. The yachts ranked from the base of the pier in ascending size, with the largest moored in the deepest water, and were named accordingly: the Macho de Monte I and Macho de Monte II. They were the personal property of General Manuel Noriega. As such, they were legitimate military targets. Moreover, they represented a possible escape route.

Two black combat rubber raiding craft moved slowly across the dark harbor toward the boat docks. The CRRCs bucked the stiff current of the ebbing tides, cutting multiple doglegs to avoid the brighter water where reflected shore light shimmered. When the boats were well up-tide from the docks, several SEALs wearing black, nonreflective wetsuits slipped over the boats' flanks and disappeared beneath the murky surface. The SEALs breathed pure oxygen through Dreäger closed-circuit scuba apparatus that emitted no telltale bubbles. Slung low on the men's bellies, the flat domes of the breathing units held a 200-minute supply of oxygen, more than enough for the present mission. But the SEALs had to be sure to stay above a depth of twenty-five feet. Deeper than that and they would suffer potentially fatal oxygen toxicity. They kicked with languid strength against the current, steering by dim chemical lights attached to their wrist compasses.

Once near the docks, the demolition men rose from the dark toward the rippling green surface of the boat slips. Each SEAL clutched a fiberglass explosives carrier, like a miniature supermarket basket. The men worked quickly in the black water. One two-man team set limpet mines under the stern of the patrol boat. The other pair of SEALs molded finger-thick rings of plastic explosive around each of the yacht's dual stainless steel propeller shafts. Noriega's boats represented a treasure house of potential criminal evidence that might be used against him in the federal drug-trafficking prosecution. He was known to conduct especially sensitive business aboard these yachts. The charges were precisely calculated to sever the shafts just forward of the screws, without damaging the hulls. After the charges were primed, the men snapped on the preset, twenty-minute timers and slid cut-rubber tubing over the switches to jam them open.[1]

In less than five minutes, the SEALs kicked back down into the muddy darkness. Once more they swam in doglegs, back toward the waiting CRRCs. Out in the harbor they rose nearer the surface, where the tide rip was less severe. But then they heard small-arms rounds smacking into the water above. They had no way of knowing the fire was simply stray bullets from the battle ashore that had begun prematurely. The men were almost to their rubber boats when the charges blew. Down in the black swirling tide, the explosions sounded like thunder.

Hidden behind sheds and warehouses on the land side of Rodman, a mobile strike force of U.S. Marines was prepared to move out. At 0045 hours, the Marines mounted up on a column of ten light armored vehicles from Delta Company, 2d Light Armored Infantry Battalion. The eight-wheeled LAVs sped out the Rodman gate and turned right onto the Inter-American Highway. Four hardshell Humvees of the Marine Security Force Company brought up the rear of the column. As the LAVs sped east, the Humvees peeled off to the left and roared up the slope to the Bridge of the Americas. Two backed into blocking positions, partly shielded by the ditch of the roadside. The other two turned into the flat parking lot at the base of the bridge, and swung around so their M-60 machine guns could sweep the grassy hillside sloping down to the Canal entrance below. The western approaches to the bridge, which was a critical choke point on the Inter-American Highway, were now effectively blocked.

The LAVs and Humvees were from Task Force Semper Fi, the U.S. Marine Corps' contribution to Blue Spoon. As the Security Force gunners traversed their M-60s and studied their fields of fire through night sights, other Marines jumped down from the vehicles and set up their roadblock. They dragged tire-bursting arrays of road jacks and coils of concertina razor wire across the three-lane highway. With these obstacles in place, the men trotted lower down the hill and set up their Claymore mines in the tall grass off the shoulders. They made certain the mines' explosive maws—"THIS SIDE TOWARD ENEMY"—pointed correctly to provide an overlapping kill zone.

While the Security Force Marines worked at the bridge, the column of Delta Company LAVs approached its first objective. The main column continued east toward the Dignity Battalion stronghold in the town of Arraijan. But third platoon scouts aboard four LAVs had been ordered to capture the National Department of Traffic and Transportation (DNTT) Station No. 2, located just off the Inter-American Highway among the jumble of cantinas and souvenir stands near the entrance to Howard Air Force Base. As elsewhere in Panama, this DNTT station had been taken over by the PDF and served as an unofficial headquarters for the local Dignity Battalion. If it were quickly captured, the Digbat unit would be decapitated.

The Marines did not expect heavy resistance from the station. For several weeks, Delta Company had patrolled this highway during increasingly confrontational Sand Flea exercises. The LAVs—*tanquitas* to the local people—were an intimidating presence. Standing high on its eight-wheeled chassis, each armored vehicle mounted a chiseled turret with a fast-firing 25 mm chain-gun cannon and a 7.62 mm machine gun. The angled armored hull could stop or deflect all but the heaviest PDF automatic weapons. During the Sand Flea exercises, the local Digbats had become adept at blocking the highway with wrecked cars and burning tires. And the Marines were prepared to blast their way through any obstacles.

It had taken the Security Force less than ten minutes to block the bridge. As they worked in the hot darkness, the city across the Canal crackled and thumped with the swelling battle.


Humvees from the 5th Battalion, 87th Infantry and the 519th Military Police Battalion sped out the front gate of Fort Clayton across the tracks of the Panama railway, and snaked along the narrow, twisting road to the raised embankment of the Miraflores Locks. The lightly armed Panama Canal Commission security guards made no attempt to resist the American combat troops. Within minutes, hardshell machine-gun Humvees guarded the power plant and the only two approach roads to the long, parallel locks. The troops fanned out and occupied the concrete, tile-roofed operations tower that dominated the lock complex. Manuel Noriega had vowed to sabotage the Canal, should America intervene militarily. But if the PDF intended to strike the vital Miraflores Locks, they would have to fight their way through Claymore mines and interlocking machine-gun fire to do so.


## 0050 Hours, 20 December

The most serious enemy threat at the northern entrance of the Canal came from the 8th Naval Infantry Company stationed in Coco Solo, the small port town facing the city of Colon across an inlet of Limon Bay, and from Dignity Battalions in the city itself. The metropolitan complex incorporating Colon, Cristobal, and Coco Solo spread across several peninsulas and headlands of reclaimed marsh on the eastern side of the bay. About 60,000 people lived in these communities, most dependent on the Canal or port for their livelihoods. The Gatun

Locks, which separated the waters of the Atlantic from Lake Gatun, lay about six miles southwest of the city.

Although equally vulnerable to sabotage, the two-level Gatun Locks lay entirely within the embrace of twin American military installations, Fort Sherman on the west and Fort Davis to the east. Just before H-hour, heavily armed units from the Army's Jungle Operations Training Center (JOTC) at Fort Sherman secured the locks. The JOTC's training cadre battalion, which was heavy with Vietnam veteran NCOs, was broken into small task force units and placed under the operational control of the 3d Brigade, 7th Light Infantry Division, which had command of Task Force Atlantic. While several of the battalion's teams secured Fort Sherman, the approach roads to it, and small nearby Army facilities, a larger, platoon-size force spread out over the Gatun Locks complex. Their Humvees, armed with M-60 machine guns, and sandbagged trucks blocked the entrance to the Gatun Panama Commission housing area, the dam spillway bridge, hydroelectric plant, and the swing bridge across the locks.

In the months leading up to the operation, Fort Sherman had been repeatedly probed by armed PDF infiltrators, often dressed in civilian clothes and posing as trespassing hunters. The marshy margins of the locks and Army bases provided an ideal staging area for saboteurs. But the experienced NCOs from the JOTC were in their element. They taught jungle offensive and defensive operations, and most of them had served several tours in Panama. Their listening posts and roadblocks effectively shielded the vulnerable lock complex from PDF and Digbat saboteurs.

The task of sealing off Colon fell to the 4th Battalion, 17th Infantry, a unit of the 7th Light Infantry Division that had been in Panama since October as part of the Operation Nimrod Dancer augmentation force, following the failed coup. Colon and Cristobal lay at the northern end of a wasp-waisted peninsula. The narrowest point, a causeway road and warehouse complex known as the "Colon Bottleneck," was the obvious spot to establish a blocking force to seal off the city from the Trans-Isthmus Highway. A composite force made up of MPs and support troops from the 4/17th, as well as assorted

The Build-Up—A Military Airlift Command C-141 lands at Howard Air Force Base, Panama, carrying equipment for the augmentation forces ordered to Panama after the failed October 1989 coup attempt. (*Department of Defense*)

December 1989—A UH-60 Black Hawk helicopter rolls off a C-5A during the build-up period. C-5As also delivered AH-64 Apache attack helicopters at night when their arrival was screened by darkness. (*Department of Defense*)

The Build-Up—A batch of Humvees roll off a C-5A at Howard Air Force Base. The Humvee proved itself in combat in Panama to be a versatile and ruggedly dependable replacement for the venerable jeep. (*Department of Defense*)

D-Day—An Air Force C-130 arrives at Lawson Army Airfield on the rainy evening of December 19, 1989, to pick up soldiers of the 75th Ranger Regiment for the initial air drops at Rio Hato and Torrijos-Tocumen airfields. (*Department of Defense*)

Rangers on a practice jump for the Panama drop. Because the drop zones at Rio Hato and Torrijos-Tocumen were less than thirty-five seconds "long," it was essential all the jumpers exited the aircraft quickly. Note the folded bench seats in the C-130 (left) and the heavy equipment carried by the Ranger beneath his reserve chute (center left). (*Courtesy 75th Ranger Regiment*)

Men of the 75th Ranger Regiment perform final equipment checks aboard a C-130 inbound to the drop zone. A few of the older Rangers were veterans of combat drops; many of the younger men had logged fewer than twenty training jumps. They were all aware that a night combat drop from 500 feet was a serious undertaking. (*Department of Defense*)

D-Day—"LAVs" of the Marines' Second Light Armored Infantry Battalion guard the streets of Arraijan on the morning of D-Day, effectively blocking the Inter-American Highway to prevent Panama Defense Forces (PDF) reinforcements from reaching Panama City. (*Department of Defense*)

D-Day—Marines of the First Fleet Antiterrorism Security Team (FAST) search for fleeing PDF and Dignity Battalion troops in the outskirts of Arraijan. The Marine at the left carries a 9 mm Colt assault weapon and is equipped for Military Operations in Urban Terrain (MOUT). Both Marines wear glint tape on their left sleeve, which is visible through U.S. night-vision devices. (*Department of Defense*)

D-Day—Howard Air Force Base. Hangar Number Three, the Special Operations Forces' headquarters at left. Note the heavy MH-53 PAVE LOW helicopters on the central apron, the AH-6 Little Bird near the hangar. During the first two days of Operation Just Cause, more helicopter sorties were flown from Howard than normally occur in a year. (*Department of Defense*)

D-Day—Fort Kobbe. Many of the troop-lift helicopters, such as these Black Hawks, had to be parked in improvised "corrals" to accommodate the unprecedented number of aircraft at the Howard Air Force Base–Fort Kobbe complex. (*Department of Defense*)

Howard Air Force Base—A CH-47 Chinook of the 1/228 Aviation takes on combat troops for a follow-on operation. The "local knowledge" of these Panama-based helicopter crews proved invaluable. (*Department of Defense*)

D-Day—Paratroopers of the 82d Airborne Division on their Pickup Zone at Tocumen Air Base. They have formed into 15-man "chalks" for the air assaults on the division's objectives. (*Department of Defense*)

D-Day—Air Force armorers load a rocket pod aboard an A-37 attack jet about to fly a close air-support mission. (*Department of Defense*)

Tocumen Air Base—This PDF Boeing 727 was used to fly in from Rio Hato the Macho de Monte reinforcements who had helped crush the abortive October 1989 coup. Seizing the Torrijos airport–Tocumen Air Base complex was a priority D-Day objective. (*Department of Defense*)

Rangers guard the perimeter of Tocumen Air Base on the morning of D-Day. Note that the Rangers, like other Special Operations Forces, did not wear protective flak jackets. The lack of lightweight ballistic body armor suitable for tropical operations was one of the few equipment shortcomings of Just Cause. (*Department of Defense*)

Rangers at Rio Hato after securing the objectives. Note the night-sight on the M-60 machine gun carried by the Ranger at the right. The ability of the Rangers to assemble and fight effectively as fire teams as soon as they landed at Rio Hato did much to crush the savage initial resistance by the PDF's Macho de Monte troops, thus minimizing U.S. casualties. (*Courtesy 75th Ranger Regiment*)

The Rangers' "armor," one of the specially modified gun jeeps deployed with the 75th Ranger Regiment. The vehicles can mount a night-sighted 90 mm recoilless rifle. Working with motorcycle outriders, the gun jeeps greatly extend the Rangers' mobility. (*Department of Defense*)

cooks, truck drivers, and riggers from the 3d Battalion, 504th Parachute Infantry Regiment, sealed the bottleneck and blocked the main road junctions to the south. The 3/504 PIR was nominally in Panama to undergo jungle training. In reality, the battalion of tough, MOUT-qualified paratroopers from Fort Bragg had been broken into company and platoon task forces and given a variety of difficult H-hour objectives along the Canal's east bank.

Sealing off Colon was an important mission. The city was a Dignity Battalion stronghold, with thousands of Noriega loyalists among the unemployed stevedores and duty-free port workers, who had fallen on hard times during the two years of American economic sanctions following Noriega's criminal indictment. The officers who had written the Blue Spoon OPLAN fully anticipated armed resistance from the civilians of Colon.

A platoon from 3/504 PIR's Delta Company was just setting up a roadblock guarding the Coco Solo hospital on the Trans-Isthmus Highway when a rusty pickup truck full of drunken but unarmed Digbats confronted the platoon leader, 1st Lieutenant Matt Miller. His unit had pushed two commandeered buses across the road as a temporary block while a squad of engineers laid out road jacks, strung concertina wire, and threw up sandbagged machine-gun emplacements. Miller's first sergeant yelled for a Spanish speaker to convince the surly Digbats "they'd better not fuck around with the Airborne."

A Puerto Rican squad leader calmly told the men in the truck that the war had started and they would not live another minute unless they turned around and drove back to Colon. The Digbats seemed inclined to argue. But the confrontation abruptly ended when a white Nissan security service van and an accompanying car, full of armed and uniformed PDF, sped up the dark highway directly toward the diagonal gap between the buses. Lieutenant Miller and the NCOs fired warning shots, but the vehicles did not slow down. The PDF drivers were used to calling the bluff of American troops in dozens of such confrontations during the antigringo demonstrations and the Sand Flea exercises.

Miller jumped behind a bus and gave the order to fire. The

platoon had two Humvees with .50-caliber machine guns mounted. They pounded the swerving vehicles. Now the whole platoon was firing M-16s. When Miller shouted for cease-fire, the van was a shattered wreck. The car had been ripped apart and lay smoking behind the van. The PDF inside were dead or dying. Without any further argument, the driver of the pickup backed away and roared off into the darkness.[2]

The word would soon be out among the Digbats of Colon that it was not wise to try to force American roadblocks. The weeks of tense but nonviolent confrontations were over. This was war.

Colon was sealed off, but the PDF's 8th Naval Infantry Company in the nearby peninsula town of Coco Solo remained to be dealt with. That assignment fell to Charlie Company of the 4/17 Infantry. They knew their enemy well, having been billeted since October in an empty wing of the Cristobal High School in the town of Coco Solo. The school was one of two identical parallel three-story concrete structures on a joint-use military facility similar to Fort Amador. The other building housed the PDF barracks, a garment factory, and a Chinese restaurant. And there were American families living here as well in a row of neat, palm-shaded bungalows just behind the high school.

Charlie Company's commander, Captain Christopher Rizzo, had spent two months developing an effective plan to take down the PDF company without jeopardizing the American civilians and the large Chinese family who lived above the restaurant or destroying the high school.

He used the repeated Sand Flea exercises, during which his company demonstrated America's "treaty rights" by throwing up a defensive cordon around the high school and housing area, to desensitize the PDF. While the Panamanian marines swaggered about the lawn separating the two buildings, Rizzo was carefully plotting fire lanes and defensive positions. He brought in two 20 mm Vulcan Gatling guns mounted on Humvees from an Air Defense Artillery unit. The PDF taunted the Vulcan crews, sitting out in the heavy tropical sun while teenage students in surfer shorts and Bart Simpson T-shirts strolled to their classes. Yet the Panamanian soldiers had better sense than to seriously provoke the gunners.

At H-hour, Rizzo sealed off the road behind the high school, using Military Police and a rifle platoon. One of the blocking squads quietly moved from house to house, evacuating the American dependent families, who took refuge on the ground floor and cinder-block garage of the furthest house. With the Americans out of small-arms range, Rizzo maneuvered a rifle platoon, the Vulcan guns, and a squad armed with AT-4 anti-tank rockets around the flank of the high school to face the PDF barracks.

All the troops wore full combat gear, including Kevlar body armor. Except for their extra ammunition loads, their appearance was no more threatening tonight than it had been during the Sand Fleas. But, no sooner had they assembled than the PDF began firing from the sandbagged windows of the barracks. Obviously, the Panamanians had received word that war had begun. Rizzo had a platoon moving parallel to the barracks, en route to the nearby PDF patrol-boat dock. That platoon returned fire with an M-60 machine gun, while the men of the attacking force dashed to their jump-off positions. The dark lawn between the two buildings was lit by tracer rounds. Sergeant David Rainer led his squad across the lawn to the cover of some palm trees. He watched in horrified fascination as PDF AK-47 tracers flew past his face and chewed up the grass between his boots.

Once the attack force was under cover, Rizzo took the battery-operated bullhorn and read from the standard text of the OPLAN surrender message, noting he was "prepared to destroy the building," if the PDF continued resisting. He then proceeded with his firepower demonstration. The two Vulcans cut loose with deafening ten-round bursts of 20 mm cannon fire. Rizzo had told them to keep firing for two full minutes, and to aim at the barracks upper windows, to terrorize the enemy without inflicting unnecessary casualties. At such close range in this built-up area the Vulcan fire was unearthly, molten slabs of tracers like glowing ingots slashing and careening in the darkness.

Under the cover of this fire, the rifle platoon advanced to

force their way into the PDF building through the doors of the garment factory. They used standard MOUT procedures, with two-man teams clearing each doorway before a squad entered a room. The first people they encountered were seventeen terrified Chinese, ranging in age from babies to a shrieking grandmother. Luckily, the troops had not fired or thrown grenades when they encountered confused movement in the dark factory room. Sergeant Rainer managed to get the civilians out of the building unharmed. He then used C-4 explosive to blow the door that separated the factory's sewing room from the PDF's gymnasium. The platoon moved gingerly into this dark, echoing hall by four-man fire teams. The air was bitter with cordite, and their rubber-cleated boots kicked spent shell casings across the hardwood floor. The PDF had just been here, but had obviously retreated further into the building.

Rainer called his platoon leader on the Tac radio and suggested another firepower demonstration, focused on the end of the building. Rizzo agreed. This time the Vulcans walked their fire down the side of the building toward the ground-floor windows. Crouching in the dark gym, the attack element could hear the concrete walls twang and shudder with the impact of the exploding cannon rounds.

Rizzo's Spanish translator had just begun to renew the call for surrender, when a white sheet fluttered from the end window of the PDF barracks. The 8th Naval Infantry Company, who had taken such pleasure in mocking the gringo Vulcan gunners assigned to guard high school students, had seen enough of war. The entire company surrendered without firing another shot.

## 0057 Hours, December 20

The commander of the 3d Battalion, 504th Parachute Infantry, was hunched uncomfortably in the blacked-out OH-58 scout helicopter. Lieutenant Colonel Lynn Moore was too tall for the cramped rear cockpit, and the aviator's helmet with radio headset and ANVIS-6 night-vision goggles further restricted his movement. But Moore forgot his discomfort and concentrated on the scene below.

His Command and Control helicopter hovered 200 meters from the compound of Renacer Prison, which spread across the cleared top of a steep jungle bluff above the confluence of the Canal and the Chagres River near the town of Gamboa. Moore stared at the prison's main lock-up, a floodlit rectangle enclosed by a high chain-link fence topped by razor wire. The cellblock was a low concrete structure along the fence line to the left. A dispensary and administrative block adjoined the cells to form a single L-shaped structure. Gravel walkways bordered a narrow exercise yard marked with chalk lines. A single guard tower with a peaked metal roof stood at the upper left-hand corner, dominating the entire fenced compound. The twin headquarters and office buildings, joined by a shaded portico of corrugated roofing, took up the remaining flat ground on the top of the bluff. A railroad line and high-voltage power cables ran between these buildings and the reinforced concrete guard barracks on a hilltop nearer the Canal.

Renacer Prison was the H-hour objective of Charlie Company, 3/504. The other companies and platoons of Lynn Moore's battalion were spread out along the Canal's east bank, about to assault four other H-hour objectives. But Moore considered the mission at Renacer the most important and dangerous his troops had been given. There were over sixty prisoners jammed into the small cellblock, most of them rebellious PDF officers and men who had survived the failed October coup attempt and subsequent brutal treatment. Moore had also been alerted that there might be two mysterious American "ecologists" among the prisoners at Renacer. He suspected they were intelligence operatives swept up by the PDF during the increased tension of recent weeks. And, like other political prisoners in Noriega's jails, they faced immediate execution when the American attack began.

Colonel Moore's battalion had come to Panama ten days before as part of a scheduled rotation through the Jungle Operations Training Center at Fort Sherman. But 3/504 had only a few days' training on the course before they were put under the operational control of Moore's old friend, Colonel Keith Kellogg, commander of the 3d Brigade, 7th Light Infantry Division. They then began a series of Sand Flea contingency exercises, which Moore figured were actual assault rehearsals rather than just demonstrations of the American military's freedom of movement rights in the old Canal Zone.

One of these Sand Fleas had involved Charlie Company at Renacer. On the night of December 16, Captain Derek Johnson, the company commander, had been ordered to load three platoons into an LCM landing craft and move down the Canal from Fort Davis near the Gatun Locks. While Alpha Company, loaded aboard another LCM, had stormed ashore at the town of Gamboa just across the Chagres River bridge from Renacer Prison, Johnson's LCM had plowed into the dock under the Renacer bluff and dropped its heavy ramp, splintering the dock's planking. He had then proceeded to march his fully armed troops boldly up the hillside and into the prison compound. They had been immediately challenged by a shouting, angry band of PDF guards, commanded by an outraged lieutenant colonel. A tense face-off had ensued, with the tall PDF colonel screaming at Captain Johnson that under the terms of the treaty Johnson had no right to bring his men onto this facility without prior consultation.

Derek Johnson was a soft-spoken young black officer built like an NFL fullback. He had listened briefly to the shrill abuse from the Panamanian officer, then cut him short. "Okay, Colonel," Johnson had conceded, "fine. We're consulting now. My troops move out again in five minutes."

The PDF commander had looked around the line of American paratroopers, decked out in full combat gear, their weapons locked and loaded. He then retreated to his headquarters to seek advice from the Comandancia. When he reappeared, he told Johnson five minutes' notice was too short, an insult to the honor of the PDF.

"Fine, Colonel," Johnson had replied. "We'll make it fifteen minutes."

Fifteen minutes later, Captain Johnson had moved his company in platoon combat formation slowly through the prison compound, then formed them up again at the guard post under the mahogany trees at the Gaillard Highway outside the PDF facility.

Moore had flown aboard this same blacked-out observation helicopter the night of the Sand Flea at Renacer. He and the pilot had watched the unfolding confrontation so intently from their hover position low over the Canal that neither man had seen the huge white freighter turn into the Bordada Gamboa channel. Then the copilot had scanned out the left side of the cockpit.

"Holy shit!" the young warrant officer had shouted.

They had almost been in the branches of the freighter's cargo booms when the pilot flared off. After the three of them had calmed down enough to speak, Moore had commented wryly, "Well, at least we'd have made history. That would have been the first time a ship ran down a helicopter."

That same night, Lynn Moore's other companies had staged similar Sand Flea rehearsals at objectives in the town of Gamboa, at the Madden Dam up the Chagres River, and at the PDF's main logistics' base at Cerro Tigre further down the canal.

Those Sand Fleas had gone down three days earlier. As tense and demanding as they had seemed, the confrontations had, after all, only been training. Tonight was combat, and Charlie Company's commander Derek Johnson could no longer depend on the ferocious appearance of his troops to intimidate the PDF guards. Two of his platoons were still going to use the LCM landing craft to hit the dock at the base of the bluff. But the actual assault element into the prison exercise yard had to get there more quickly. So the twenty-two men of Team Oswalt would be landed from two UH-1 Huey helicopters inside the fenced compound, right at the steel cellblock door.

Assaulting such a small landing zone at night, probably under fire, demanded unusual courage and skill from the helicopter crews. The Hueys would have to come in low over the Canal, shoot up the bluff, and clear the high obstacle of the power lines before swooping almost straight down into the prison exercise yard. But Moore was confident the crews from the 1st Battalion, 228th Aviation Regiment based at Fort Kobbe, were up to the demanding task. The unit was permanently stationed in Panama and its air crews knew the country and the flying conditions well. The pilot of the lead Huey, Chief Warrant Officer Michael Loats, and his copilot, Warrant Officer Duane Treadway, had practiced flying steep approaches to tight LZs. But for safety reasons, they had never actually flown into such a narrow landing zone among actual rotor-snapping obstacles such as power lines, light poles, and high chain-link fences. Moore was a qualified helicopter pilot himself, and he knew the forty-degree glide slope into the prison yard was within the skills of a veteran pilot like Loats. But Moore also realized that delivering Team Oswalt to the doors of the prison would require a straight approach with no evasive maneuvers. If the PDF were alert and shooting at the choppers, the pilots would simply have to grit their teeth and get on with the job.

Above all, this had to be a precisely timed operation. Led by Moore's Command and Control ship and a sniper chopper, the two Hueys from Fort Sherman would assault the LZ at exactly 0100, thirty seconds after their fire support AH-1 Cobra gunship from Task Force Hawk blasted the guard quarters on the nearby hilltop. The Cobra would be the first aircraft on station, arriving at 0059 from Fort Kobbe to the south. Derek Johnson and the bulk of Charlie Company would storm ashore from the LCM at 0100, and rush up the bluff to lay down fire support. A third Huey carrying the ten company scouts would hit the prison guard post on the Gaillard road and seal the compound entrance. Finally, a sniper, sitting in the door of a second OH-58, would neutralize the guard tower outside the northwest corner of the fenced prison yard. The sniper would fire precisely, aiming his shots on an angle to avoid the Team Oswalt men below, or the scouts landing 500 meters away.

It was a complex plan, but certainly well within the capabilities of the troops involved. The element of surprise was important, of course, but not absolutely essential. The coordinated use of sudden, overwhelming force *was* vital, however. Two SEAL reconnaissance teams had been watching Re-

nacer Prison from hidden observation posts on nearby hilltops
for the past four days. The SEALs were probably the best recon men in the world. Their team leader had exfiltrated before dawn that morning, and that afternoon, at Fort Sherman,
had presented Moore with a detailed target report, including
excellent infrared photos of the prison compound. The SEAL
officer had assured Moore that at H-hour the bulk of the PDF
guard contingent would be in their barracks, not the fenced
prison compound.

That had been excellent news. But there had been other,
later information that eroded Moore's optimism. In the middle
of their final flight briefing on the pick-up zone at Fort Sherman that evening, Colonel Keith Kellogg, the brigade commander, had taken Moore aside.

"Intel just intercepted a PDF radio message," Kellogg whispered. "They're saying, 'The party's on for one o'clock tonight.'"

So much for tactical surprise.

And there were other nasty surprises. Colonel Moore had
spent a year in Vietnam, following his graduation from West
Point. He was well acquainted with Murphy's Laws of Combat,
especially No. 11: "Good weather ends when the operation be-
gins." Tonight was no exception. A thick overcast hung low
over the Isthmus of Panama, with the tops of the taller hills
along the Canal swallowed by clouds. And there were rolling
banks of dense fog just above the water. Given this weather, it
was no surprise their fire-support Cobra was late arriving from
Fort Kobbe.

But they couldn't wait for the Cobra. The two OH-58s led
the three Hueys down the Canal. Moore's pilot banked hard
left to hold hover a hundred meters southeast of the prison.
The sniper helicopter crossed above them and slid into hover
forty meters from the guard tower. Chief Warrant Officer
Loats led his two-chopper flight straight in toward the bluff,
while the scouts' Huey continued down the Canal, then
banked left around the prison compound to assault the guard
post on the road. Loats' Huey was almost at the power lines
and there was no sign of the Cobra. The disparate aircraft
were not linked by secure FM, so Moore had insisted on mini-

mal radio traffic until contact was made with the enemy.[3]

"Joker 31 is on short final," Loats called. "Going in." His voice was dry and precise.

Moore clicked his mike button twice to acknowledge. There was still no sign of the Cobra, so the Hueys were hitting the LZ without fire support.

Specialist George J.C. Theophle III sat on the right door-gunner's seat of Joker 31, the lead Huey, training his M-60 at the dark bluff. He had his night goggles perfectly adjusted, and could see good depth and detail out there around the dimly lit prison guards' barracks. Before leaving Fort Sherman, Loats had had the crew remove the sling seats in the troop bay. The eleven guys from the 82d Airborne sat on the open door sills, their feet hanging out with their boots touching the skids. This team had positioned their three SAW gunners and two guys with 203 grenade launchers on the right side. The guys in the left door had strict orders not to fire to avoid hitting the cellblock.

As they cleared the power line and tilted steeply onto final, Theophle realized they were not going to get any cover fire.

"Hit the guard post," Loats ordered.

"Roger that, sir," the gunner replied. He cut loose with his M-60, walking the bursts through the narrow windows of the concrete structure. As soon as he fired, he saw PDF in other windows return the fire, the green tracers leaving sparkler trails in his goggles. The men seated in the door beside him opened up with their SAWs and 203s. The grenades were deflected by the rotor wash and exploded short of the barracks.

They were steeply tilted now, and Theophle caught a glimpse of the trailing Huey just clearing the wire. The chopper's skids seemed to touch a cable, and there was a blinding green explosion of sparks. But the chopper cleared the power line and was behind them on the final glide slope. Now the lights were out all around the prison. And the black sky was filled with crisscrossing tracers. Theophle knew they were going to be hit and probably shot down. All he could do was keep firing. He heard a metallic snap and saw a rotor spark orange about halfway out to the tip. But the pitch didn't change so they were okay.

Then they were down inside the fence. He kept firing to the right as the soldiers tumbled from the door. Through his headset he heard the pilots talking. He saw soldiers running on the ground. He saw the clouds of hot, crazy tracers. They climbed away, banking to the left, out into the darkness of the Canal. Somehow they had not been crippled.[4]


Lynn Moore watched the two Hueys tilt into the prison yard, drop their troops, and climb away through the lashing bands of PDF fire. Miraculously, neither helicopter was shot down. The men of Team Oswalt were moving with disciplined precision, despite the small-arms fire that plunged around them. Then Moore saw movement to his right. The Cobra was out there in the mist, dipping and bobbing like an angry, prehistoric insect. A long gout of flame poured from the gunship's 20 mm cannon, probing and stabbing at the PDF quarters.

"Keep on that target," Moore called the Cobra pilot. "Just keep suppressing that fire."


Derek Johnson's LCM was hard against the dock, the landing craft's propellers churning up creamy water at the stern. Lines of troops clawed and lunged up the slope to the railroad embankment. Lieutenant Charles Broadus, commander of the fire-support platoon, urged his SAW and M-60 gunners forward to take the guard quarters under fire. But the troops ran into the unexpected obstacle of a wire fence that no one had seen the night of the Sand Flea. The team was slowed down as Claymores were called for to blow the wire.

In the dark prison yard, the demolition engineer, Staff Sergeant Wagner, low-crawled through the fire to the steel doors of the cellblock. Men around him were hit. Someone was standing and firing an M-60 back at the guards' barracks, appearing in the strobing muzzle flashes like a parody of Rambo. Wagner jammed his three half-kilo blocks of C-4 explosive into the corners and center of the door frame, verified that the primer cords were intact, then pulled the pin on the igniter. He forced himself to count puffs of smoke before crawling away through the broken glass and gravel. When the door blew, it sounded louder than any ten-pound charge in training.

The unwounded members of Team Oswalt were on their feet. It was high man, low man, through the smoking door, just like in MOUT training back at Fort Bragg. The 3d Squad of the 2d Platoon blasted the guardroom door and swept into the main cellblock. In the pulsing light from the fire outside, the paratroopers saw strange, jumbled mounds on the concrete floor. Then they realized they were looking at mattresses. The prisoners had upset their cots and taken dubious shelter beneath their stained, thin mattresses. They were terrified, but otherwise unhurt.


The third platoon moved up from the railway embankment, through the fire-support positions, and through the breach blown in the chain-link fence to assault the headquarters and office buildings. The guards from the cellblock had fled the assault and had sought refuge in the headquarters. As one squad advanced, they saw two PDF soldiers carrying AK assault rifles dash beneath the shade portico joining the two buildings. An M-60 gunner stopped, swung his weapon, and opened fire, just as the enemy soldiers were leveling their AKs. The two PDF were blown backwards, their limbs flailing in the hail of fire.

Sergeant Kevin Schleben led his squad into the dark headquarters building, searching for PDF guards. As soon as he entered the central corridor, he choked on a lungful of Chemical Stun (CS) gas. Shouting at the men behind him, he backed away, face streaming with tears, his nose and eyes burning. The men had their gas masks on within a minute and Schleben led them back into the building. In the dim glow of his red flashlight he spotted a smeared blood trail on the polished tile floor. Schleben moved forward, cautiously following the blood spoor down the corridor and out the back door of the headquarters.

He ripped off his mask and dropped into a crouch at the end of the building. Only four meters away around the corner, two PDF soldiers also crouched in the darkness, one of them was bleeding from his wounded leg. They both clutched assault rifles and were gazing intently at the three guys from the first squad who were moving away under the portico toward the office block.

"Down!" Schleben shouted. He spun and fired his M-16 just as the PDF soldiers raised their weapons. Both men died before they could spring their ambush.

Captain Derek Johnson was frustrated by the inability of the Cobra to silence the fire from the thick-walled guard barracks on the hilltop to the right. Finally he called the chopper off and sent two squads ahead through the brush along the rail embankment, covered by the M-60s of the fire-support platoon. From their firsthand recon during the Sand Flea, Johnson and his men had a much better grasp of the objective than the Cobra crew. When the men were in position, they opened up with AT-4s, blasting the walls and windows of the guard barracks.[5]

"Just keep hitting them 'til they stop returning fire," Johnson radioed the squad leader. "We've got plenty more AT-4s where those came from."

Lynn Moore sat in the narrow rear cockpit, watching the attack unfold. He had chosen Derek Johnson's Charlie Company for this difficult mission because he knew the young captain was unflappable and his troops were trained to an edge of tough proficiency. But Moore had not anticipated the sheer scale of violence erupting below. The Renacer Prison was ripped by tracers and pounded with the flashing blasts of heavier weapons. Suddenly the jungle hilltop looked exactly like a fire base under attack in Vietnam's III Corps that Moore had helped relieve on another hot, smoky night two decades before. But this war, he knew, was different. This one we had come to prepared to win.

# II

# The First Day

# 7

# The Long Fight to Dawn

The Rangers at Rio Hato had quickly overwhelmed the initial PDF resistance on the drop zone.

Two of the attacking V-150 armored cars had been reduced to smoking rubble halfway down the runway. The third APC, a V-300 with a 90 mm cannon, had turned in flight from the impromptu antitank section that had formed up so suddenly among the Rangers who had just hit the ground and shucked off their harnesses. The vehicle sped north and bounced across the grassy fields west of the long runway, skirted the low barracks of the Herrera-Ruiz Military Institute, and turned west onto the Inter-American Highway. An AH-6 Little Bird pursued the armored vehicle, harassing it with minigun fire. But the helicopter pilot was under orders not to fire his 2.75-inch rockets near the Institute.

Once the V-300 was on the highway, however, it became a prime target for the Spectre. The Air Papa fire-control officer called off the Little Bird, and the big gunship swung into a tight orbit above the road. Despite the overhanging acacia trees, the weapons operators got a good lock on the fleeing vehicle. Just as they fired the first 105 round, however, the V-300 momentarily disappeared beneath a clump of hardwoods. The cannon round smashed harmlessly into the trees and exploded with a savage orange blast. But the second round did not miss. When the oily fireball cleared, the road was littered with smoldering chunks of metal.

Colonel Buck Kernan established his Tactical Operations Center on the eastern side of the runway. He was satisfied that the PDF's heavy firepower had been accounted for. Three ZPU 14.5 mm antiaircraft guns had already been destroyed. Two V-150s and a V-300 had been eliminated, and scouts across the runway reported that the remaining armored cars stood abandoned in the motor pool near the tower.

Two companies of the 3d Battalion were now maneuvering in disciplined teams to secure the airport itself and clear the runway for the first C-130 with the regiment's gun-jeeps to land. These troops would secure the airport perimeter, capture the PDF communication center (intact, it was hoped, so that Kernan's Intel section could eavesdrop on PDF radio traffic), and set up strong roadblocks on the Inter-American Highway.

The 2d Battalion was now ready to assault its objectives. Alpha Company was moving toward the broad wooded compound of the Military Institute. There had been no fire from the rows of low cinder-block barracks and classrooms. But the scouts reported many vehicles parked near the instructors' barracks. There were people in there, Kernan knew, and he guessed they included a whole gaggle of the teenage cadets who Southcom J-2 had predicted might be there over the Christmas holiday. Kernan had marked the Institute compound a No Fire Area on his fire-support plan. And the advancing troops were constrained by stringent rules of engagement to only fire at armed combatants. There would be no preliminary preparation of the school buildings with LAWs or 203 grenades prior to the actual clearing.

Charlie Company had formed up to move south through the narrow gullies of chalky soil and assault Noriega's luxurious El Farallón beach villa. Delta operators from the Joint Special Operations Task Force had shadowed the villa over the past week and had reported no indication that Noriega was in residence. But that didn't mean the bastard wasn't there. The spooks had noted that a squad of PDF troops had arrived two days earlier with a Christmas tree and had been observed in the living room decorating it with satin ball ornaments, tinsel, and flashing lights. In any event, the Rangers' orders were to secure the villa and to search it for criminal evidence.

The 2d Battalion's Bravo Company had drawn the roughest assignment, clearing the fenced compounds of the 6th and 7th Rifle Companies, the Macho de Monte. During the final briefing at Lawson Army Airfield, some of the younger troops had relished the prospect of "kicking ass" among the PDF's "macho men." The officers had not disabused them by explaining that *macho de monte* was Spanish for tapir, a stout, long-snouted tropical beast known for its shy and gentle disposition. These elite PDF units had adopted the tapir as a mascot because of the resemblance between the squat, short-legged animal and their V-150 and V-300 armored cars. But the "Macho" image was useful in target identification. The main two-story barracks in the 7th Company's compound was decorated with gaudy murals of stylized cartoon tapirs in skull-and-cross-bones berets, firing .50-caliber machine guns from V-150s charging through the jungle. The murals bore the legend, "Super Tanque Macho."

If there was going to be a tough fight, it would come from troops in those barracks. The assault plan called for Bravo Company to fan out by platoon at the southern end of the runway, cross the broken ground and gullies along a fire-division line west of Charlie Company, and blow breaches in the chain-link fences enclosing the barracks compounds. A "Colt" element from the Air Force Combat Control Team would move with the Bravo platoons to coordinate fire from the Spectre and Little Birds. This was a straightforward Ranger assignment, but the men had to exercise unusual fire discipline with their heavier weapons. Only 200 meters separated the far end of the compound from the tin-roofed houses of the fishing village, El Farallón del Chirú, which spread along the wide white-sand beach to the southwest.

Kernan knew there was the potential for heavy civilian casualties at Rio Hato if the Rangers of the 2d Battalion did not display this unusual fire discipline. When clearing their objectives, they couldn't simply lay back and let the airborne firepower do the work. Any enemy holding out in those buildings would have to be subdued by brave young soldiers on the ground.

Sergeant Dan Brown had completely recovered from his rough landing. After the brief, savage encounter with the armored vehicles, he moved without further incident to his assembly area. Within ten minutes the six-man fire team Brown led had formed up and was ready to proceed to the final assault staging point, under the grassy bluff of the enemy barracks compound.

Brown's platoon had been briefed to assault the 7th Rifle Company barracks, a cluster of one- and two-story cement-block buildings with corrugated orange roofs, set among tall old sea pines and spreading acacias. The buildings' exteriors were painted in soft pastels and decorated with bold, primitive murals and slogans in garish, primary colors. These distinctive features were prominent in the aerial photographs and detailed target folders the Rangers had studied back at Lawson. And Dan Brown was confident his men could recognize their objectives, once they breached the fence.

As the platoon advanced south across the end of the runway and through the knee-high grass, Brown made sure his fire team was correctly spread on line. The M-60 gunner was beside him in the center, with the 203 grenadier on the other side, then the SAW man and a rifleman on the flank. On his other side, the team sniper, carrying a 7.62 mm M-24 with a night scope, protected the team's right flank. Their platoon leader had ordered them forward in leapfrogging rushes, with each squad covering another's movement.

They were almost through the broken ground and on Position Gloria, the assault jump-off point in a tree line shaped like an arrowhead, when the team was fired on from the left. They were instantly down in the grass, the team line pivoted toward the threat, weapons ready.

"Hold your fire," Brown ordered. There was something about the sound of the weapons shooting at them that made him uneasy. Another burst of fire confirmed his suspicion. Those were M-16s.

"It's the Colt team," Brown yelled. "Just stay down and move right."

As the team crab-crawled away from the gully, Brown spread the word down the line that they had blundered too close to the sea and near the defensive perimeter of the Colt team deployed there. He was glad his men were Rangers. A straight-leg outfit might have cut loose with its M-60, SAW, and probably the 203 as well, raking the Colt team in the gully. Friendly fire casualties were a constant threat in this type of operation, especially when you worked with non-Ranger support units.[1]

Brown found a strip of glint tape another squad had laid down to mark the proper access of advance. He took a quick compass azimuth reading, determined the tape was correct, and motioned his team forward. They left the cover of the trees and dashed into a clump of high grass bordering a paved road near the compound fence. The four other fire teams from his platoon were already deployed along the fence line. Another platoon had taken up a fire-support position behind them and would stay in reserve to evacuate casualties if necessary.

A couple of men went forward to breach the fence quietly, but were having a hard time with their wire cutters on the thick, galvanized chainlink.

"Go on up and blow it, Brown," the platoon leader ordered.

Dan Brown ripped open the Velcro tab on his demolition kit and pulled out a half-kilo block of C-4. He scurried across the road and set his charge against the low concrete base of the fence, then pulled the pin on the thirty-second timer. When the charge blew, a whole ten-foot section between two metal uprights was shredded.

A squad down the line blew their own breach and the platoon moved through the gaps and up the grassy slope to take cover in the pine trees around the first barracks. The guys from the 4th Psychological Operations Group had already "read the PDF their rights" on the bullhorns, but the enemy showed no sign of surrender. So the Rangers were authorized to use deadly force in clearing the barracks.

Their methods were brutally direct. While one squad laid

down automatic weapons fire on a barracks' window, concentrating on the upper floor, another squad fired two or three grenades into the lower windows. Meanwhile two fire teams sprinted forward, blew open the end door, and threw hand grenades inside. They burst through the door, high-man, low-man, as soon as the grenades went off.

Sergeant Brown led the first team into the enemy barracks. That building was empty and it took only a few minutes to clear it. His team went to the rear of the column for the next barracks. That building too was empty. His team moved through the bullet-pocked, smoking rooms and took up an assault position for the next building. The other platoon had run into opposition across the parade ground. They were laying down a lot of M-60 and 203 fire. And Brown heard the distinctive heavy snap of AK-47s and saw their neon green tracers.

When he pushed his team through the next building, a recreation hall, they stumbled over the wet, still bodies of four dead enemy soldiers who had been killed by the squad's 203s. They lay with their weapons, crumpled beneath the shattered remains of a pinball machine. Outside in the fresh air, Brown's men rested, waiting for the support squad to move up for the assault on the last buildings. There were discarded assault rifles and camouflage uniform blouses on the gravel walk. Apparently, some of the PDF were bugging out as the Rangers advanced.

Brown looked up and tried to decipher the bold slogan of an exhortation printed on the wall above his head. It was something about Saint George the military warrior looking favorably on the brave soldiers of the PDF. The slogan was signed, "M.A.N.," Manuel Antonio Noriega. The two-story company headquarters through the pine trees nearby was covered with murals of tanks and gallant soldiers and similar slogans. There was even a white-bearded Santa Claus painted in the one window, decked out in camouflage jungle fatigues. Above the Machos' Santa was yet another Noriega slogan, *Lealtad o Muerte* (Loyalty or Death).

They had pushed the PDF into the last two buildings of the compound. Clearing them would not be easy. Brown led his

team out of cover and up against the end wall of the first barracks. The 1st Squad dashed through the darkness to the left
and took up a parallel position, crouching at the end of the
opposite barracks. Their support element began raking the
upper-floor windows of the two buildings with M-60s, SAWs,
and 203s.

Dan Brown decided to peek around the corner to make sure
the other squad was ready for the assault. But before he could
move, some hot, unseen violence threw him to the ground, a
good five feet from the end of the building. He tried to raise
his M-16 but his left arm wouldn't move. In the glare of the
sudden firefight, he saw the flash suppressor of an enemy
weapon protruding from a window in the opposite building.
The gun fired again, raking the ground around him. He was
hit in the left thigh. He tried to aim the M-16 with his right
hand, but before he could fire, two Rangers had him by his
web gear and were dragging him back into cover.

Across the dark alley, Rangers were also hit. Two wounded
men thrashed in pain. One lay still. Now the support squads
had moved up and were pounding the enemy barracks with
sustained machine-gun and grenade fire.

"Shit," Brown swore, "Goddammit to hell." He ran his right
hand across his shattered left wrist. His watch was gone. The
arm felt lumpy and sticky hot. But the wound in his thigh was
only superficial. Now the pain began, after the numbing shock
of the impact.

A Ranger tried to sling him over his shoulder, but Brown
pushed him back.

"Get on with the op," he told the man. "I can evacuate
myself."


Alpha Company surrounded the Military Institute with two
platoons in fire support, and moved the other two platoons
forward by squad rush to assault the barracks. The officers
and NCOs had made sure all the Rangers understood their
orders: No fire prep, no grenades.

When the first Rangers kicked down the door and dashed
into the darkened bunkroom, their weapons swinging low,

they found over a hundred Panamanian boys in their underwear huddled around their cots. The acrid stench of urine was
heavy in the darkness.

The men from the 3d Battalion were not so timid assaulting
Noriega's beach villa. When no one answered the bullhorn
summons to unlock the thick wrought-iron and glass front
door and surrender, a sergeant stood up and leveled his 203
to blow the door off its frame. Inside the men found a frightened old maid hiding in the scullery. A civilian watchman was
down behind some plastic garbage cans in the carport. Neither
one was injured. The maid showed the Rangers to Noriega's
bedroom. There were lots of mirrors and dozens of porcelain
figurines of young girls' heads. A hat rack was heaped with
floppy pastel beach sombreros. On the headboard of the king-
size bed stood a painted ceramic sculpture of a Hindu love
goddess.

There was no sign of Noriega himself.

It was after two in the morning when Vincente Sanchez stood
in the darkness near his Santa Clara beach cantina, watching
the big American transport planes landing at Rio Hato. For
the past hour, soldiers of the Defense Forces had stumbled by,
fleeing up the dark beach. Some wore their uniform trousers
but no shirts. Some were wounded, hobbling in pain. None
carried a weapon. At Rio Hato, the fight was over.

In the noisy glare of Santa Ana, Kurt Muse huddled with the
wounded men from Delta Force between the parked PDF vehicles and the chipped cement wall where they had taken refuge.
Snipers on surrounding buildings were still trying to hit them
with plunging fire, but the small party from the crashed helicopter had found a relatively secure sector. When the fire
slackened, a Delta man sprinted into the street, holding his
PRC-90 radio to his mouth with one hand and an infrared
strobe with the other. A Little Bird buzzed up the dark street

and hovered a moment, then did a bumblebee dance signifying it had marked the survivors' position.

The man dashed back to the shelter. "They're sending tracks
for us," he said.

Overhead the Spectre was back, its weapons flickering
among the fat clouds, backlit by the flames from below.

After a long time, they heard the grating rumble of tracked
vehicles turning off Avenida A.

"We're okay," Kurt Muse told one of his seriously wounded
rescuers. "It's the cavalry."[2]

The men of Charlie Company, 1st of the 508th, kept low in
their cover, waiting for orders to storm the breach blown in
the Comandancia wall. Three times they had to evacuate their
doorways and stairwells, falling back by squads on Captain
Flynn's orders as the Spectres were brought back in to hit machine-gun posts and snipers in the buildings of the Comandancia.

Once as they pulled back along one of the stinking narrow
"piss alleys" off Avenida A, grenades came bouncing down
from the tenement roof above. The men scattered and regrouped further up the street.

After the Spectres had hit the Comandancia with repeated
blasts of the 105 mm No. 6 gun, the men of Charlie Company
moved forward once again to their assault positions facing the
breach in the side wall. The wooden shops and tenements
among the higher buildings near the Comandancia had burnt
down to heaps of flaring embers and twisted, red-hot girders.
Still, there was small-arms and rocket-propelled grenade fire
from inside the shattered buildings of the Comandancia.

Sergeant Hans Dengner moved his squad into the stairwell
of a heavily damaged apartment building. He had two M-60
gunners with him and several men with LAWs and 203 grenade launchers. As the men sorted out their weapons and
ammo loads, a heavy machine gun opened up from a corner
building in the Comandancia, ripping through the stairwell.
The weapon was firing from so close that its rounds struck
with the power of a jackhammer. Sergeant David Lynch, a fire-

team leader, crouching on the first landing, had the floor cut out from under him. The entire wall caved in and he tumbled into the rubble, unconscious. In the dusty confusion, a soldier named Hicks yelled that he saw movement near the corner of the narrow street. Dengner took a soldier with him to cover Hicks. As they dashed down the shattered sidewalk, Dengner heard a metallic ping. Then the street exploded with a blinding flash. A grenade had detonated nearby, wounding all three soldiers.

Sergeant Robert Sure knelt in a second-floor window of a wooden tenement, down the street from the breached wall of the Comandancia. He was firing his M-24 sniper rifle at PDF in the windows of a three-story building just inside the walls opposite. Suddenly he was thrown off his feet by a blasting orange explosion. He looked down through the shattered wooden landing and saw two American soldiers stagger into the street, drenched with blood. The wounded men were howling with pain.

A squad leader, Sergeant First Class Jim Almeda, staggered along the sidewalk, then went down on his knees before toppling forward. "I need a medic," he said woodenly, as if reading from a script. "I need a medic," he repeated.

Weird purple smoke bellowed from the shattered doorway. Soldiers rushed into the room and pulled out a dead soldier. The man's arm had been blown completely off. In the glare of the muzzle flashes in the roiling smoke, it took Sure a moment to recognize the dead guy was one of the youngest men in the outfit, a PFC named Vance Coats, a quiet kid from Montana. Medics had the most severely wounded man down on a stretcher now. Sure saw it was another sergeant, Michael Deblois. He had been riddled with shrapnel and looked as if he'd been ripped up by some kind of a machine.

Second Lieutenant Joseph Minus, Jr., the platoon leader, held Deblois down, grappling at his web gear. Minus yelled at the soldiers around him to help, then grabbed the medic's scissors and ripped the sleeve of the wounded man's BDUs up to the shoulder in order to jam a field dressing against a gaping shrapnel wound.

"Somebody get a tourniquet on his leg," Lieutenant Minus shouted. The blood pool from the leg wound was spreading on the sidewalk, wide and dark. As the officer worked frantically to save his sergeant, other soldiers crept out to help if they could. Then Lieutenant Minus looked up and shouted at them to get back under cover and keep an eye on those fucking high-rise windows above.

When Sure moved to another firing position, the soldiers in the street told him the PDF had either fired an RPG or managed to toss a hand grenade into the tenement room, which had cooked off one of the 90 mm recoilless rifle rounds in a rucksack beside the heavy weapon. That accounted for the strange smoke and all the shrapnel.

But despite these losses, Charlie Company was now firmly established around the breach. Whenever PDF gunners fired from windows of the Comandancia or the high-rise building on the corner, American snipers would keep them pinned down while teams of 203 grenadiers would maneuver to fire their 40 mm fragmentation rounds through the windows. Once the Marine LAVs had repositioned along Fourth of July Avenue, Charlie Company could call their direct 25 mm chaingun fire onto the Comandancia windows. As the night wore on, the enemy fire was steadily suppressed.

Charlie Company had taken casualties but was still a coherent combat unit. The men waited through the long night for the order to advance through the breach. After a while the word came down that there would be no clearing of the compound until reinforcements arrived. The Mech had been chewed up worse than Charlie Company. And one Mech platoon had been peeled off to search for the survivors of some spook helicopter that had gone down on the other side of the prison. Then the Tac radio net announced PDF soldiers, many of them wounded, were streaming from the gates of the Comandancia that had been left unguarded by the diverted Mech platoon.

A man from Charlie Company crouching in a doorway wiped the crusted sweat and soot from his face. "Shit hot," he muttered. "Just let the fuckers go away and leave us alone."

A man listening nearby wasn't sure if the speaker was serious or sarcastic. But it didn't really matter. What was important was making it through the long night to dawn.

The fires had started again down off Avenida A. Here, near

the Comandancia, burst water pipes in the tenements had dampened the blaze. The men of Charlie Company knelt in the shattered plaster and broken glass as the rusty water rained down from above. A squad on the right flank watched young looters smash through the security grill of an undamaged bodega, and emerge lugging cases of Soberena and Panama beer. Some of the looters were sucking straight gin and rum from the bottle. In the glare of the fires, the scene looked like something out of a ghetto riot back home.

A Panamanian in a greasy T-shirt and stained fatigue trousers limped around a corner wearing only broken flip-flops on his bleeding feet. He held his hands above his head, more like a religious supplicant than a surrendering enemy. "Help me," he said in good English. "I've been a prisoner since the October coup." The man nodded toward the roofs of the prison compound down the street. "Won't you help me, please?" A soldier wrapped him in a poncho and led him back to the POW collection point on the other side of Fourth of July.

The company officers and platoon sergeants moved purposefully from one position to another, despite the sniper fire. They checked their men for wounded and distributed extra ammunition. They also brought reassuring news. The final assault on the Comandancia would not begin until morning. The men could stand down now and slake their thirst with tepid water from their canteens. And those who still had an appetite could eat.[3]

Captain George Kunkel and Chief Warrant Officer Fred Horsley had remained hidden and somehow out of harm's way as the savage battle for the Comandancia progressed. They had managed to crawl a safe distance from their burning Little Bird helicopter, but machine-gun fire from PDF positions in the dark buildings above had driven them back from their first attempt to climb a low wall and move through an alley up toward Fourth of July. They heard the tracks of the 4/6th Mech rumble by, but there was no way they could talk to the men inside the APCs. Sometime after two in the morning, there was a lull in the fighting and they crawled back to the wall. Kunkel was in better shape than Horsley, so the captain volunteered to scale the obstacle, sprint across the street, yelling the password, "Bulldog," and attempt to link up with a friendly unit.

When they got to the base of the wall though, they saw the top was protected by two strands of razor wire. Kunkel ripped off his Kevlar flak jacket and draped it across the wire. He looked cautiously around the dark courtyard, then pulled himself up.

Horsley was crouched in the shadows, his injured back throbbing now like a drilled tooth. There was movement in the nearby weeds and he spun to level his short-barreled CAR-15 assault rifle. But the man who emerged from the brush was a soot-streaked PDF soldier with his hands in the air. The man had deep shrapnel gashes in his arms and legs, and there was blood on the back of his neck.

He spoke passable English. Everybody inside that section of the Comandancia, the soldier explained, was either dead or had already escaped. "I want to surrender," he said.

Kunkel was over the wall and picking his way through the rubble of a blasted building when he was challenged by an American soldier yelling in Spanish.

"Bulldog," Kunkel repeated. "I'm an American."

A squad of grimy, sweat-soaked infantrymen emerged warily from a dark doorway.

"Hey, sergeant," one of the GIs said, "we got one of the helicopter guys."

Two soldiers went back with Kunkel to guide Horsley to safety. But Horsley insisted on helping the wounded PDF soldier over the wall first. As they were perched there, the Spectre gunship swept back over the street and cut loose with its 20 mm cannons, raking the buildings twenty meters behind them. Horsley managed to vault over the PDF prisoner, who was now hung up in the wire. After the Spectre had passed, Kunkel and Horsley dashed back and dragged the man down. The razor wire slashed the prisoner's flesh, but he didn't complain.

A few minutes later, the three of them were in the command track of Company D, 4/6 Infantry. In the glow of red flashlights, a medic worked on the wounded prisoner. Horsley and Kunkel drank tepid cans of Pepsi, listening to the small arms and shrapnel pelt the armor hull. It sounded like hail in a bad storm.

\*     \*     \*

Up on Quarry Heights, the crews of the two M-551 Sheridan tanks parked on the lip of the hill stared down with mounting frustration. The Tac radio net was crowded with fire-mission requests from the Mech soldiers and infantrymen down in those burning streets. But neither of the tank gunners in the adjacent Bull 1 and 2 firing positions had a good sight picture on the Comandancia. The smoke from the burning buildings was just too thick.

Private First Class Marcus Davis, the gunner at Bull 1, traversed his 152 mm main gun turret slowly, gazing into his optics scope intently. The crosshairs and range lines shimmered against the sheets of flame and greasy smoke.

"No good, Sarge," he told his commander. "We shouldn't shoot if we don't see a good target."

The men waited as the noisy radio crackled. In a few hours it would be light, and then they could fire.

Fort Amador was loud with the clatter of approaching helicopters. The GIs on the ground were waiting for Alpha Company, 1st of the 508th, the main assault unit for the barracks and bunkers of the PDF's 5th Rifle Company. They were scheduled on two lifts of Black Hawks, each helicopter jammed with twenty combat-equipped soldiers for the short ride over from Fort Kobbe across the Canal. Landing Zone Gator lay inside a broad grassy gully that ran west from the seaside road and divided the fairways of the golf course. The officers who had planned the air assault had picked this LZ with care, the low terrain gave good cover and concealment from the PDF bunkers on the far side of the golf course.

Unfortunately, the operation planners had not anticipated the ferocity of the battle at the Comandancia, only a thousand meters across the bay to the north. As the Black Hawks from the 1/228 Aviation Regiment swung out over the Amador causeway to give the isolated PDF unit on Flamenco Island a wide berth, the line of blacked-out choppers came under fire from El Chorrillo. The six Blacks Hawks kept a good formation despite the tracers rising toward them from the burning city. But the flames and muzzle flashes were washing out the lead pilots' night-vision goggles, eroding depth perception.

The choppers settled onto final approach, thumping down between the tall coconut palms and mango trees bordering the gully. In the dark shadows, neither the pilots nor the door gunners could judge altitude. Everybody was nervous from the unexpected groundfire. When some crew chiefs shouted "Go!" to the soldiers jammed like subway commuters in the open troop bays, the Black Hawks were still ten feet in the air. One soldier, clutching three heavy rucksacks, was about to leap after his buddies when the door gunner grabbed him. The chopper had already climbed twenty feet.

The men crashing down into the damp grass below were angry and confused when they struggled under their rucksacks and weapons to form up for the assault.

The second lift from Kobbe kept the same tight formation, under the chiding guidance of Captain Bradley Mason, the commander of the Black Hawks' Aviation company. The battalion's chaplain, Captain Allen Boatright, was on the third chalk of this second lift, jammed in with the sweating soldiers. As the choppers swung out over the dark bay and turned in again for their final on the LZ, the sky around the aircraft was laced with red and green tracers.

The crew chief wedged next to the chaplain shouted over the thump of the rotor: "Pray for me."

"Are you kidding?" the chaplain yelled back. "I haven't stopped praying since I got on this thing."

Despite the initial confusion on the LZ, Alpha Company quickly formed up at the caddy shack into its assault teams, then moved through the security position Captain John Hort's Headquarters Company had established around the American family quarters. A final helicopter lift brought in a 105 mm howitzer, dangling from a sling. The howitzer would be used with the .50-caliber machine guns on APCs and the AT-4 anti-tank rockets of the SCAT platoon in firepower demonstrations meant to convince the PDF to surrender.

Lieutenant Colonel Billy Ray Fitzgerald, the battalion commander, established his tactical operations center on the veranda of an unoccupied American house. He waited for the specialized teams to report their objectives secured before beginning the main assault on the fortified barracks across the fairway. To make Colonel Fitzgerald's evening more interesting, he learned Major General Marc Cisneros, commander of Southcom's Army forces, was now at Fort Amador.

The specialized units were running into trouble. A hunter-killer team armed with AT-4s that Captain Hort had dispatched past the officers' club and on to the far side of the PDF lines to take out the V-300 armored car and the ZPU-4 antiaircraft gun guarding Noriega's headquarters in Building 8, had been spotted by the PDF troops rallying behind the building. The four Americans were now pinned down, trapped in the jumbled granite boulders of the seawall.

Alpha Company's 1st Platoon had been dispatched north along the bayside road to secure the U.S. Navy headquarters area and evacuate the American dependents housed there. But when the platoon approached the compound's fence, they were challenged by the American MPs guarding the area. In the confused confrontation, the MPs opened fire, forcing the 1st Platoon scouts to take cover. Once more, the MP platoon leaders' poor grasp of the operation had almost precipitated a disaster. It took almost half an hour for the confusion to be settled and that flank of the base secured.

Colonel Fitzgerald was not amused.

At the southern neck of the causeway, the blocking team had now reinforced their TOW Humvees with Claymores and concertina wire. They were tweaking their night sights when they heard an Air Papa Spectre orbiting overhead, announce that it had "acquired" a pair of V-150s that had infiltrated the causeway from Isla Naos. The enemy armor was almost inside the American position, the Spectre warned. The men at the roadblock scanned the dark road with their night sights, but saw nothing. A soldier backed his Humvee sharply to get a better fire angle for the TOW tube.

Then the Spectre called with obvious frustration that the GIs on the ground *had* to see the V-150s because one of them was backing around alongside the seawall.

"No, no! Repeat, negative," the sergeant at the roadblock

Colon-Coco Solo—The barracks of the 8th Naval Infantry after the assault by U.S. forces. This is a good example of the effective use of "firepower demonstrations." Although the building was badly damaged, there were few PDF casualties. (*Department of Defense*)

Panama City—"Hardshell" Humvees carrying M-60 machine guns on circular mounts proved an effective deterrent against looters once the vehicles were deployed in large numbers throughout the city. (*Department of Defense*)

The face of battle—This soldier from the 5th Mechanized Infantry reflects the tension and exhaustion the morning after the long battle to secure the Comandancia. Note the glint tape on his left sleeve, and his flak jacket. The soldier behind him in the hatch of the M-113 armored personnel carrier is beneath the badly exposed .50-caliber machine gun. (*Department of Defense*)

Panama City—A U.S. soldier takes cover from a PDF sniper. Drive-by shootings and sniper attacks during the first two days of Operation Just Cause kept U.S. combat troops occupied, preventing them from systematically suppressing the widespread looting that hit the capital. (*Department of Defense*)

Troops of the 82d Airborne Division take cover from snipers in Panama Viejo. (*Department of Defense*)

Panama City—Soldiers of the 7th Light Infantry Division help clear a Dignity Battalion stronghold in the outskirts of Panama City. The "Digbats" put up fierce resistance in some areas. Had PDF officers not fled but instead rallied this irregular militia, American casualties would have been far greater. (*Department of Defense*)

Mopping up—A soldier of the 82d Airborne Division guards the perimeter at Panama Viejo after D-Day. The disorganized resistance by PDF stragglers and the Dignity Battalions kept the 82d Airborne on the defensive during most of December 21. Note the infrared-reflective tabs at the rear of this soldier's helmet and the LAW antitank rocket to his right. (*Department of Defense*)

Occupation duty—Another paratrooper of the 82d at the Panama Viejo perimeter, reading hometown newspaper coverage of the invasion. The small American flag pinned to his left sleeve was more than a chauvinist decoration: The PDF wore similar uniforms, and the flag served to prevent friendly-fire casualties. (*Department of Defense*)

Guns for Money—U.S. troops sort some of the thousands of weapons exchanged by Panamanians for no-questions-asked cash, one of the most successful of the many Psychological Operations conducted during Just Cause. Many of these weapons were turned in by wives and children of Dignity Battalion members, effectively undercutting the potential of an armed pro-Noriega resistance. (*Department of Defense*)

Weapons cache—Some of the weapons seized by the Rangers at Rio Hato in the huge PDF arms cache. These assault rifles, heavy automatic weapons, and light artillery were of Soviet-bloc origin and packed in crates marked "Purifier," "Battery," and "Drilling Equipment." The discovery of these weapons led intelligence officers to speculate Noriega planned a quasi-military alliance with the Colombian drug cartels. (*Courtesy 75th Ranger Regiment*)

Captured weapons—A small portion of the massive PDF arsenal seized by U.S. forces. The armored vehicle (center) is a Gage-Cadillac V-300 with a 90 mm turret-mounted cannon. Several of these dangerous armored cars were destroyed by U.S. air strikes. The multi-barreled antiaircraft weapon (right) is a Soviet-built ZPU-4 14.5 mm like those destroyed by the AC-130 Spectre gunship at Rio Hato. (*Department of Defense*)

Contraband cash—Some of the several million dollars in suspected drug money seized at Noriega's headquarters in the Comandancia. The packaging around the bundles of money bore the address "General Manuel Antonio Noriega." (*Department of Defense*)

Aftermath—A member of the 1/508 Parachute Infantry Regiment guards the "ruins" of the Comandancia. The precision of the U.S. firepower is evident in the building at the left. Although the AC-130 Spectre gunship pounded the structure, each incoming round blasted directly through the roof, leaving the walls undamaged. The fieldstone wall (right) was the one breached by U.S. paratroopers. (*Department of Defense*)

Aftermath—The streets of the Santa Ana barrio near the Comandancia following the widespread looting of Panama City's central commercial district. Many of the abandoned cartons had contained Japanese luxury goods. Note the complete lack of battle damage, another indication that U.S. firepower was used with great discipline. (*Department of Defense*)

Aftermath—The El Chorrillo barrio after the devastating fire that swept the neighborhood on the morning of December 20, 1989. Despite the impression that vast areas of Panama City were fire-gutted after U.S. "bombing," this picture shows the total extent of the El Chorrillo fire. Antiaircraft positions and snipers in the high-rise apartment (center) were struck with great precision. La Modelo Prison and the Comandancia can be seen (upper right). The wooded slopes of Quarry Heights (left) dominate the barrio above Fourth of July Avenue. (*Department of Defense*)

Noriega in custody—A haggard, dejected General Manuel Antonio Noriega is escorted aboard a U.S. C-130 by Drug Enforcement Administration officers to begin the flight to Miami on January 3, 1990. (*Department of Defense*)

shouted into his radio mike. "That's us here. We're in Humvees."

He dashed around to the hood of his vehicle and played his red flashlight across the diamond pattern of glint tape.

"Roger, copy," the Spectre replied.

The men on the ground crouched lower, twanging with the terrible awareness they had almost been taken out by the unseen gunship overhead.

A clearing team led by 1st Lieutenant Paul Vinyard had better luck. They burst into quarters numbers 152 and 153, the "witch houses" where Noriega kept his Brazilian sorceresses. Although they didn't find the general, they did capture two PDF guards and secure a cache of incriminating documents. One of their most interesting discoveries was a crude voodoo doll made of corn dough, punctured with pins and severed knife blades. When they ripped the doll open, they discovered a folded newspaper photograph of Guillermo Endara, the legally elected president of Panama.

While the assault units waited, the heavy weapons for the firepower demonstrations were maneuvered into position. But before this demonstration could begin, the men who had secured the front gate called for more medics. The PDF prisoners who had been wounded attempting to escape were bleeding to death down there. But Fitzgerald wasn't going to dispatch medics, who might be fired on by the enemy still dug into their bunkers and barracks across the open golf course. He sent an uninjured PDF MP prisoner with a surrender ultimatum across the fairway into Building 4, the 5th Rifle Company's headquarters. The man never returned.

Fitzgerald personally inspected the assault units, making sure they knew their objectives and the Rules of Engagement. It was time for the first firepower demonstration.


While the men of the 508th prepared for the assault on the PDF barracks, an OH-58 observation helicopter from Task Force Wolf banked through the dark sky, its crew searching the enemy buildings for targets. Captain Tim Jones had the controls while his copilot, Chief Warrant Officer Andrew Porter, scanned the line of barracks on the Canal side of Fort Amador. Jones turned back toward shore and ran parallel to the seawall to give Porter a better line of sight. Suddenly a cloud of tracers rose from the PDF barracks. The little helicopter staggered and lurched hard right, crashing into the Canal.

Porter was unconscious, seriously injured. Captain Jones struggled desperately to free his copilot as the helicopter sank. But the task was impossible. Jones managed to kick to the surface and swim ashore to the seawall rocks. He crawled among the granite boulders and tried to make his way south, away from the fire coming from the enemy buildings.

After a long time, someone shouted at him in Spanish. He realized it was better to surrender to the PDF and become a hostage rather than risk being shot at such close range. Reluctantly he stood up among the slippery boulders and shouted. "*Aqui* . . . I'm here. Don't shoot."

"Hey, okay." The soldier came out of the shadows, leveling an M-16. "It's okay, we're Americans. We're the Airborne."

Team Buck was now in forward fire-team deployment to begin the assault on Building No. 5. After consulting with General Cisneros, Colonel Fitzgerald gave the order for the tracks to pound the barracks with .50-caliber fire. Following this initial fire, the loudspeakers echoed across the golf course, informing the PDF that had only been a "small demonstration." There was no reply from the PDF. Fitzgerald ordered the howitzer rolled forward. At 0310 hours the big gun blasted, its barrel almost horizontal at zero elevation. The round blew the upper right-hand corner off Building No. 5. There was still no reply from the PDF.

Fitzgerald consulted with his officers, then gave his orders. The escalating fire demonstrations would proceed with M-60 and .50-caliber machine guns, followed by the 105 mm howitzer. Each enemy barracks, beginning with Building No. 9, would be assaulted in turn. But he cautioned them to avoid hitting the granite-block tomb of General Omar Torrijos-Herrera, which stood near Building 8. Fitzgerald hoped this combination of firepower demonstration and battlefield preparation would drive any enemy from the bunkers and barracks and shepherd them north along the seawall toward the blocking positions already established near the front gate.[4]

\* \* \*

For the American military dependent families at Fort Amador, the terrible night seemed endless. The machine-gun fire from the Comandancia bounced and ricocheted across the mud flats, striking houses along the bay side of the fort. And the fact that many of the husbands of the women huddling with their frightened children were also under fire elsewhere in the city made the situation seem even more frightening. Susan Keller lay under her dining room table, with her two children beside her. The windows on the golf-course side of the house had all been smashed by enemy fire. Every time bullets crashed into the plaster overhead, her prayers were interrupted and she was forced to begin again. The night became a timeless struggle. Somehow she knew if she could just complete her prayers the enemy fire would stop.

Down the street, Kathleen Torres-Cartagena, the wife of the Southcom Signal Brigade commander, kept her three children under cover behind a jumble of living room furniture. When the howitzer outside fired, the windows shook and plaster dust settled through the air. PDF tracers sailed through the darkness and smacked the corner of her house. On the veranda, American troops had moved her washer and dryer outside from the utility room to provide cover. The loudspeaker team was located there. Kathleen began counting slowly each time the amplified voice told the PDF across the fairway they had five minutes to surrender before the next artillery round was fired. When the countdown reached one minute, then thirty seconds, she drew the children close to her and tried to cover their faces.

But her eleven-year-old son Emilio tried to squirm away. "Ah, Mom," he complained, "let me up. I want to see the howitzer."

Lieutenant Colonel Jerry Murguia forced himself to concentrate on the Execution Checklist and avoid morbid anxiety about his wife and children down in Fort Amador. Most of the men in this bright, airless room had family there. They were professional military and had to put their personal concerns aside. Murguia could only hope the PDF's 5th Rifle Company would not continue to resist.

Overall, the operation was proceeding more smoothly than anyone had dared hope. When he got the report that item number 26 on the checklist—neutralizing the Balboa DENI station—had been completed only ninety seconds after the time allotted in the OPLAN, Murguia began to believe the entire operation would succeed.

He read the terse tactical computer printout that had been transmitted via secure fax from Fort Clayton. Troops of the 5/87th Infantry had surrounded the DENI building, located on a traffic circle in the center of the Balboa business district, the heart of the old Canal Zone. When the American troops had come under fire, and after the PDF refused repeated surrender demands, Colonel Mike Snell, the brigade commander, had authorized Task Force Wildcat to use their 90 mm recoilless rifles. But he had ordered them to avoid all collateral damage. Snell also authorized the use of the Spectre gunship to silence the PDF in the building.

Five minutes later, the Balboa DENI station was a smoking shell. There was a Christmas creche ten meters from the building on the lawn of the traffic circle. The sheep and goats inside this fenced religious display were shaken up, but otherwise uninjured. There were no survivors among the PDF in the building.


In the echoing dark arrivals hall of the Torrijos Airport terminal, the hostage standoff had reached a critical point. The airport security manager had volunteered to act as a mediator between the barricaded PDF and the Rangers of Charlie Company, 3d Battalion. He repeatedly walked the twenty meters of no-man's land between the baggage office where the Rangers crouched behind their SAWs and shotguns and the Customs area where the PDF held their terrified hostages. He assured the Panamanian soldiers there would be no retributions, that they would be treated fairly as prisoners of war. Finally, the men agreed to leave their hostages and walk with the manager behind the baggage carousel where they could be disarmed and searched by the Rangers.

The tense confrontation ended quietly. After the prisoners were searched and flex-cuffed, the Rangers shepherded their civilian detainees upstairs to the second-floor restaurant. To their surprise, the soldiers from the ground floor found over 300 civilians thronging the dark departure hall. They were passengers from incoming flights—stranded in the limbo of the arrivals hall when the airdrop began—who had success-fully hidden from the PDF. Most of them were Panamanians. A few were nervous Colombians, muttering that the gringos' operation was one of the most elaborate drug raids in history.

A young Ranger lieutenant convinced the restaurant man-ager to start cooking food for the hungry children. The officer apologized that he had only U.S. dollars to pay for the food and explained that he would need a receipt.

"That's okay, Lieutenant," the restaurant manager said. "In Panama we use American money."

The officer nodded in tired acknowledgment. Fighting a war in a glistening, modern airport terminal, then paying for cheese-burgers with a twenty-dollar bill, was a bit much for one night.

While the hostage negotiation sputtered down to its resolution, the airport terminal was shaken by the roar of twenty-eight C-141 Starlifters plowing through the dark sky 800 feet above Run-way 03. The planes dropped hundreds of tons of heavy equip-ment on multiple green cargo chutes. This was the scheduled supply drop of the 82d Airborne Division. Most of the cargo pallets were heaped with wooden ammunition cases and bundled cardboard boxes of MREs—Meals, Ready to Eat—cinched down by green webbing. But eight of the planes each carried more exotic cargo: a fifteen-ton Sheridan tank. The Sheridans were chained to girdered pallets mounted with rollers.

With the rear cargo ramp lowered and the hydraulic door fully retracted, the loadmasters deployed an extraction chute for low-velocity air delivery. The squat armored toads were dragged out the cargo ramp into the dark sky. Then the ten-canopy cluster of cargo chutes burst open and each tank swung like a giant pendulum. One by one they crashed into the marshy ground east of the Torrijos runway with a watery thump, and disappeared beneath the tall kuna grass. One tank was destroyed when its parachutes malfunctioned.

At 0211 hours, eight more C-141s flashed low over the runway. This was the first serial of 82d Airborne paratroopers. Accepting the prerogatives and responsibilities of rank, Major General James H. Johnson, the division commander, was the first soldier to jump into the dark slipstream. He was followed by over 900 more paratroopers, most of them from brigade and battalion headquarters packages.

The commanders of the 82d's combat brigade were on the ground. But the bulk of their troops were still en route from Pope Air Force Base. As Johnson assembled his headquarters in the newly liberated Torrijos arrivals hall, it became painfully obvious that the helicopter air assaults on the PDF installations at Panama Viejo, Tinajitas, and Fort Cimarron would have to take place well after daylight.

General Manuel Antonio Noriega said goodbye to Gloria on a quiet street in Parque Lefevre. The frightened young woman ran down the dark sidewalk and disappeared behind a wall. Again, Noriega tried to convince Captain Castillo to return to Ceremi. This time the General reasoned that he had forgotten his wallet there, which contained sensitive information. Ivan Castillo managed to persuade Noriega the trip was too dangerous.

They drove to Lieutenant Pinto's house in the northern suburbs, and went in once they were sure the small bungalow was not under surveillance. The first person Noriega telephoned was his mistress, Vicky Amado. Noriega stuttered and trembled as he spoke to her, but then pulled himself together, braced by a full water-glass of whiskey. Next Noriega telephoned Major Eduardo Lopez Grimaldo, the suave official spokesman of the PDF. Grimaldo was a normally unflappable operator who had always been able to cast the best light on the most catastrophic events. But his public relations aplomb was shattered by the invasion. He was weeping on the telephone and told Noriega he planned to seek asylum at the Cuban embassy.

Around 3:00 A.M. Noriega grew increasingly nervous, certain there were Delta Force commandos in nearby gardens.

The three men got back in the Hyundai and drove aimlessly around the suburbs. At a quiet police station off Avenida Simon Bolivar, Captain Castillo was told that UESAT special forces men had just been there, asking the officers if they had seen the general.

Noriega shook visibly when Castillo told him this news. *"Mierda,"* Noriega swore. "Harari has turned those bastards against me."

Michael Harari was a shadowy Israeli operative with both underworld and espionage connections. It had been Harari who had helped arrange the Israeli military training mission that had established the UESAT special forces. Ever since the failed October coup, Noriega had been convinced that Harari's role had always been duplicitous, somehow part of an elaborate CIA scheme to topple him.

Noriega's confused and ambivalent anti-Semitism now erupted. (He kept large framed photos of both Israeli general Moshe Dayan and Adolf Hitler on his office wall and seemed to revere the audacity of both men.) For a moment he railed against Jews in general, and Harari in particular. Then he abruptly reversed himself and ordered Castillo to take him to the luxurious home of another Jewish associate, arms dealer Jorge Krupnik. This wealthy colleague, Noriega said, had his own cadre of bodyguards, so tough and loyal that no one from the UESAT or Delta Force would dare assault the sprawling villa on Avenida 3 Sur.

The little Hyundai sped through the night. In the distance, the Comandancia and El Chorrillo smoldered like a foundry.

Two gunmen pounded on the door of Raymond Dragseth's apartment around 3:00 A.M. The Defense Department computer science school teacher was wide awake. His fifth-floor apartment in Punta Paitilla was midway between the battles raging at the Comandancia and at Paitilla Airport. When Dragseth opened the door, his wife Victoria stayed back in the living room, watching fearfully from an archway. The men had AK-47 assault rifles and automatic pistols. The man who spoke was a thin, light-complected European. His Spanish was cultured with a slight Cuban accent.

He announced they were members of the Defense Forces who had been sent to search for Americans. Dragseth was ordered to accompany them. He tried to argue that he was only a high school teacher, that they were making some kind of a mistake. But the shorter of the two gunmen, a mestizo wearing dark glasses and a straw hat, only smirked. He thrust the barrel of the assault rifle into Dragseth's chest.

Victoria Dragseth watched out the window as her husband was pushed into the back of a civilian car. A total of four gunmen climbed in with him, and the vehicle sped away. She would never see her husband alive again.


Lieutenant Colonel Ed Whitt studied the tactical area chart of Panama that took up an entire wall of the Air Operations Center in Building 703 at Howard Air Force Base. The clear plastic overlay showed scores of aircraft symbols moving across the isthmus. Air traffic controllers seated at radar consoles behind him monitored a steady stream of C-141s and C-5s, approaching Howard from the Bay of Panama. Aircraft were landing and taking off every few minutes. But the entire base was blacked out, the operation on the busy cargo ramp was conducted completely in the dark.

Colonel Whitt checked his schedules and his Execution Checklist, making sure that the air-support packages, both fixed-wing and rotary, were on their proper stations. The next item for consideration was the inbound empty C-141s that had just dropped cargo and 82d Airborne paratroopers at Torrijos. They had to refuel at Howard before continuing on to the States. But he needed to get them in and out of the fuel pits quickly, because he had a long serial of other C-141 Starlifters inbound from Fort Ord, California, with a brigade of reinforcements from the 7th Light Infantry Division.

The only alternate refueling field for the big jet transports was Torrijos itself. But that objective had not yet been officially secured. The contingency refueling plan—to be executed if the Howard runway came under attack—called for a huge C-

5 carrying multiton bladders of JP-4 to land at Torrijos and serve as a giant mobile gas station. But Whitt certainly hoped that would not be necessary. Tocumen-Torrijos was littered with hundreds of troop and cargo parachutes that might be sucked up by the engines of any aircraft landing in the dark. No matter what, Whitt had to keep the Howard runways and cargo ramps open.

So far there hadn't been any fire-support requests for the A-37 and A-7 attack jets holding station in fixed orbits northwest of the base. But there was plenty of traffic on the helicopter fire-support net. Then the Tac net crackled with a fire-support request from someone using the call sign "Dragon 31." The voice spoke clear English with a slight Spanish accent, nothing unusual with so many Hispanic members of the American forces. Dragon 31 wanted a "fast mover" bomb and rocket mission on a precise, six-digit set of coordinates. He said his unit was under fire and needed that mission ASAP.

But when Whitt went to the wall chart to double-check the coordinates, he discovered they lay directly in the center of the main runway of Howard Air Force Base. Dragon 31 might well have been under fire. But he certainly was not an American.


Major Wanda Bisbal was working through the most difficult night of her Air Force career. As commander of Howard's 6th Aerial Support Squadron, she was in charge of the entire downloading and refueling operation. The scene on the cargo ramps bordered on chaos.

A C-130 from the Ranger Rio Hato airdrop had landed and parked short of the ramp. They had a wounded man on board, a Sergeant Tom Whelling, who'd been hit before he could jump. The man was still in his parachute harness, and the crew chief was concerned because Whelling had live grenades and a LAW antitank rocket that seemed to have been torn ajar by the rounds that hit him. Before the medics could evacuate the wounded Ranger, the aircraft commander wanted ordnance men on board to handle the explosives. Major Bisbal managed to sort that problem out, but the C-130 reported another dangerous situation. It had been riddled by enemy machine-gun and small-arms fire across the wings. JP-4 jet fuel was raining down from multiple bullet holes.

Sergeant Dan Molar rushed out, clutching a handful of emergency epoxy putty. With jet fuel pouring down over his head and soaking his fatigues, Molar stood on a workstand, chewing the epoxy to soften it, then jamming it up into the bullet holes in the wing above.

He would have looked like a madman to anybody who did not understand the situation. But then, the whole ramp looked crazy. Major Bisbal knew, however, appearances were deceptive. C-141s and C-130s trundled along, their wingtips almost overlapping, as airmen with hooded flashlights walked them through the labyrinth. Forklifts and big articulated download-ers spun and rumbled through the heaps of ammunition crates, Humvee tires, and ration boxes. Young soldiers from the 7th Light Infantry filed from planes, their faces tense and fearful under their floppy camouflage helmet nets.

Major Bisbal made another circuit of her ramps and paused near the northern end. She recognized why the disembarking infantrymen had seemed so somber. The tents of the Medevac hospital spread around the tarmac just past the fuel pits. Black Hawk and Huey dustoffs landed and took off constantly. Teams of volunteer stretcher bearers carried the wounded to the open-sided triage tents. Most of the casualties were PDF, some terribly disfigured, near death. But many of the wounded were Americans. The nurses and surgeons did not discriminate by nationality, only by the nature of the wounds.

Those who were beyond hope were sedated and carried to a large general purpose tent that seemed to exude a strange aura of silence amid the clatter of the cargo ramps. This was the "expectant tent." This was where the mortally wounded were taken to die.

# A Long Morning of Combat

The 2,176 paratroopers of the 82d Airborne Division departed Pope Air Force Base in three separate serials over a period of three hours and jumped on the Torrijos drop zone as their serials arrived. The division headquarters led the first drop of eight C-141s, jumping at 0211 hours. Twenty-eight C-141s of the heavy-equipment drop preceded the first troop serial by almost half an hour. Back at Pope, deicing proceeded slowly in a steady freezing rain. Two Starlifters straggled into Torrijos at 0350 and dropped their paratroopers. Ten minutes later, three more chalks unloaded. Almost an hour passed before another two airdrop planes arrived. Finally, at 0515 hours, the last Starlifters banked low over Panama Bay, descended to 500 feet, and dropped their paratroopers.

This was hardly the mass drop of the Division Ready Brigade the Blue Spoon planners had envisioned. They had hoped to have three combat battalions on the ground and ready to air assault their objectives by 0230. Now they were three hours behind schedule. En route to Panama, some of the Starlifters had even been intercepted by a Cuban MiG-21 in international air space off the Yucatan Peninsula. The MiG had fired a warning burst of cannon fire past the nose of one C-141, more a gesture of angry defiance than a valid military action. It was as if the Cuban pilot was telling the Americans

191

their massive airborne operation was no longer a secret, that the PDF would be waiting for them on the ground.[1]

At least all of the drops had been made before dawn. But several of the aircraft had missed the centerlines of their drop zones and disgorged their paratroopers well to the east of the runway in twelve-foot-high elephant grass and swamps. The ensuing confusion would have simply been one of the inevitable glitches of combat if PDF and Dignity Battalion snipers in the Tocumen barrios had not made the situation dangerous. Some troops, on edge from the long frustrating wait in the freezing rain back at Pope, inadvertently fired on other Americans thrashing through the thick cane grass, their boots deep in the sucking mud.

Once on the ground, a few of the chalks degenerated into noisy chaos as the dark, narrow paths in the grass became tangled with shroud lines and muddy canopies. It was hot and dark. Clouds of mosquitoes tormented the men, and people were out there shooting at them. The situation was ripe for what the military terms "fratricide." Luckily, the hundreds of confused and nervous young paratroopers made it out of the grassy marsh with no one wounded or killed.

Since Operation Just Cause, Army malcontents and journalists have argued that the 82d Airborne Division's airdrop at Torrijos was totally unnecessary, a grandstand play. The Rangers had already secured the airport, the critics argue, so the twenty incoming C-141s could have safely air-landed; but the division's senior officers persisted with the drop simply to earn the glory of a combat jump for their beloved outfit.

Although this myth has become widely accepted, indeed one of the fundamental elements of civilian criticism of Operation Just Cause, the airdrop was in fact a military necessity. When the orders were given to press on with the drop, both the Military Airlift Command and General Johnson's staff were confident that the twelve chalks remaining at Pope could be deiced quickly after the first serial departed and then could join up into a single, large second serial. The commanders were trying to preserve one of the basic principles of airborne warfare: maximum numbers on the ground. This was a corollary to an even more elemental principle of war: mass. Simply stated, dropping combat-equipped paratroopers was the quickest and surest method of massing maximum numbers of usable troops on the ground. And, had the large second serial been able to form, the airdrop would have preserved the night schedule for the air assault of the division's D-day objectives.

Had Joint Task Force South changed the OPLAN with the straggling serials en route from Pope, however, and ordered the planes to land instead of airdrop their troops, a number of impossible requirements would have arisen. First, the Rangers would have had to guarantee that there were no operable air-defense weapons within effective range of the runway. Then, someone would have had to provide runway and taxi ramp lights. Finally, the long runway and taxi ramps would have to have been carefully "policed" for the hundreds of T-10 and cargo parachutes from the Ranger and heavy-equipment drops. The critics neglected to note that air-landing C-141s would have had to take off again quickly; twenty Starlifters parked on open ramps would have been a tempting target for PDF mortars in the nearby barrios. And one parachute canopy sucked into a single Starlifter engine on takeoff might have provoked a disastrous crash that would have blocked the run-way, preventing the other aircraft from landing.[2]

The "unnecessary" Torrijos airdrop, however, has become an article of faith in the antimilitary canon. Ironically, the same people who criticized the 82d Airborne and the Air Force for the fiasco of the protracted air landing at Point Sa-lines during the Grenada invasion—C-130s and C-141s stalled on the runway caused incoming transports to abort for refuel-ing at Barbados—ridicule the 82d for precluding a repetition of this mess by planning an airdrop. But the division's leaders and the Air Force were determined to avoid another Grenada.[3]

As the fighting continued through the long first night, a pat-tern emerged in Panama City. The American forces were con-centrated at certain key objectives, not spread evenly around the capital. The sheer size of the metropolitan area, home to over a million people, which stretched ten miles from the

Bridge of the Americas to the eastern industrial suburbs on the road to Tocumen along the Pacific, precluded immediate imposition of American control. Entire neighborhoods lacked any kind of official authority, American or Panamanian. PDF soldiers in civilian clothes—and many still in uniform—as well as heavily armed members of Dignity Battalions, moved openly in many sectors of the city.

A few hours after the fighting began, a squad of uniformed PDF soldiers in full battle gear roared down Avenida Balboa in a pickup truck and a Land Cruiser and stopped under the palm trees near the American Embassy. Using the concrete barrier of the seawall as a shield, they proceeded to blast the Embassy chancery with rocket-propelled grenades. The RPGs smashed through the chancery's outer wall and exploded near the ambassador's office on the third floor. Inside, the Marine guards returned the fire as best they could with M-16s and shotguns. But the Embassy guard was badly outgunned. Had the PDF elected to exploit their fire-power advantage, they could have blasted their way into the Embassy and slaughtered the guards and foreign service personnel. Instead, the PDF soldiers knocked out a few more windows with their AK-47s and drove off into the night.

The Marriott Caesar Park Hotel was another target for disjointed PDF vengeance. The high-rise luxury hotel stood beside the modern Atlapa Convention Center in a middle-class neighborhood on the bay front east of Paitilla Point. For the prosperous rabiblanco community, the Marriott was a gathering place of social importance, only one rung lower than the Club Union. The Marriott's pool, spa, tennis club, and ballrooms attracted the newly prosperous middle class. Holding a wedding reception or bar mitzvah at the Marriott was a status symbol, an indication that a family had reached financial prosperity, if not social prominence. And the Marriott was also a mecca for visiting gringos. The American news media used the Marriott as their headquarters, and both CBS and ABC News maintained production offices there.

So it was not surprising that the Marriott Hotel was raided

by masked Dignity Battalion gunmen soon after H-hour. They quickly overpowered the hotel security guard and swept into the handsome atrium lobby, rushing past the gaudy Christmas tree and menacing the desk staff with assault rifles and grenades. They demanded to see the guest register, so they could locate Americans. The gunmen seemed particularly interested in American reporters.

Luckily for CBS News correspondent Juan Vasquez and producer Jon Meyersohn, they were in the bureau office on the mezzanine, talking to the network in New York, not in their rooms. They turned off the lights, locked the door, and huddled in the darkness, listening to the shouted orders and screams as the Digbat thugs rounded up hostages. Ironically, Vasquez, who is bilingual, had a hard time understanding the gunmen's Spanish because the Muzak speaker in the corridor outside droned incessantly with Christmas carols. Lindsey Gruson of the *New York Times* was rounded up, as was the wife of Patrick Chauvel, a veteran photographer on assignment for *Newsweek*. Chauvel himself was out in the dangerous streets, shooting pictures of the fighting around the Comandancia.

Juan Vasquez kept his telephone line open throughout the ordeal, and at one point was talking to Dan Rather in New York while gunmen in the corridor outside debated whether it was worth it to break down the door of the CBS bureau. But the initial terror of the Digbat raid was somewhat dispelled when the hostages taken from the Marriott to a nearby Digbat center by the first gunmen were released within two hours and allowed to return to the hotel.

This first hostage seizure, combined with the noise of the savage fighting at Paitilla Airport, just three blocks from the Marriott, and the absolute bedlam of the assault on the Comandancia convinced most reporters to remain within the relative safety of the hotel. As Juan Vasquez later candidly admitted, many reporters familiar with Panama were not in the country during the first critical forty-eight hours of the operation, "And even those of us in chaotic Panama City had to weigh our desire to cover the story against the instinct to run for cover."[4]

Other American reporters in Panama were equally constrained. The sixteen-member Pentagon press pool of print and electronic media reporters, photographers, and the inevitable clutch of technicians had been activated the night before in Washington and flown to Howard Air Force Base on an Air Force transport. Fred Francis, an NBC newsman, had an entourage of five, including his camera crew and a satellite team struggling with twenty boxes of equipment that weighed over a ton. The most lightly equipped newsmen were the print reporters, some of whom had come straight from social functions in Washington to the Andrews Air Force Base assembly point and were still dressed in wool suits.

The concept of a Pentagon press pool to be officially escorted by the U.S. military into combat operations had evolved after the Grenada invasion, when the task force commander had forbidden the news media access to the island. But in Operation Just Cause, General Maxwell Thurman was also concerned that premature activation of the media pool would breach operational security. Therefore, the reporters did not arrive at Howard Air Force Base until almost dawn on D-day. The fighting in the streets of Panama City was still too intense to permit ground transportation, and the pool's bulky equipment load was too much for the UH-1 Huey helicopter that had been reserved for their transport. They had to wait for a CH-47 Chinook to be taken off another mission to provide transport. Once the Chinook was loaded, however, they were "escorted" not to the scene of the fighting around the Comandancia or at Fort Amador, but to Fort Clayton, where the American chargé d'affaires John Bushnell, who had just witnessed the swearing in of the Endara government, proceeded to give the frustrated reporters a lecture on Panamanian history. While waiting for Mr. Bushnell at the Southcom news center, the reporters were invited to watch CNN's coverage of the fighting taking place three miles away on the other side of Quarry Heights. The reporters were not amused. Their editors back in Washington went berserk.

After vehement protest, Southcom Public Affairs managed to twist the arm of Task Force Aviation. Another Chinook was dragooned as the pool's transport and they were flown to Fort Amador, where they were allowed to watch one of the final firepower demonstrations involving the 105 mm howitzer against holdouts in the PDF barracks across the golf course. But the pool was not given access to combat GIs or American wounded.

Once again, the circumstances of the invasion prevented the news media from accurately reporting the sheer scale of the violence and the stubborn resistance put up by some Panamanian units.[5]

Back at the Marriott Hotel the initial relief felt by the Americans after the release of the first hostages was shattered when a second wave of drunken Digbat gunmen burst into the lobby. This time CBS producer Jon Meyersohn was not so lucky. He was grabbed along with an American businessman and ABC producer Robert Campos. This new group of hostages was badly manhandled by the gunmen and dragged roughly from the hotel.

What made the second hostage seizure especially frightening were the rabid antigringo messages still inexplicably being broadcast over Radio Nacional. The station had remained on the air throughout the night. It broadcast a message from General Manuel Noriega (taped the week before for just such a contingency), urging the Dignity Battalions to report to their staging areas and crush the gringo invasion of the sacred soil of the fatherland. In the same apocalyptic tones, the PDF announcer proclaimed that the Digbats guiding principle would be *"Yanqui Visto, Yanqui Muerto!"* (Yankee Seen, Yankee Dead!).[6]

After the second hostage seizure, the Marriott's managers took most of the American guests, including many of the news media, to a secure refuge in the basement laundry room, which was difficult to find and located behind several securely locked steel fire doors. They remained there throughout the day, waiting for the hard-pressed American troops to rescue them.


West of the Canal, Marine Task Force Semper Fi was one of the best led, smoothest functioning elements of the whole operation. The Marines proceeded to "take down" their objectives exactly on schedule, despite initial strong resistance. By

H-hour, Marine security forces had blocked the Bridge of the Americas, denying the PDF access to Panama City from the west; in the south, Marines secured the Veracruz Bridge, denying enemy access to Howard Air Force Base and Fort Kobbe; and in the north, they secured the swing bridge across the Canal, thus protecting Fort Clayton and the Miraflores Locks.

At the DNTT station near the Howard front gate, the scouts of the 3d Platoon, Delta Company, 2d Light Armored Infantry Battalion, quickly crushed PDF resistance. Unfortunately, the platoon suffered several casualties. One, Corporal Garreth Isaak, was killed by a burst of assault rifle fire from a PDF officer hiding in the last room of the station to be cleared. Despite their losses, the Marines proceeded on to their next objectives, clearing PDF positions in the town of Arraijan, ten kilometers to the west. Although more media coverage was given to the Army operations in Panama City, the actions of Task Force Semper Fi were critical to the success of Operation Just Cause. Had the well-equipped and certainly well-motivated PDF and Dignity Battalion forces been able to maneuver near Howard Air Force Base and to hit the crowded runway with 81 mm or 120 mm mortars, the outcome of the entire operation might have been different.[7]

At Fort Amador, the fighting progressed slowly. Lieutenant Colonel Fitzgerald's initial plan of driving the PDF down the line of barracks seemed to be working. But the firepower demonstrations had so far not stimulated the mass surrender he had hoped for. It was obvious that his men would have to clear each of the buildings, beginning with the barracks at the southern end of the PDF compound.

But the problem of the ZPU heavy machine gun and the V-300 armored car guarding the Canal side of Noriega's headquarters in Building 8 remained unsolved. The hunter-killer team pinned down in the rocks of the seawall reported that the ZPU had probably been the weapon that had shot down the OH-58 scout helicopter earlier. Fitzgerald could no longer permit the PDF to use this machine gun or the armored car. He called in fire support from the Air Papa Spectre gunship.

The AC-130 made one orbit above Fort Amador, then

swung out over the Canal onto its gun run. It flew parallel to the Amador seawall just beneath the low scudding clouds. As the gunship approached the line of PDF barracks, its 20 mm Gatling guns and 40 mm cannon opened up with a long stream of fire.

Aboard the gunship, the fire-control officer was aware that American forces were maneuvering on the far side of the barracks, and that there were U.S. troops pinned down somewhere in the rocks of the seawall. He was concerned that ricochets between the concrete buildings might injure U.S. troops nearby. So he elected to walk the fire carefully along a narrow strip beside the road to destroy the two targets. The fire-control officer watched the cannon rounds sparkle on the screen of his low-light television, impacting in dense clusters on the V-300 and the unmanned ZPU.

"Devil Six," he called Fitzgerald, "All you got down there now are smoking, twisted hulks."

Lieutenant Colonel Fitzgerald and his headquarters staff now felt confident they could proceed with the building clearing.

As the squads from Alpha and Bravo Companies worked through the PDF barracks, they found the floors littered with uniforms, boots, and several wallets containing military identity cards. In Building 8, Noriega's headquarters, the young soldiers burst into the general's private office and played their flashlights around his conference room. One soldier stopped when he encountered the double glass-fronted display case bulging with scores of ceramic and porcelain toads. One grotesquely bug-eyed toad was painted in a striped camouflage pattern and bore Noriega's patriotic credo: *"Soy Nacionalista . . . Ni Un Paso Atras"* (I am a Nationalist . . . Not One Step Backward.) The toad's humanoid right hand was raised with the middle finger extended. In the bookcase the troops found biographies of Adolph Hitler and histories of the Nazi SS. There were figurines everywhere, many of military figures in uniform, including Hitler, Field Marshal Erwin Rommel, Charles de Gaulle, and Robert E. Lee. Beside the bookcase stood a beautiful Louis Quatorze hardwood settee on which rested a clutch of uniformed teddy bears, some replete with berets, miniature parachute harnesses, and ammunition belts.

One young soldier, his face streaked with cordite soot, hefted a teddy bear and tossed it on the floor. He glanced around the room, then spit on the fine mauve carpet. "What the fuck *is* all this shit?" he asked no one in particular.

When the troops dashed out the Canal side entrance of Building 8, they encountered the abandoned ZPU heavy machine gun. The weapon sat on its wheeled carriage, the multiple barrels still pointing across the waterway. The grass and asphalt beside the gun position looked as if they'd been dug up by an excavating machine. But the gun itself was untouched. Down the line of buildings they found the V-300. It stood tall on its eight high tires. The ground next to it was also slashed and shredded by the Spectre's cannon fire. But the armored vehicle had not received a single hit.

Major Ed Dearborn, the battalion executive officer, stroked the camouflage paint of the V-300. "So much for the twisted, smoking hulk," he said bitterly.[8]

Clearing Building 4, the PDF MP headquarters, the soldiers from Alpha Company encountered a weird sight. At the dispatcher's desk stood an empty wheelchair. But there was no sign of the man who had occupied it.


As the smoky dawn broke over El Chorrillo, automatic weapons fire still continued from several buildings in the Comandancia compound. Apparently the PDF holdouts would fire a few bursts, shoot several RPG rounds at the American positions in the surrounding streets, then reposition themselves in another building. But this resistance was soon crushed. With daylight, two Sheridan tanks positioned on Quarry Heights had a clear line of fire. Now PFC Marcus Davis could see individual windows in the enemy compound through the optics of his main gun sight. The Sheridans began firing 152 mm high-explosive antitank (HEAT) rounds. The heavy projectiles pounded through the reinforced concrete of the general staff headquarters, leaving wide, cratered holes. One by one the PDF gun positions were silenced. As the Sheridans fired, a pair of Apache gunships hovered out over the bay, probing the

Comandancia with their laser range finders. Three times the Apache gunners detected movement in the shattered buildings. Three Hellfire missiles flew with flat, geometric precision straight through windows to explode in the interior rooms.

Hot daylight now flooded the streets of Santa Ana. Again the loudspeaker teams crept forward through the broken glass and shattered masonry to urge the surviving PDF forces inside the Comandancia to surrender.

As the day grew brighter, PDF stragglers and Dignity Battalion snipers who had been harassing the U.S. assault troops from the wooden tenements in El Chorrillo began to fall back. They were taken under fire from the Humvees and Marine light armored vehicles along the raised roadway of Fourth of July. Some of the Panamanian forces replied with RPG fire. Others sought refuge in the wooden tenements deeper in the barrio. Those still in the street fired wildly at the American helicopters buzzing overhead.

Father Javier Arteta, pastor of the Nuestra Señora de Fatima parish, the principal Catholic church of El Chorrillo, had been up all night attending the wounded from the streets around the Comandancia. He was thankful that the fires that had burnt in the shops and wooden tenements along Avenida A had not spread into the heart of El Chorrillo. But then, a little before seven that morning, he saw armed Dignity Battalion men dashing from house to house along Calle 26. Moments after several armed men fled from house number 31, which stood fifty meters from the church, the house erupted in flame. The pattern was repeated along the entire block. The priest was dumbfounded; members of Noriega's Dignity Battalions, who had ruled this barrio with a harsh hand for the past two months were now burning down the people's houses. Father Arteta had no way of knowing if the Digbats were acting under orders, or simply starting the fire as a diversion to cover their escape from American soldiers.

For over an hour, the people tried to fight the fires, using buckets of water. Then a strong wind began, and the inferno spread quickly. The blast-furnace heat of the burning wooden buildings had created its own wind, sucking in oxygen to feed a sudden firestorm. As Father Arteta watched in stricken horror, the entire block took fire. Then the flames jumped a narrow lane, and the tenements on the next street were ablaze.

The loudspeaker up on Ancon Hill blared a warning that everyone had to evacuate El Chorrillo. Father Arteta helped evacuate some elderly parishioners who had taken refuge in the church during the terrifying night of gunfire. He fled with them before the advancing wall of fire. One old man shook his head repeatedly. Did Noriega order this? he asked.

Father Arteta watched the flames advance through the poor, densely populated barrio. *"Yo no sé,"* was all he could answer, "I do not know."[9]

At Torrijos Airport, the 82d Airborne Division's brigade and battalion staff officers who had dropped with General Johnson at 0211 had other problems to consider that were far more pressing than potential civilian criticism of the airdrop. The OPLAN called for the Division Ready Brigade, composed of the 1st and 2d Battalions, 504th Parachute Infantry Regiment, and the 4th Battalion, 325th Airborne Infantry Regiment, to attack three separate battalion objectives: the PDF strongholds at Panama Viejo, Tinajitas, and Fort Cimarron, in predawn helicopter assaults. Obviously, the delayed airdrop meant that these air assaults would also be delayed. Further, the incoming chalks were crossloaded, so that no single serial would drop all the troops from a given battalion, who then might be quickly assembled at the proper helicopter pickup zone on the runway to preserve the timing of a predawn air assault. As the night progressed, General Johnson and his colonels accepted the grim reality that the helicopter assaults so carefully planned for the hours of darkness would now occur in broad, dangerous daylight.

And there could be little doubt that the division's first three D-day objectives were dangerous.

Objective number one was the PDF garrison at Panama Viejo, located on the bay shoreline in the eastern outskirts of Panama City. The fenced compound housed the PDF Cavalry Squadron, an armored platoon from Battalion 2000, and, since the failed October coup, the headquarters of the UESAT Special Forces. The two-story PDF barracks stood beside a historical park of sixteenth-century Spanish colonial ruins, which included a handsome dressed-stone tower flanked by stately old palms and hibiscus hedges. The structure had once done double duty as a carillon and a lookout point for marauding pirates, an important attribute, considering that the site had been frequently raided by buccaneers, most notably the Englishman, Captain Henry Morgan. There were two landing zones at Panama Viejo, LZ Bobcat located in grassy wasteland near a soccer field several hundred meters from the coastal highway, and LZ Lion on the narrow beach just west of the barracks. Both were within effective range of the 14.5 mm ZPU-4 antiaircraft machine gun set up to defend the garrison from just such air assaults. The Digbat Venceremos Battalion—trained and equipped by Cubans—had its assembly point at Panama Viejo. The 2d Battalion of the 504th would assault this objective.

Objective number two was at Tinajitas, the hilltop garrison of the PDF's 1st Infantry Company, "Los Tigres." Although these troops' loyalty to Noriega was in doubt because they had failed to come to his aid during the October coup, the 200-man garrison was armed with heavy mortars and machine guns. Equally ominous, the Digbats' San Miguel el Archangel Battalion supported the company from staging areas in the sprawling slums of San Miguelito beneath the steep hills. The Tinajitas garrison lay about five miles inland, just off the Trans-Isthmus Highway. An air assault at night would have stood a decent chance of achieving tactical surprise. But there was no way for helicopters to approach this hilly garrison undetected during daylight. Tinajitas was the objective of the 1st Battalion of the 504th.

The division's third D-day objective was Fort Cimarron, headquarters of Battalion 2000, some of whose 400 troops had been chewed up at H-hour by the Special Forces and the Spectre gunship at the Pacora River bridge. This unit was probably the best trained and equipped in the PDF; it had almost twenty V-150 and V-300 armored vehicles, heavy mortars, multiple rocket launchers, and heavy machine guns. Fort Cimarron was the target of the 4th Battalion of the 325th Airborne Infantry Regiment.

These air assaults would be made in multiple lifts aboard

nine UH-60 Black Hawk helicopters, four from the 228th Aviation permanently stationed at Fort Kobbe, whose pilots knew the area intimately, and the other five from the 123d Aviation, attached to the 7th Light Infantry Division in California. The chopper crews had seen their first combat air assaulting Fort Amador at H-hour. Waiting for the 82d to arrive, the crews had been able to stand down in relative security at field refueling points on the Empire Range west of the Canal. The two companies of Black Hawks had been given some of the most demanding assignments in the Blue Spoon OPLAN: four multilift night combat air assaults in five hours. The first assault at Fort Amador had gone well, with no aircraft receiving groundfire damage. And the rigorous schedule for the three remaining operations had been relaxed with the late arrival of the 82d Airborne. But the aviators had lost the protective mantle of darkness. They would now have to fly three assaults into heavily defended landing zones in daylight.

Each lift of Black Hawks would be escorted by an AH-1 Cobra gunship. And the landing zones would be "over-watched" by a heavy attack team of two AH-64 Apache gunships working with an OH-58C observation helicopter. In principle, the assault forces had plenty of fire support. But there was a lingering uncertainty as to how well the Black Hawks and their crews would hold up against concentrated groundfire. Certainly the first combat test of the Black Hawks six years before during the Grenada invasion had been disastrous. During daylight operations, Black Hawks had been shot down by heavy machine guns and several had collided and crashed during an air assault on a garrison objective similar to these. When it became obvious that the 82d Airborne's air assaults would have to go down after dawn, the helicopter crews abandoned the jubilation of their success at Fort Amador and became somberly quiet.

The last paratroopers jumped onto the Torrijos drop zone at 0515. They joined men who had landed earlier and formed up in their units as best they could. Those who were not on the first air assault (Panama Viejo), had been assigned to derig heavy-drop Humvees and equipment, police up parachutes, or establish perimeter defense. The derigging and sorting out of cargo pallets in the heat and cloying mud of the mosquito-ridden marsh was a frustrating job. But no one volunteered to leave this duty and replace injured men from the 2/504 who were forming up on Pickup Zone South at the end of the Torrijos runway.

As dawn broke, painting the fat tropical clouds in shades of gold and orange, most of the air assault troops for the first two objectives had been sorted out and assembled on the grassy runway margin into eleven-man chalks. A lone command-and-control Black Hawk, carrying the Air Assault Commander and extra radio equipment, came thumping over the misty bay and turned into the hot eye of the rising sun to land. Officers of the 2d Battalion converged on the chopper to prepare for the first lift.

At 0650 hours, with the sun just clear of the jungle mountains inland, paratroopers from companies A, B, and C, as well as elements of the battalion staff and scouts, climbed aboard the nine Black Hawks. The men were humped beneath the familiar heavy rucksacks, and burdened by belts of extra M-60 ammunition and antitank rockets. Like the paratroopers on the other air assaults, they were seated facing outward in both open doors, their weapons held at ready, restrained by a single green web safety strap.

The first lift rose in two columns. The five Black Hawks headed for LZ Bobcat flew parallel to the Inter-American Highway, above the truck and bus garages and the walled factory compounds that spread east from Panama City along both sides of the highway. Although the poor barrios below were known Dignity Battalion strongholds, the helicopters were not fired on.

The four helicopters headed for LZ Lion on the Panama Viejo waterfront swung over the bay with their escort Cobra keeping station ahead on the right flank. The bay below was streaked with the mauve colors of sunrise, flat calm at slack water after low tide.

As the two lifts converged on their landing zones, the OH-58 scout helicopter of the over-watching attack team buzzed low across the objective, swung west along the mud flats of LZ Lion, then turned inland toward LZ Bobcat. The grassy fields of LZ Bobcat lay between barrios of narrow unpaved lanes separating nondescript cinder-block houses, each with a leafy, postage-stamp-size garden. The observation pilots almost missed an extremely important target. Hidden in a weedy junkyard surrounded by a cement wall plastered with graffiti, they spotted two camouflaged V-300 armored cars and five two-and-a-half-ton PDF trucks. The assault lifts were due on the LZs in three minutes. If the V-300s got loose with their 90 mm cannons, the operation would end in disaster. The attack team did not hesitate. With the observation helicopter illuminating the junkyard with its laser target designator, the evil-looking Apaches banked low over the barrio and rumbled to a hover, their rotor wash blasting down mango trees and corrugated roofing below. One chopper cut loose with its 30 mm Area Weapon System chain gun, shredding the trucks with 300 rounds of heavy armor-piercing ammunition.

The pilot/gunner of the second Apache spotted his laser target designator on the first armored car and activated his Hellfire missile Point Target Weapon System. His console screen blinked with a positive laser range of 416 meters and displayed the solid symbol of a positive lock-on. The first missile howled away on a cone of orange flame and dull white smoke. Two seconds later, the mottled green hull of the targeted armored car swelled like an overripe fruit, burst, and rose several feet in the air, surrounded by a ball of burning diesel fuel. Its turret with the long cannon flipped through the smoke and clattered down among the rusty wrecks in the junkyard. Only seconds later, the second armored car was hit by a Hellfire. It disappeared in a cloud of flaming debris. As the attack team swung back toward the landing zones, the junkyard was covered by a dense pall of black smoke from burning tires.

Approaching the two landing zones, the Black Hawks suddenly came under fire from both the PDF barracks on the seafront and, unexpectedly, from the gardens and muddy lanes of the surrounding barrio. The tracers sailing up from the dense groves of banana, mango, and kumquat trees were the telltale green of AK assault rifles. A few heavier red tracers rose from the garrison: a badly aimed burst from a ZPU. The Cobra escorting the LZ Lion lift made a run on the two-story barracks on the seafront, its 20 mm cannon probing for the ZPU. After that run, the air-defense weapon fell silent.

But the Apaches and the Cobra escorting the Black Hawks into LZ Bobcat refrained from firing on the densely clustered houses, half-hidden behind floppy banana leaves. As the Black Hawks flared for landing, the doorgunners were close enough to see individual PDF soldiers firing from the gardens and windows of cinder-block homes. Despite the intense groundfire, the five Black Hawks stayed in a good trail formation, landed their troops squarely on the LZ, and climbed away keeping a proper interval. There was none of the dangerously erratic flying that had plagued the Black Hawk operations in Grenada.

The paratroopers spread out by fire team and began moving through the high grass toward the surrounding neighborhood, trying to take enemy gunners under fire with automatic weapons and 203 grenades. The fire from the nearby gardens and houses ebbed briefly as the helicopters climbed away, then rose sharply. Long bursts of AK tracers snapped through the grass. Mortar rounds smacked down now; fortunately the enemy mortarmen were just as stymied by the tall grass as the Americans. Other weapons joined in a crossfire. The paratroopers were pinned down. In the shoulder-high kuna grass, it was impossible to get a good line of fire on the enemy weapons. Then Sergeant Michael Alexander of Charlie Company stood up and pinpointed a cluster of houses to the left where the worst of the crossfire was coming from.

"Somebody get me a damn 203," he yelled.

Sergeant Alexander sighted the grenade launcher on the window of a cement-walled bungalow. He fired one round, reloaded, and fired again. The PDF weapon fell silent. Still standing, despite the rounds slashing through the grass around him, he fired a white phosphorous grenade to mark a PDF automatic weapon for the company's machine gunners. Within ten minutes, the enemy fire around the landing zone had been suppressed and the soldiers could move off toward their objective.

On the beachfront LZ Lion, the enemy fire was equally intense, but the helicopters approaching from the bay were not caught in a crossfire. The Black Hawks flared into a low hover along the narrow rocky beach bordering the bayside Via Cincuentenario. Jumping from the doors, the troops hunkered down behind the grassy knee-high bluff between the highway and the mud flats. There were thick-trunked old acacia trees here that also provided good cover from the small-arms fire coming from the houses on the other side of the coastal road.

The second lifts into the two LZs also came under fire. And this time, the PDF gunners had learned how to lead a deceptively slow-moving helicopter. Several of the Black Hawks flaring in to settle on the thrashing kuna grass of LZ Bobcat were hit by small-arms fire. But the pilots held a steady low hover as the paratroopers jumped from the doors. Once more the five aircraft climbed away in good formation.

At LZ Lion on the bayside, enemy gunners also scored hits. The lead pilot spread his formation slightly to avoid the worst of the fire from a two-story building beyond a weedy field across the road. The paratroopers in the lead chalk jumped down behind the low bluff and took cover. But the troops leaping from the three Black Hawks hovering over the mud flats were not so lucky. Many of the heavily laden soldiers sank deep into the spongy black mud, some up to their armpits. They flailed wildly to free themselves. As the doorgunners reported the soldiers' plight to the pilots, the helicopters dropped back to low hover so the soldiers could grab the landing gear and be pulled free.

But some of the men had already thrashed toward shore and were bogged down by even softer mud. Then a remarkable event occurred. Even though small-arms fire still crackled from the PDF barracks along the bay front, and from some barrio houses inland, Panamanian families streamed out of the shelter of their own homes, dashed across the open road, and set up a human chain to drag the mud-caked paratroopers to shore.

The first wounded prisoners captured as the 2d Battalion maneuvered toward their attack positions around the PDF barracks explained why fire from the garrison had been relatively light while fire from the nearby barrio had been unexpectedly heavy. Just before H-hour, the UESAT soldiers, PDF Cavalry troopers, and most of the men from the Battalion 2000 armored platoon had changed into civilian clothes, taken their weapons, including several light mortars and plenty of extra ammunition, and spread north into the poor neighborhoods of Panama Viejo. Of those who had remained in the garrison overnight, all but a handful took up positions in surrounding buildings just before dawn.

By the time the third lift of four Black Hawks landed on LZ Lion, organized resistance from the surrounding neighborhood had ended. When the men of the 2d Battalion encircled the fenced PDF compound on the bay front and called for surrender, the ten men remaining inside shuffled out with their hands in the air. Inside the paratroopers found scores of discarded PDF uniforms but few weapons. They did find several empty wooden 60 mm and 81 mm mortar-round cases, however. The PDF had not fled in disarray, but rather dispersed to continue fighting in the streets of the city. The only encouraging find in the garrison was the fully loaded ZPU-4 heavy antiaircraft machine gun. The weapon's multiple barrels were pointed down the beach toward the mud flats of LZ Lion. There were a dozen spent shell casings around the carriage tires. Either the Cobra had killed the gunner, or the soldier had fled at the menacing sight of the little gunship. Had that gun remained in operation, the helicopter landing and the eventual assault of the garrison compound might have been a bloody disaster.

Within two hours, the objective was technically secured. But the bulk of the PDF forces had escaped the encirclement and fled with their weapons into the Dignity Battalion stronghold of the surrounding barrios. They had automatic weapons, and they had mortars. Capturing this garrison had been accomplished with only a few casualties, but holding it and moving out to secure the neighborhood might well prove costly.

*     *     *

While the 2/504 assaulted Panama Viejo just after dawn, the battle had already erupted in the steep hills of scrub jungle and banana groves around Tinajitas. Another attack team of two AH-64 Apaches with an accompanying OH-58C left Howard Air Force Base and flew east to take up an over-watch position near the PDF 1st Company garrison. As the three helicopters swung low and slow above the treetops, they spotted a uniformed PDF squad on a bare hilltop north of San Miguelito, grouped around several light machine guns. The choppers were flying in trail formation at seventy knots, only a hundred feet above the trees. Under orders not to fire on the PDF unless fired upon, the crews stared directly into the faces of the Panamanian soldiers. Without warning, the PDF opened fire. The OH-58 scout broke hard left, but was raked with 7.62 mm rounds and began trailing a thick mist of fuel.

The pilot of the lead Apache felt his aircraft shudder as several long bursts of tracers pounded along the fuselage, some spiraling away as ricochets when they struck armor plate. His instrument panel blazed with a cluster of warning lights, indicating his right engine and hydraulics had been damaged. The right engine's RPM and fuel flow gauges went crazy. When the pilot/gunner in the forward cockpit traversed the 30 mm chain gun toward the PDF, the weapon jammed. The ammunition bay and hydraulic controls had been chewed up by enemy automatic weapons fire. If this had been a Black Hawk or a Huey, the aircraft probably would have crashed, killing the crew. But the Apache had been designed to absorb this kind of punishment and return to base on a single engine. The lead pilot did exactly that, banking hard left and climbing to follow the OH-58.

The number two Apache had not been hit. The pilot shuddered into an abrupt hover as the gunner swung the chain gun onto the enemy squad. He painted the clearing with his laser rangefinder and locked the target data into the fire-control computer of his chain gun. One long burst of 160 cannon rounds was sufficient. When the Apache roared over the hilltop clearing, none of the shattered bodies on the ground was moving. A lone survivor scrambled off the hilltop and fled into a banana grove.

Twenty minutes later at Howard Air Force Base, the damaged Apache maneuvered precisely among the scores of helicopters and set down on the pad outside Hangar 1. The ground crew counted twenty-three bullet holes in the fuselage and right engine cowling, as well as multiple ricochet nicks in sections of armor plate around the cockpits. The number two gear box had taken several hits, as had the main rotor blades. The tail rotor driveshaft was deeply gouged and bent. The AH-64 Apache gunship had just survived its most extreme combat test.[10]

As the battle-damaged attack team departed Tinajitas, it handed off over-watch responsibility to an incoming team, warning them the PDF had set up machine-gun positions in the garden clearings and banana groves on the hilltops ahead. The lead scout moved forward on a fast recon and called the information on enemy gun positions to the Air Assault Task Force commander over the secure FM net. The commander was aboard the command-and-control Black Hawk, then at Pickup Zone Center at Torrijos where the soldiers of the 1st Battalion, 504th Parachute Infantry Regiment, were loading the first lift for Tinajitas. The new Apache attack team was worried that the Air Assault commander did not understand the gravity of the situation. No Black Hawk could take the pounding that Apache had absorbed and stay in the air. If one of the Black Hawks loaded with troops strayed over one of the PDF gun positions, the helicopter would probably be destroyed with all on board.

At 0830 hours, seven Black Hawks took off from Pickup Zone (PZ) Center on the Torrijos runway carrying the first lift of 1/504 soldiers. The battle damage these helicopters had received at Panama Viejo was limited to small-arms hits on non-critical sections of the airframes. No vital engine or hydraulic components had been lost, although one pilot's windscreen had been cracked. Two others at Torrijos were down for emergency maintenance. One of the Black Hawks had received groundfire damage to its hydraulic system. The aircraft commander was a woman chief warrant officer named Debra

Mann, one of two female Black Hawk Pilots-in-Command in Panama. The other PIC was 1st Lieutenant Elizabeth Dreiling, and First Lieutenant Lisa Kutschera was a copilot in the Black Hawk company from Fort Ord. Both Lieutenants Dreiling and Kutschera were flying on the Tinajitas lift. Despite the multiple small-arms hits Debra Mann's aircraft had received, she calmly flew the battered helicopter back with the rest of the lift. She promised the Air Assault commander that she would have the aircraft ready for the second lift into the Tinajitas landing zones. He knew that he might have to take up her offer. As the Air Assault radio net crackled, the crews learned that the PDF were waiting for them in the steep hills around Tinajitas.

Six Black Hawks headed for Landing Zone Leopard, an open field around an abandoned mine off the Trans-Isthmus Highway that lay northwest of San Miguelito and due south of the Tinajitas garrison. A single Black Hawk trailed them, headed for LZ Jaguar on an open hillside beneath the wooded compound of a Bahai temple. Given the steep terrain and dense clusters of villages along the highway, LZ Leopard, the main landing zone, was well below the Tinajitas garrison, but it was the only open ground in the sector wide enough to accommodate multiple helicopters.

It was known that the PDF garrison had almost 200 men, equipped with ten heavy mortars and another ZPU-4 antiaircraft gun. The exact strength and armament of the local Dignity Battalion was unknown. With two Apaches patrolling overhead and two Cobras escorting the lift, the ZPU was less a threat than mortars dispersed and hidden in the surrounding villages, which like the houses in the Panama Viejo barrio were cloaked with floppy banana groves and big old mango trees. It was a lot easier for the PDF to fire from this concealment than it was for the gunships to locate the enemy.

As the helicopters flew along the coast and crossed north through the industrial suburbs of Panama City, people in the yards below waved white handkerchiefs and pounded on cooking pots, just as they had done during the anti-Noriega demonstrations during the past two years. But when the assault column crossed the Inter-American Highway and passed near

San Miguelito, the people down below were firing weapons, not waving handkerchiefs. Once more the helicopters were hit by small-arms fire. The lead chalk was relatively immune from this Digbat groundfire, because the inexperienced gunners below had not yet mastered the knack of leading helicopters flying at 130 knots. But the trailing aircraft did receive more small-arms hits. And paratroopers were wounded in two of the Black Hawks.

As the helicopters approached, the true nature of the problem facing the assault force became obvious. Hundreds of civilians were out alongside the highway and crowding the muddy lanes of the surrounding villages, watching the approaching helicopters as if the assault were a sporting event. PDF soldiers in uniform and Digbats had mixed in with these civilians. When the Black Hawks passed overhead, the armed Panamanians below would dash out from a crowd, fire a full magazine at the American aircraft, then run back for cover into the gardens and under the shade verandas of the homes below. The Black Hawks' doorgunners showed amazing discipline by refraining from firing their M-60 machine guns, which might have taken out the enemy gunners, but which certainly would have killed or wounded hundreds of innocent civilians. Many of the doorgunners were temporary replacements from the 82d Airborne Division. It was hard for them to hold their fire while the men from their own unit, jammed into the Black Hawks' troop bays, were being hit even before they reached the LZ. But when one gunner spotted a pickup truck racing down a rutted lane with three men firing assault rifles from the back, he carefully aimed his M-60 machine gun and killed the enemy gunners with two bursts.[11]

Flaring in above the tall grass of LZ Leopard, the Black Hawks came under intense fire from both sides. Mortar shells began to walk toward the hovering Black Hawks. More paratroopers were wounded, trying to leap from the open doors. Now the doorgunners could see PDF firing from rusty old abandoned buses to the right of the LZ. As the six Black Hawks climbed away, they took more small-arms hits. Fortunately, the self-sealing fuel cells sealed quickly, and the hardened engine shells deflected the small-arms fire.

The densely clustered housing below presented no obvious targets to the circling Apache over-watch team. While the Black Hawks were taking fire on the LZ, the gunships had to wait in frustration. But a Special Operations MH-6 AHIPS that had joined the fight was nimble enough to dart low over the rooftops and engage individual PDFs with its chattering mini-gun. The small helicopter, flown by 1st Lieutenant John Hunter and Chief Warrant Officer Wilson B. Owens, made one low pass too many. Just as the gunship flew over a cluster of houses, a PDF soldier stepped out and hit the aircraft squarely with an RPG round. The MH-6 exploded in a fireball, instantly killing both aviators.

As the Black Hawks returned to Torrijos to pick up the next lift of paratroopers, the crews counted their casualties. Three airmen had been hit, one of them seriously. Captain Tom Muir, the flight leader, had been struck in the head going into LZ Leopard. Fragments of an AK-47 round that shattered his windscreen shredded his scalp and he was bleeding profusely. There was blood sprayed across the windscreen and instrument panel. His young copilot took control, completed the landing, and led the column back out of the hot LZ.

Back at PZ Center at Torrijos Airport, the troops waiting in the heavy sun heard the report that their LZs were hot. Some men swore quietly, cursing the bastard officers who had fucked things up again. Other men prayed with quiet determination. And others stared numbly at the incoming helicopters. When the Black Hawks set down, the call went out for medics. The young paratroopers climbing on board gazed with terrified fascination at the scarlet smears of fresh blood on the green aluminum deck. They noted the precise, round bullet holes in the choppers' bellies. But no one balked or faltered. They climbed through the doors and humped the weight of their rucksacks into the chopper, then sat shoulder-to-shoulder as the aircraft climbed back into the hot morning.

The new flight leader took the second lift into LZ Leopard along a different approach route, hoping to avoid such heavy groundfire. But this lift was hit just as badly as the first. Despite the renewed groundfire, the second and the third lifts deposited their troops in the high grass of the landing zone.

By now three companies of paratroopers had assembled and managed to suppress the organized resistance around the landing zone. One company moved straight up Cerro Tinajitas, toward the PDF garrison, while the other two maneuvered east and west to seize the surrounding hilltops in order to bring the garrison under direct line-of-sight fire. It took two hours for the troops to gain their objective, two hours of humping rucksacks up the steep hills through the humid morning, occasionally harassed by sniper fire from the houses beside the highway.

When the troops finally swept into the fenced PDF compound, they found the 1st Company had abandoned the garrison. As with the other objectives, the Americans discovered discarded uniforms. They also found three 120 mm heavy mortars, two set up to fire on the landing zone below. One was aligned on an azimuth of 255 degrees, directly at Fort Clayton. Luckily, the heavy round in the mortar tube was hung up, a misfire. The exhausted paratroopers, their nerves strung tight by the intense fire they had survived, began the nasty task of searching the slums for snipers.

Staff Sergeant Louis Olivera woke up with flies on his face. The sun was brutal. Strange shrill birds cackled in the jungle branches overhead. He had never been this thirsty. Somehow, he had fallen asleep outside. Then he remembered. He was on an op, at Rio Hato. But somehow he had just fallen asleep. The Sergeant Major would not be happy. It was not a good idea to go to sleep in combat.

Then he remembered all of it. His hand went up to his head, where the PDF AK round had seared his scalp. His skull was still intact. The thick Kevlar helmet had deflected the bullet.

He tried to move. But there was no strength in his crushed chest, no power in his frozen limbs. He lay, watching the flies move across the caked blood of his BDUs. There was a rifle nearby, an M-16 with a weird green ribbon tied to it. The ribbon was some kind of unit symbol. He realized the Macho de Monte soldiers who had ambushed him had tagged his weapon as a trophy. Like war was some kind of a game. They probably thought different now.

A long time later, a patrol from Alpha Company found him lying crumpled in the brush. As the medics worked on him, Olivera stared at the soft blue of the Pacific, wondering if he would live to see his family.

# III

# Victory

# 9

# Objectives Secured

American Rangers and Airborne forces gained control of the Torrijos International Airport and adjacent Tocumen Air Base before dawn. But the surrounding industrial suburbs and villages to the east were still in the hands of the PDF and Dignity Battalions. Clearing these areas was not an immediate priority for the 82d Airborne. Rather, the division's officers were anxious to press on with their original three air-assault objectives. A brigade of the 7th Light Infantry Division was due into Howard Air Force Base, and these troops had the unglamorous and dangerous mission of fanning out through the city and environs and crushing what military planners euphemistically call "pockets of resistance." But the 7th LID's airlift from Fort Ord had been delayed by dense fog in northern California, just as the 82d's air column had been held up by ice at Pope Air Force Base.

This meant the Special Operations forces that had seized key isolated objectives at H-hour would have to hold out unreinforced much longer than anticipated. For the SEALs at Paitilla Airport, the enemy resistance from the surrounding neighborhood had decreased to sporadic sniper fire. They had secured the airport perimeter as best they could, considering that thirteen of their original assault force of fifty-four were either dead or wounded. They set up their M-60 machine-gun positions and deployed their AT-4 and LAW gunners, then hunkered down to wait out the night. The SEALs were physically and emotionally battered, shocked by the death and maiming of their teammates. They were angry beyond expression, but resisted the urge to unleash that anger on the few Panamanian civilians who incautiously ventured near the airport. Around them the gleaming high-rise towers of Paitilla point were now blacked out, dark monoliths silhouetted against the flaming caldron of the Comandancia to the west.

At the Pacora River bridge, ten kilometers east of the international airport complex, Major Kevin Higgins and his small Special Forces detachment faced the task of holding the bridge against PDF Battalion 2000 troops who had survived the initial attack on their truck convoy. Higgins used the first lull in the firing to reposition his men, so that they could cover the opposite river bank, as well as the bridge itself. Whenever the enemy fired across the river, Higgins' men replied with 203 rounds and small arms fire. Twice the Spectre made 20 mm cannon runs, chopping up the brush on the steep muddy eastern bank. After the second Spectre pass, the enemy troops were observed pulling back from the river. Even in retreat, however, these disciplined soldiers moved well in the darkness and were difficult to detect with night-vision goggles.

The next threat came from the west, not from the PDF troops across the bridge. The Air Papa Spectre reported four vehicles moving in a "military-type convoy" toward the bridge from the built-up area near the airport. These vehicles were now cresting a low rise a kilometer from the bridge. Higgins seized a night sight and adjusted the focus to maximum magnification. But he couldn't be certain whether the vehicles were military or civilian. And the orbiting Spectre gunship was momentarily obscured by low clouds, so that its powerful low-light television sensors and infrared search and track (IRST) system were unavailable to help him. Instead of ordering his men to fire directly on the vehicles, however, Higgins grabbed his PRC-77 radio.

"Put some tracers over them," he ordered the M-60 team deployed on the right flank of the road.

The gunners immediately fired four well-aimed bursts of cherry-red tracers that sailed through the night and clipped the branches of the umbrella-shaped hardwoods on the hillside above the road cut. The vehicles stopped immediately and began to maneuver wildly, backing and turning on the concrete highway. They sped back over the hill crest west, and were out of sight within a minute. Whoever they were, they had chosen not to fight.

The big gunship could not stay on station indefinitely. Only minutes after the Spectre droned away toward Howard Air Force Base to refuel, a three-man enemy team sprinted from the cover of the knocked-out convoy directly onto the bridge. They carried a 60 mm mortar tube and wore gas masks. Either they were going to lay down a mortar-bomb smoke screen to cover a larger assault across the bridge, or they intended to strike the American positions with CS gas. It was obvious to Higgins, however, that the enemy did not realize how close his own men were to the bridge. The PDF troops were courageous but ineffective. Three SAW bursts from Higgins' right-side element stopped the enemy team on the bridge. One PDF soldier was killed outright, one lay wounded, and one managed to leap from the bridge onto the opposite bank.

When it was clear that no larger enemy force intended to follow the mortar team, the Special Forces medic, Sergeant José Roman, retrieved the wounded Panamanian soldier. The man was hit in the legs, but would survive. As Sergeant Roman worked on the wounded soldier, he and the Panamanian spoke quietly in Spanish. The man explained that their lieutenant had not warned them of the American invasion. Instead, they were mustered the night before and ordered to prepare to put down a "civil disturbance" that had broken out in the town of Tocumen near the airport.

The wounded soldier cursed this officer. He and his comrades were professional soldiers, he said, but they had been treated like delinquent children, unworthy of the officer's trust. Once he was certain his wounds were not life threatening, the man handed Sergeant Roman his $240 Christmas-bonus check. "Hold it for me, my friend," the Panamanian soldier told the American medic. "The guards in the prison camp will just steal it from me."

The Special Forces medic agreed to hold the check and promised to visit the wounded man at whatever hospital he was sent to.

An hour passed and there was no other sign of PDF probes. The sky to the east finally began to pale with the watery green light of false dawn. But it was still quite dark down on the river bank. Now Higgins sent out a small recon team armed with 203 grenade launchers and automatic weapons to make certain no more PDF infiltrators were moving toward the bridge. The dark water gurgled below. The insects whined. Overhead the Spectre rumbled and whistled through the clouds. The recon team called in enemy KIAs, but no "live ones."

Then a scout whispered hoarsely on the radio net that there was more movement on the road. Everyone was down behind their guns, straining to focus on the new target. Higgins was one of the first to identify the approaching figure.

The enemy soldier coming toward them carried no shoulder weapon. He rode a bicycle, not an armored vehicle. He seemed determined to cross the bridge, and might simply have been en route home to his family, hoping to escape the destruction he saw behind him in the ruined convoy. When he pedaled up onto the concrete apron of the bridge, Sergeant Roman shouted in Spanish for the man to stop. He kept pedaling, and Roman shouted again. At the last moment, the Special Forces security team fired at the bike's tires, and the man fell unharmed to the pavement of the bridge span.

"Don't shoot me," he yelled in Spanish. "I am Cabo Hernandez of the Battalion 2000."

As the Americans searched and flex-cuffed the prisoner, the man seemed confused. "You are gringos," he finally said. Still confused, the soldier explained that he had spent the night at his girlfriend's house and was returning to his own home to change into a clean uniform before pedaling back to Fort Cimarron. In the darkness, he had not seen that the convoy was riddled with cannon and small arms fire. He had mistaken Sergeant Roman and the security team for PDF troops guarding the parked trucks.

"Didn't you hear any firing in the night?" Roman asked.

The man shook his head vehemently.

"That must be one hell of a girlfriend," a Special Forces trooper wryly noted.[1]

As the pastel dawn colored the hills to the east, they heard the thump and stutter of helicopters approaching from Panama City. Then Higgins' radio operator reported that Major Gill Perez, Higgins' friend from Fort Bragg, was calling in. Perez was leading a relief force of forty-five Special Forces troops aboard six choppers. He wanted clearance to land.

"Roger that," Higgins said. "We've got a cold LZ for you, Gill."

The siege of the Pacora River bridge was over. Major Higgins and his handful of men, protected by the devastating firepower of the Spectres overhead, had sealed the eastern approach to the airport and Panama City from the armored infantry of the PDF's Battalion 2000.


In the terminal of Torrijos International Airport, almost 400 civilians crowded the second-floor departure lounge, watching the hot dawn flood through the tall plate-glass windows. Most of them still had their carry-on baggage, bright clumps of vinyl and imitation leather dumped at their feet, adding to the bizarre appearance of this disparate band of people whom the Rangers officially designated "detainees." The civilians were not prisoners, of course, but they weren't free to leave, either; the surrounding barrios were far from secure. So they simply waited in the incongruous limbo of the ultramodern airport terminal. There weren't enough seats for everyone, but the Rangers guarding this unexpected throng of refugees made sure women with small children and the elderly were given priority.

Many of the stranded passengers were Panamanians returning for Christmas from jobs or school in the United States, and their family members who had gathered at the airport to greet them. Now that it was clear that the initial battle was over and that the airport was not about to be counterattacked, the young children who had come to greet their older brothers and sisters could no longer restrain their curiosity. They began opening the brightly decorated Christmas presents, the bounty of Miami Walmart and Toys R Us stores. Soon young kids in shorts and T-shirts were dashing about, proudly displaying their Ninja Turtles and radio-controlled dump trucks to the tired Rangers in full battle gear who stood guard in the departure hall.

On the taxi ramp leading to the runway below, lines of paratroopers moved shoulder-to-shoulder in slow formation, heads bent, searching for spent shell casings, bits of web equipment, and of course stray parachutes—the dangerous "objects" that produce Foreign Object Damage to jet engines. The airport would not be ready to receive the first air-landed reinforcements and cargo until this sweep was complete. From the departure lounge, the strange ritual of huge soldiers in camouflage helmets and fatigues silently pacing in long curved lines intrigued the watching children. Like the young observers of any war, the kids in the departure lounge soon formed their own little FOD sweeps, and patrolled the broad expanse of gleaming tile floor, searching for cigarette butts and the odd M-16 or AK-47 souvenir shell casing.

The foreign object damage hazard at Tocumen-Torrijos remained a menace to aircraft for several days. After the airport perimeter was secured, CH-47 Chinook helicopters of the 1/228 Aviation were employed to lift sling-loads of cargo that had been heavy-dropped into the swamp southeast of the Torrijos runways. One Chinook, flown by a warrant officer named Standish, sucked up a parachute canopy at an altitude of thirty feet above the kuna grass. The parachute wrapped around the huge forward rotor, destroying its lift. The Chinook rolled sharply onto its right side, the 98.6-foot diameter disks of its twin rotors swinging perilously toward the ground. Chief Warrant Officer Standish wrestled with the controls and somehow managed to right the big helicopter before the rotors smashed into the ground. But the movement was so violent that one of the door gunners, a sergeant named Norris, found himself momentarily hanging nearly vertical in his monkey-strap safety harness.[2]

While the 82d Airborne's assault was progressing on Tinajitas, the division reported to Joint Task Force South that the immediate Tocumen-Torrijos Airport perimeter had been secured. But General Johnson suspected the surrounding roads and settlements were still hostile. This suspicion was confirmed an hour later when a convoy from Delta Company, 2/504, departed the Torrijos terminal area en route to link up with the rest of the battalion at Panama Viejo.

The column of sixty soldiers rode in five hardshell Humvees, escorted by two Sheridan tanks. The lead Sheridan had just crossed a narrow bridge over a drainage canal when it encountered a roadblock of two burning automobiles. What made this roadblock truly dangerous was the pile of squat blue household gas propane tanks scattered between the burning cars. Suddenly, a heavy force of PDF and Dignity Battalion troops opened fire from nearby buildings, raking the convoy with automatic weapons and RPG-18 rounds. The lead tank cut loose with its main gun, destroying an automatic weapons position inside a shuttered bodega. Gunners on the Humvees returned the fire as best they could. The troops on board the vehicles dismounted and laid down a screen of small-arms and 203 grenade fire. But the convoy was taking wounded and was in a bad position. The grenade fire set off several of the propane gas tanks, and men were burned by the fireball. The vehicles backed away, screening the withdrawal with .50-caliber covering fire. Now the convoy concentrated its fire on the obvious PDF ambush positions. Another Sheridan main gun round scored a direct hit. But the sniper fire was still intense.

Specialist Alejandro Manrique Lozano, a Delta Company antitank gunner, was hit squarely with automatic fire and killed instantly. Several of the men were badly burned. Nevertheless, the commander of Company D was prepared to push through the smoldering remnants of the roadblock and run the sniper gauntlet. But his convoy was ordered back to Torrijos to link up with another convoy from the 1st Battalion, forming up to relieve the assault force at Tinajitas.

As the 2d Battalion dug in around the historic ruins of Panama Viejo, the paratroopers continued to receive sniper fire from the nearby houses. Over a three-hour period, ten separate civilian vehicles rolled along the seaside road, spraying the Americans with fire from AK-47s and Uzis. Most of these vehicles never made it past the first American position. By late morning, the unit was in desperate need of more 203 grenade rounds, and the road was littered with the burning hulks of pickup trucks and vans. The stench of burnt flesh fouled the humid midday heat.

While these drive-by shootings continued, a fairly well aimed mortar barrage began to fall inside the American lines. The troops who had been filling sandbags and stretching concertina wire took shelter below the old stone ramparts of the colonial ruins. Then the call came out on the tactical radio net: A V-300 armored car was approaching up a shady side lane, using the mortar barrage as cover. Two antitank squads moved forward and took ambush positions on either side of a gas station. When the armored car was within range, a soldier braced his shoulder on a broken concrete wall and fired his AT-4. The armored car burst into flame. One crewman managed to escape, his uniform smoldering.

This corner of Panama City was a long way from being secured.


A little after noon, the troops of the 4th Battalion, 325th Airborne Infantry Regiment, began the assault on Fort Cimarron. Eleven Black Hawks were now operable. Fortunately, the assaults on the two landing zones south and west of the Fort Cimarron airport complex were not contested. Within an hour, the battalion's three combat companies were on the ground and searching for the remnants of PDF Battalion 2000. Bravo Company made contact with a strong PDF force, hiding in the village of Paso Blanco, south of the Fort Cimarron garrison. The scout platoon surrounded the village and took the enemy under fire. Alpha Company maneuvered around the Fort Cimarron garrison and engaged remnants of the PDF force there. Once the base was surrounded, an AC-130 Spectre was called in to take out individual barracks with its automatic weapons. A Psy Ops team attached to Alpha Company warned the PDF that every building would be destroyed if they didn't surrender. But the enemy inside the concrete barracks was either brave or too terrified to leave the dubious shelter of the buildings.


The SEALs at Paitilla Airport were finally relieved by paratroopers of the 82d Airborne Division, who arrived aboard several lifts of Chinook helicopters in the midday heat. As the men of SEAL Team Four waited in their defense positions around the perimeter, hungry, thirsty, and ragged from lack of sleep and the spent adrenalin of the long, savage night, they heard the hollow boom of the approaching heavy choppers. Then the Chinooks swept across the glare of the Bay of Panama and flared in for an assault landing above the line of civilian hangars along the eastern edge of the long runway.

The rotor wash blasted down so powerfully that several of the single-engine Cessnas that the private security guards had tried so vigorously to defend the night before were flipped violently in the invisible mechanical hurricane. The planes lay crumpled on their backs, more useless rubble cluttering the airfield. As the Chinooks hovered, the downwash of the rotors pounded the corrugated metal roofs of two private hangars until the roof beams gave way and the metal panels collapsed like sections of giant cardboard boxes. Finally the big green helicopters settled on the runway and the troops spilled out to dash for cover.

The SEALs watched them with silent contempt. Eventually the paratroopers trotted up, then stood to gape with awestruck embarrassment at the heaps of burned-out aircraft before the open maw of the bullet-shredded PDF hangar. The older NCOs recognized the pattern of carnage from the chewed-up sod and asphalt of the parking apron before the hangar. They had heard the news that the SEALs had somehow stepped in shit here. Now they saw exactly what had happened, and how bad it had been.

Tiredly, the men of SEAL Team Four gathered up their weapons and equipment and ambled toward the waiting helicopters. One by one they paused to look back at the blackened wreckage of the aircraft and at the Airborne troops taking up positions on the perimeter that had cost so much to secure.

One young SEAL turned to his chief petty officer, a veteran of Grenada, and asked the question many of them wanted answered. "Where were all those bastards when we needed them last night?"[3]


At 1515 hours that afternoon, big CH-47 Chinooks arrived at Torrijos from Fort Howard, ferrying the first troops of the 2d Brigade, 7th Light Infantry Division, who had arrived at the air base overnight. As soon as the "Lightfighters" had formed up into assault task forces shepherded by hardshell Humvees, they began to fan out into the surrounding villages, hunting for the PDF and Digbats who had ambushed the convoy earlier that day.

Up in the Quarry Heights tunnel, Lieutenant Colonel Jerry Murguia and his fellow officers on the Current Operations A Team logged the arrival of the 7th LID units with a mixture of relief and apprehension. The Blue Spoon OPLAN depended on these troops to prevent the Dignity Battalions from consolidating into viable combat units and to maintain order among the civilian population in Panama City. The plan's original concept had been sound: While the battalions of the 82d Airborne conducted their air assaults to neutralize the regular PDF forces at Panama Viejo, Tinajitas, and Fort Cimarron, the light infantry of the 7th Division, who had been rigorously trained in MOUT, would spread through the wide metropolitan area to establish roadblocks and secure key government buildings and infrastructure, such as power plants and water works. The Airborne was to have been the point of the spear, and the 2d Brigade of the 7th LID, the reinforcing muscle.

Unfortunately, due to the freak ice storm at Fort Pope and the stubborn fog in California, both these units had arrived too late to fulfill their missions as originally conceived.

Murguia read the latest secure fax situation reports from JTF South, noting that, as should be expected, the 82d Airborne were conducting their air assaults effectively, despite heavy resistance and the lack of protective night cover. And the latest reports also indicated that the troops from Fort Ord were moving out toward their objectives in the city as soon as they could be airlifted over from Fort Howard. But in both cases the deployments lacked the originally conceived "shock and mass," which were valid principles of war. Had the Airborne units been able to strike in darkness, surrounding the PDF garrisons, the enemy forces would probably not have been able to disperse. And had the whole brigade of the 7th LID arrived at Howard soon after H-hour and been able to deploy across the city before dawn, the Dignity Battalion forces now conducting these drive-by shootings and sniper attacks would probably have been neutralized before they could react.

Certainly the widespread looting now being reported along Avenida Central and Via España could have been prevented with three thousand more American infantrymen manning roadblocks and cordoning off the poorer barrios. Murguia looked across the muggy room at the large situation map. The operation had gone remarkably well, considering the valid old adage that the best written plan always went up in smoke when the first round was fired. But there simply had been no way to control the raw forces of nature that had effectively grounded the heavy mass of American combat forces at their U.S. bases.

He understood that the will to fight and cohesiveness of the PDF had been effectively crushed in the first hours of savage combat after H-hour. But he also realized that the opportunity to quickly deploy the overwhelming military force needed to completely subdue the PDF and the Dignity Battalions and to pacify the country had been missed.

Looting was a tangible result of this missed opportunity. Already officers around the Operations table were commenting that the scenes of unchecked looting and the perceived anarchy of the sniper attacks—as broadcast around the world by CNN—were giving the operation an unwarranted black eye, distorting the truly remarkable success that had otherwise been achieved since H-hour.

One rather scholarly colonel noted the irony of the situation. When General Carl Stiner had been named to command JTF South, he had discussed Blue Spoon's execution at length with the Southcom J-3 staff. He brought up the lessons learned from Urgent Fury, the U.S. invasion of Grenada.

"There's a couple things we really have to watch this time around," General Stiner had said. "We've got to keep a lid on looting, and we can't let the press turn sour on us."

Jerry Murguia now recognized that both of Carl Stiner's admonishments were as perceptive as they were futile.[4]

The pattern of sniper attacks and drive-by shootings persisted wherever American troops were engaged throughout the city. This unexpected resistance effectively pinned down the American forces, fixing them near their original D-day objectives.

But resistance at the Comandancia was finally crushed in mid-afternoon. Charlie Company, 1/508, was reinforced by a company of Rangers from Tocumen Air Base. Together the 200 tired soldiers swept the shattered buildings of the PDF headquarters compound. Because there had not been any fire from the Comandancia for hours, the final assault did not require much preparation. A weary sergeant from Charlie Company fired two 90 mm recoilless rifle rounds through the breach in the wall, and another soldier blasted the area inside with 203 grenades. The company went in by squad rushes, the 1st Platoon leading.

There was no further attempt to use the loudspeaker to call for surrender. But if any PDF were encountered, the men were ordered, they should be given the chance to surrender. The paratroopers and Rangers had divided the compound down the middle, with Charlie Company taking the southern sector. As they swept through the shell-blasted barracks and offices, the biggest problem they encountered was the carpet of broken glass. Many of the men had no gloves, and their hands were badly cut as they crawled up dark stairwells and across corridors.

The only serious resistance the soldiers of Charlie Company met was in the shattered quarters of the Macho de Monte. As they approached, the Americans saw a wounded PDF soldier trying to hang a white towel out a window. But his comrades dragged the man back inside and cut loose with a burst of AK fire. The paratroopers lobbed grenades through the window, and swept inside as the blast still echoed. They took several wounded prisoners among the dead.[5]

Room by room, building by building, the Americans worked through the walled compound. This tense, exacting clearing operation continued through the hot afternoon.

At Fort Amador the building clearing had proceeded through the long morning and into the afternoon. Clumps of isolated PDF troops surrendered as the Americans approached their bunkers or the rooms where they had taken refuge. As follow-up teams swept the barracks again, they encountered PDF who had successfully hidden from the first sweep. One squad found two Panamanian soldiers wedged into an air-conditioning vent. Major General Marc Cisneros took a personal interest in the operation. For almost two years he had been forced to swallow insults and harassment from these troops. He wanted to be certain no one escaped.

In midafternoon, the soldiers swept across the northern end of the fort and past the rickety old American Legion Post on the edge of the Canal. The Headquarters Company scout platoon had seen enemy soldiers fleeing in this direction the night before, toward the pier and sailboats in the yacht club moorings. When the American infantrymen cleared the yacht club bar and came down onto the pier, they found thirty-two unarmed Panamanian soldiers hiding in the boats. They had been led there by a young American-trained lieutenant. As the prisoners were being processed, this lieutenant shook his head in disgust. He'd lost two of his friends in the firing the night before.

"Why did you have to be so brutal?" he asked. Again he shook his head. "I never thought you people would do this to us. Why did you have to use so much power?"

The American lieutenant processing the prisoners was tired. He had been shot at several times during the night. He stared at the Panamanian officer and finally spoke. "What do you mean we used too much power?" he asked. "You're still alive aren't you?"

Among the prisoners recovered from the boats was the legless PDF dispatcher who had abandoned his wheelchair in the MP office in Building 4. Fortunately, his friends had carried him to the refuge of the yacht club. He quickly pointed out that he was an American military dependent, married to an American soldier stationed at Fort Clayton.

"You guys almost shot me last night," he said, happy to have his wheelchair back.

"Yeah," a tired sergeant replied, "I guess we did."

With the American forces and the surviving PDF otherwise occupied, effective law enforcement ceased to exist in Panama City. Under Noriega, the National Police had been incorporated into the PDF. Now there was no one to patrol the streets of the capital. And these streets contained some of the richest shopping districts in Latin America. Only hours after the last Spectre gunship had pounded the Comandancia, Avenida Central and Via España were jammed with looters. They came in small tentative bands at first. Fearful lookouts kept watch while several men smashed the windows and jimmied open the grates of appliance and electronics stores.

Then armed Dignity Battalion members showed up, and used their guns to blast open shop doors. The crowds in the streets swelled now. By midafternoon, thousands of Panamanians, many of them mestizos and blacks from the barrios, swarmed into the shopping districts. Soon the streets were crowded with men carrying boxed refrigerators on their shoulders or pushing freezers and washing machines down the center of the roads. Looters showed up in cars and trucks to pillage the big Gago supermarket near Via España. A human chain of looters linked up in a stairwell beside an untouched Catholic art store to pass down furniture from a household goods warehouse on the second floor above.

There was not much squabbling or many angry confrontations among the looters. Occasionally a man would menace a young boy who had luckily found a small color television set or an elaborate stereo boom box. But most of the people in the streets were too intent on finding their own treasure. One man was seen pushing a wheelbarrow heaped with frozen chickens, beefsteaks, and a case of gin down the middle of Avenida Central ("El Central"). He was met by a relative who piled two handsome brass floorlamps precariously on top. At the next corner, they encountered yet another relative who added a sewing machine and a portable color television to the family loot.

By midafternoon on Wednesday, December 20, Dignity Battalion officers who had done well in the initial looting returned to the commercial center to encourage the newcomers. Take as much as you want, they told the people in the street. The rabiblancos deserve it. They betrayed our country to the gringos. The looting was to continue unabated for the next thirty hours. When it was over, the once thriving retail commercial center of Panama City had been stripped clean. For months after the invasion, unemployed men and boys offered their pilfered loot for sale to motorists stopped at traffic lights. One man would have bottles of Taster's Choice coffee, another panty hose. Very little of the pilfered liquor was ever sold.

Early that evening three Special Operations helicopters—an MH-6 AHIPS gunship and two MH-60 Pave Hawks—hummed purposefully along the Avenida Balboa waterfront and slowed to a hover before a towering high-rise building in Punta Paitilla. Like a curious insect, the AHIPS gunship moved closer to the eastern corner of the building and hovered just outside the windows of the eleventh floor. These were the offices of Radio Nacional that had been taken over in the night by the PDF.

The Pave Hawks hovered above the building's flat roof and disgorged two teams of Delta Force troopers. One team used bolt cutters to sever cables at Radio Nacional's microwave antenna. The other team broke into the building and assaulted the offices. They used stun grenades and warning shots to force the PDF announcers and technicians to surrender. Then the Delta troopers blasted the station's studio with plastic explosives. The windows blew out and smoke stained the building's facade. But the charges had been well placed and the fire did not spread.

The strident voice of the PDF went silent.[6]

While the capital of Panama was wracked by combat between U.S. forces and the PDF and its Dignity Battalion allies, General Manuel Noriega, the self-proclaimed Maximum Leader, had not yet found a safe refuge. Despite his confidence that Jorge Krupnik's bodyguards could protect him, the sound of battle from the nearby waterfront convinced Noriega that U.S. forces were about to assault the house. Ulysses Rodriguez, husband of Noriega's secretary Marcela Tason, joined him at the Krupnik villa.

After several formerly loyal PDF associates and government officials refused him sanctuary, Rodriguez convinced Noriega to hide in the modest bungalow of Rodriguez's sister, located in a nondescript neighborhood in the outlying Campo Lindbergh district.

They drove in Marcela Tason's small Japanese sedan. On the

way to the small flat, they passed mobs of looters ransacking shopping centers. Some of the suburban streets were barricaded with parked commercial trucks and guarded by nervous rabi-blanco men and boys, hefting shotguns and hunting rifles. Look at them, Ulysses told Noriega, they're afraid of our Dignity Battalions. But the general seemed oblivious to the chaos around them.

In the tiny bungalow in Campo Lindbergh, Noriega was confronted with an unexpected problem. There were no curtains on the windows, so he had to crawl on the tile floor whenever he talked on the telephone in the living room. As the city crackled and thumped with gunfire and heavy weapons during the long afternoon of D-day, Manuel Noriega lay on a narrow couch, staring at the ceiling, a glass of whiskey on the floor beside him. Late that afternoon, Rodriguez suggested Noriega contact a homosexual friend who could convincingly disguise Noriega as a woman. The general considered this suggestion carefully, but then rejected it because the friend would undoubtedly betray him.

Once again, Manuel Noriega showed an astute cunning. Within hours, the White House announced a reward of one million dollars for anyone bringing information that led to Noriega's arrest.

In a private air-charter terminal at Miami International Airport, two civilian pilots of a Gulfstream jet led a tall, disheveled, and unnaturally pale young man to the counter of the U.S. Customs Service. One of the pilots produced a computer message half the size of a normal page, which stated the man they were escorting was a U.S. citizen named Kurt Frederick Muse. The customs inspector read the cryptic blocks of numbers and digits at the bottom of the form. He stamped the page and returned it to the pilot.

"Welcome home, Mr. Muse," the inspector said.

He watched the three men leave, once again the tall, stooped American walking slowly between the two younger pilots. Muse's cheeks were soot streaked and unshaven. His eyes were sunk deeply in his gaunt face and rimmed with crusty red. His T-shirt and greasy blue jeans had been torn by barbed wire and were spat-tered with rusty orange blood. He looked like a prematurely old wino who had fallen down a railway embankment.

Kurt Muse walked slowly through the Miami sunshine, his head swiveling to take in the bizarre sights of the normal com-mercial world of America. There were big shiny cars moving on the airport freeway. Catering trucks disgorged stacked pallets of food trays. Children with toys held their mothers' hands, cross-ing the sidewalks to the parking lots. There was no gunfire, no flame or smoke.

Less than twelve hours before, he had been rescued from La Modelo Prison. Now he was physically back in America. But his mind was still jumping between the flaming streets of El Chor-rillo and the Dante-esque spectacle of the MASH unit near the runway at Howard Air Force Base. When he closed his eyes, his vision was filled again with the flash and roar of the Delta Force soldier's plastic explosive blasting the barred door of his cell. The crack and thunder of heavy machine guns and the Spectre's heavy cannon echoed in his head.

Muse could smell the sweat, biting-sour surgical wash, and the curdled stench of blood in the post-op tent at Howard as he had bent over the stretchers to thank the wounded Delta men who had saved him.

One of the Delta soldiers, both legs in casts, his face criss-crossed with thick black stitches, had grabbed Muse's arm. "Moose," the man whispered hoarsely, "it's really good to see your face."

Muse had choked up, and finally stammered his eternal grati-tude. What could he say to these young men who had risked so much to save him?

Now he found himself, dressed in a clean shirt, the crusted blood washed from his face, sitting in a chilly, air-conditioned Denny's restaurant, staring at a clean round plate with a paper doily on which sat a perfect, heavy patty-melt.

One of the pilots asked him if he would care for a beer.

Muse almost broke down crying again. It had been a long time since he'd even thought about a beer.[7]

\*     \*     \*

In the Colon–Coco Solo area of operations the battle had reached a kind of stalemate. The only serious offensive threat from the PDF had been crushed when the troops of the 4/17 Infantry had routed the PDF's 8th Naval Infantry Company at Coco Solo. But the city of Colon itself had not yet been cleared of small PDF units and of the hundreds of heavily armed Dignity Battalion members cut off there.

U.S. forces had completely sealed the Colon bottleneck. The final remaining objective was the Cristobal DENI station, which was reportedly held by up to thirty PDF stragglers and perhaps a hundred more Digbats. But these forces had nowhere to go, with the bottleneck sealed.

This stalemate, however, led to a power vacuum similar to that in Panama City. Once the initial fighting tapered off, hundreds of looters swarmed out of the Colon slums and attacked the rows of Connex cargo containers stacked along the docks of the duty-free port. People were seen struggling back to Colon, humped under huge bundles of sports clothes, gunny sacks of shoes, and, of course, cases of liquor.

Under the rules of engagement, the American forces were initially not allowed to fire at unarmed looters. But as the looting in the Colon duty-free port got completely out of hand, the Americans were authorized to fire warning shots, then to fire near the looters, and finally, to shoot to wound.

This situation was further confused with the report that the PDF remaining in Colon had freed all the jail prisoners and armed dozens of hardened criminals willing to swear their allegiance to Noriega. This report was borne out when groups of civilians armed with AK-47s and RPG launchers appeared among the looters. It was impossible to tell if these men were recently armed criminals or Digbats. But they certainly represented a threat.

However, the effective strength—and definitely the morale—of these "troops" was cut by the Navy SEAL sniper team set up on the roof of a port building at the south end of the bottleneck. The SEALs had a spotting scope, as well as an M-24 7.62 mm sniper rifle. They also had one of the new .50-caliber long-range sniper weapons, which was in effect a single-shot version of the devastating .50-caliber machine gun. This weapon was precisely accurate out to a thousand yards. The SEALs spotted a group of civilians armed with assault rifles and festooned with ammunition pouches and rocket grenades. Technically, these "armed civilians" fell under the shoot-to-wound category. But it was impossible to merely *wound* with a .50-caliber sniper rifle. When three of the four Digbats were struck squarely in the torso and killed, falling one after the other like shooting-gallery targets, the scale and tempo of the looting quickly dropped.[8]

The surgical wards of Brooke Army Medical Center in San Antonio, Texas, and the Wilford Hall Hospital at nearby Lackland Air Force Base were crowded with the wounded from Operation Just Cause. Many of the most serious cases, including the mortally wounded soldiers from the fighting at the Comandancia, had been treated at the Gorgas Army Hospital on Quarry Heights. But those wounded troops medevacked to Howard Air Force Base were "backfilled" aboard empty C-141s returning to the States. This was a useful combat expedient as there simply were not enough available Air Force Nightingale air ambulances to handle the more than 300 injured and wounded men.

But the C-141 Starlifters were not adequately equipped to care for the gravest cases. Despite heavy sedation, many of the casualties endured the three-hour ride to San Antonio clinging to the edge of agonized consciousness. One medic who made several round-trips from Howard to Lackland described the Medevac flights as "long, bloody nightmares."

But Ranger Staff Sergeant Louis Olivera did not complain. He was grateful to be alive, but deeply curious how he had survived his terrible wounds. His right shoulder was shattered. One lung was riddled and had collapsed. And there was a deep furrow ripped through his scalp from an AK-47 bullet fired at close range, which had fractured his skull but somehow missed his brain. After the first surgical team had worked on his wounds and Olivera was conscious again, a doctor came to his bedside to explain the nature of Olivera's injuries. The shoulder would require more surgery, he said, but the chest wound had been re-paired.

"What about my head?" Olivera asked, still groggy from the anesthesia.

The doctor blinked and nodded, at a loss for words. "You're a lucky young man," he finally said. A nearby fatal bullet fired by a Macho de Monte soldier had been deflected slightly by the lip of Olivera's Kevlar helmet. And by chance, the round had been a tracer, which had cauterized the deep wound as it tore through the flesh of his scalp. If it had been a normal, copper-jacketed round, the young sergeant would have proba-bly bled to death from the head wound alone.

"Well, sir," Olivera said weakly, "I guess I'm lucky."

"Yes, sergeant," the doctor replied, "I guess you are."

The wounded SEALs from Paitilla were cared for in one cor-ner of the surgical ward. Navy Special Warfare Group Two had dispatched one of their senior medical corpsman chief petty of-ficers to help the Army medics and to keep up the wounded men's morale. The chief found himself faced with a grim assign-ment. Several of the SEALs had been maimed by the savage gunfire that raked the parking apron outside the PDF hangar at Paitilla. But miraculously, Corpsman Alfredo Morino, who had been hit in the head and lost a four-inch chunk of skull, had somehow survived and was expected to recover.

A couple of the men had infected bone fractures in their legs, suffered when the enemy rounds had shattered on the asphalt and ricocheted. It was important to arrest these bone infections, which meant frequent dressing changes. This was an agonizing process, and the wounded thrashed as the chief worked as quickly as he could.

He knew there was only so much pain even these tough SEALs could endure without lapsing into shock and losing the will to survive. But the chief also realized they could not be indefinitely sedated. He soon found himself screaming at the thrashing men as he stripped back the clotted surgical dress-ings. They howled back in outraged agony, filling the ward with shrieked, obscene invective.

To visitors on the ward, these sessions appeared like some cruel, barbaric ritual.

\*　　\*　　\*

Late the night of December 20 in Panama City, a convoy from Bravo Company, 2/504, left the Panama Viejo perimeter and crawled west along Via Cincuentenario toward the Marriott Hotel. The battalion had received orders to secure the Marriott where an undetermined number of American citizens were reported being held hostage. These orders had an unusual genesis: American reporters in the Marriott had kept contact with their networks and bureaus in the United States. Influential news executives had harangued the White House and the Pentagon to rescue their employees "held hostage" in Panama City. Among the confused reports, no one seemed to have noted that the American citizens were in a safe refuge, not held prisoner by gunmen. The handful of Americans actually held hostage were nowhere near the Marriott.

Nevertheless, the paratroopers of the 82d were ordered to undertake the dangerous nighttime relief of the hotel. To do so they had to traverse several kilometers of PDF and Digbat ambush.

No sooner had the convoy of hardshell Humvees left the American lines, when they came under intense small-arms fire from buildings along the bay front. Following their MOUT training doctrine, the troops rushed the enemy position while the Humvees laid down heavy covering fire. The first ambush had been cleared. Now the dismounted troops moved in squads, darting from one shadowed side street and driveway to the next, ahead of the Humvees.

Only 300 meters down the dark road, however, a large truck careened from a side lane and rolled toward the column of paratroopers. Men in the truck fired light machine guns and AK-47s. A passenger in the cab threw a grenade and emptied an automatic pistol at the Americans. The paratroopers scattered, taking cover along the sidewalk before firing at the speeding truck. Somehow the vehicle escaped the fire and continued east. But Bravo Company's 3d Platoon in the column trail had more time to prepare for the speeding truck. Specialist James Smith dashed into the middle of the road and took careful aim with his 203 grenade launcher. The first round exploded on the cab's passenger side. Somehow the driver managed to control the vehicle. Smith calmly reloaded a second grenade and fired again. The round blew the driver apart and the truck crashed into a palm tree. When the troops searched the vehicle, they found only dead inside.

Once more en route to the Marriott, Bravo Company came under sniper fire. The unit had already lost three wounded and the men were not prone to leniency. An Air Papa Spectre gunship was called in and directed to attack sniper positions on the roofs of nearby houses. When the Spectre departed, more PDF dead lay along the route of Bravo Company's advance.

The unit swept up the curved driveways to both entrances of the hotel. Bravo Company cleared the first three floors in by-the-numbers MOUT squad rushes. The tired, angry paratroopers ignored the Marriott security guards, who assured them there were no PDF or Digbats in the hotel. The men were in no mood to listen. They'd seen friends go down wounded in the street on the way here. Some assholes in Washington had told them to clear the fucking hotel and they were going to fucking well get on with it. When they encountered locked room doors on the first two guest floors, the paratroopers simply blew the doors off the hinges.

A little after midnight, Bravo Company called back to battalion that the Marriott hotel was secure. It was agreed that the American citizens, now freed from their basement laundry room, would be evacuated in the morning by another convoy, this one consisting of four hardshell Humvees, an escorting Sheridan tank, and two aluminum-paneled catering trucks from the airport.

As the tired troops took up their positions in the tasteful Spanish colonial atrium lobby, snipers in the neighborhood began sporadic fire. But the enemy only fired small arms. For the first time in almost twenty-four hours, no heavy weapons blasted in Panama City.

D-day had ended. Organized resistance by all the principal PDF units and the Dignity Battalions had been crushed. Armed pockets remained to be mopped up in Colon and in the western towns. But by midnight on December 20, all the major Blue Spoon objectives had been secured.

# 10

# 21 December 1989–
# 3 January 1990

---

# Mopping Up

The morning of December 21 dawned quietly in Panama City. But the relative tranquillity was soon broken by the rumble of mortar fire from the northeast suburbs. PDF and Digbat holdouts near Tinajitas used up the last of their ammunition to harass the paratroopers of the 1/504 on their hilltop perimeters. Soon the rattle of cannon fire and the heavier thump of rockets replaced the sound of the mortars. Helicopter gunships and A-37 attack jets swarmed over Tinajitas to suppress the mortars.

In the city itself, the sniper fire around the Marriott Hotel continued sporadically, not enough to hurt anybody, but certainly a nerve-wracking irritant for the tired troops of the 2/504 guarding the hotel. The relief convoy that would evacuate the American citizens from the Marriott to the battalion perimeter at Panama Viejo was overdue. For the men of Bravo Company, 2/504, this was just one more screw-up in the "hostage" situation. They had taken casualties fighting their way through the ambushes the night before, only to find the American citizens in no immediate danger, certainly not under the gun of the PDF or Digbats. Now the company was fixed in this stationary position, unable to maneuver and effectively engage the snipers and the occasional van or pickup truck that roared by to harass the hotel with bursts of small-arms fire. The men were tired and jumpy.

So they were in no mood to deal with the three sweaty and soot-streaked newsmen who showed up at the front entrance of the Marriott a little after 0800. Patrick Chauvel, a veteran French photographer on assignment for *Newsweek,* was accompanied by two other photographers, one Italian, one British. They wore their telltale multipocketed newsmen's vests and were crisscrossed with the straps of extra camera bodies and lenses. The paratroopers guarding the front entrance had orders to keep the building sealed until the American citizens were evacuated. There had been intelligence reports—probably nothing more than rumor—that Digbats might try to infiltrate the hotel and disrupt the evacuation. Chauvel and his colleagues protested that they were guests at the hotel, and even showed their room keys. They were tired and filthy from the long night in the streets. Moreover, they wanted to get their film packaged for shipment out of the country.

After Chauvel began photographing the troops guarding the front entrance, an officer challenged him, and an angry confrontation ensued. Finally, the photographers crossed the street and waited near the entrance to the Atlapa Convention Center parking lot. The situation was tense, but certainly not dangerous.

But under the shade canopy of the hotel entrance portico, the troops suddenly began dashing for cover, pointing their weapons toward the bayside road, half a block away. The rumbling sound of armored vehicles and the roar of heavy engines was loud in the still morning. The tactical radios crackled with a confused flurry of messages.

From Chauvel's position across the street, he could easily see the approaching convoy: two Sheridan tanks leading three Marriott Catering airport service trucks, trailed by a hardshell Humvee mounting a .50-caliber machine gun. The tracks of the small tanks clanked loudly on the concrete pavement. The Marriott trucks had been reinforced with a sandbagged machine-gun position mounted on the hydraulic ramp above the cab that normally extended to reach the galley service doors of airliners. The cabs of the Ford trucks were bright red, and the lead truck had a plastic Santa Claus mounted on its grill. This was the long-awaited evacuation convoy.

Chauvel and the other photographers called to the troops up on the hotel entrance, then began snapping pictures. The Frenchman left his position near the convention center and walked down the road to talk with the troops riding on the slowly advancing lead tank. One of the paratroopers told him it would be great if his picture appeared in *Newsweek*. Chauvel was assuring the man that would be no problem, when suddenly the morning was shattered with the blast of automatic weapons and small arms.

Machine-gun rounds and M-16 bullets splattered the pavement around him. He spun around and saw a window on the hotel second floor disintegrate under a burst of automatic weapons fire. The firefight reached a sudden crescendo, with troops in the convoy firing at the hotel and the soldiers at the entrance returning the fire with everything they had. Chauvel suddenly realized there were no PDF or Digbats involved in this battle. Somehow, the soldiers at the Marriott had mistaken the convoy for a PDF armored attack, and the men in the convoy obviously thought they were being ambushed just as the battalion's troops had been the night before. The line-of-sight angle from the lead vehicles to the hotel allowed a deadly exchange of fire, but prevented the two sides from seeing each other very well.

Chauvel, who had been under fire in most of the Third World's recent wars, stopped shooting pictures and sprinted for cover. He never made the safety of the convention center wall. Hit in the abdomen by several small-arms rounds, he was knocked to the pavement, his cameras flying ahead of him.

"Photographer down," he yelled. "Help!"

In the bedlam of the firefight no one heard him. He lay bleeding in the hot sun for a long time. The convoy was still firing. And men up at the hotel entrance were dodging and weaving, snapping off bursts of M-16 and machine-gun fire. Bullets snapped and howled above him. Finally, the firefight tapered off. The two sides made contact by radio and the grim realization set in that the whole incident had been one prolonged friendly fire episode.

When medics carried Chauvel into the hotel, he saw the British photographer being carried in an ornate Spanish colonial chair by two paratroopers, as if he were a king seated on a throne. The man had been lightly wounded in the leg. He asked Chauvel how he felt.

"I am fucked," the Frenchman said.

He knew he had lost a lot of blood and did not expect to live through the morning. But that afternoon, at Gorgas Army Hospital, he came out of surgery, and stared down at a long stitched incision across his belly, which terminated in a plastic drain tube. The Army surgeons explained they had resectioned his intestines, removed multiple bullet fragments, and cleaned up his digestive track, removing the eggs he had eaten for breakfast.

"You should make it," the surgeon assured him.

But another newsman caught in the crossfire between the American forces was not so fortunate. Spanish photographer Juan Antonio Rodriguez Moreno of the Madrid newspaper *El Pais* had been killed by the friendly fire.[1]

The American citizens were finally evacuated from the Marriott at 1255 hours. The convoy returned to Panama Viejo without further incident. A CH-47 Chinook was waiting at the edge of the water, its two huge rotors turning. The evacuees were herded on board, and the big aircraft began to climb away even before the tail ramp was closed. Fifteen minutes later, the Chinook landed at Howard Air Force Base.

Ironically, some of the newsmen who had been evacuated at such great cost were back at the Marriott within twenty-four hours, covering the war from the windows of their hotel rooms.

By the afternoon of December 21, the mopping up operations around the Comandancia had progressed to the point where the American forces could begin to move into the commercial district of El Central and attempt to suppress the looting. Once again, however, sniping and drive-by shootings by the Dignity Battalions kept the U.S. troops confined to the immediate sector around the base of Ancon Hill.

Near the Comandancia, American medics and graves registration specialists had undertaken the grim task of clearing away the burnt skeletal remains of PDF soldiers and innocent civilians who had died in the fires that had burned out during the first night of the operation. Captain Allen Blake Boatright, chaplain of the 1/508, worked with the medics. He was holding up fairly well to the task, and had loaded sixteen charred skeletons into body bags. Local residents were helpful, indicating which of the remains were PDF or members of the Dignity Battalions and which were civilians. Then an old lady led Boatright through a heap of black timbers and cracked masonry to locate a final body. What he found was a tiny blackened skeleton, the remains of a baby. The bones were so charred they turned to ashes as he tried to lift them. For the first time in all the long hours of the operation, the chaplain began to cry.[2]

The removal of charred remains from the burned-out buildings around the Comandancia by American medical personnel and the placing of these remains in body bags was the starting point of the bitter controversy over the number of civilian dead in Operation Just Cause. The body bags collected around the Comandancia were subsequently turned over to Panamanian authorities, who numbered them and added the data to the new government's casualty list. The body bags were then buried in individual graves at the Corozal Cemetery outside Panama City. Other remains of civilian and military dead that were not burned beyond recognition were retained for several days in hospital mortuaries and only buried if no family member came forward to identify the dead.

Nevertheless, the rumor that "thousands" of civilian dead were thrown by callous U.S. forces into multiple mass graves persists to this day.

At Rio Hato, the Rangers had cleared a wide perimeter around the PDF garrison and set up multiple roadblocks along the Inter-American Highway. As teams fanned out through the compound and searched the buildings, the Rangers encountered a truly staggering arms cache. Entire buildings were stacked from floor to ceiling with weapons and ammunition crates, all of Soviet-bloc or Chinese Communist origin. Many of the heavier weapons, including recoilless rifles and ZPU-4 antiaircraft machine guns, were found in cases marked "Surveying Tools" or "Drilling Equipment." Since most of the weapons were still packed in protective grease, Colonel Buck Kernan estimated that Rio Hato was simply a transshipment point. Either Noriega intended to arm a greatly expanded Dignity Battalion force, or he intended to sell or barter the weapons to the militias of the Colombian drug cartels with whom he had established an unofficial alliance.

American forces eventually recovered arms caches totaling 51,386 weapons, which included recoilless rifles, mortars, heavy machine guns, and assault rifles. Over 600 tons of ammunition was also discovered in the arms caches.

No SAM-7 or SAM-14 shoulder-fired antiaircraft missiles were discovered.

On the second day of the operation, the American forces began a "Guns for Cash" program. U.S. troops with loudspeakers drove throughout Panama City and other secured towns announcing an amnesty under which anyone voluntarily turning guns or ammunition over to the American forces would be paid on the spot, in cash, no questions asked. The program was a resounding success. Even while the looting continued along Avenida Central, men and women, and some children, trudged to the foot of Ancon Hill and lined up at the collection point to turn in M-16s, P-65 and AK-47 assault rifles, pistols, and hand grenades. At one collection point in Balboa, a nervous "former" Dignity Battalion sergeant rolled up with a flatbed truck heaped with assault rifles of various calibers and a jumble of ammunition magazines. The American sergeant in charge took one look at the piled arms and told the man not to expect to be paid the announced rate of $300 per assault rifle. An intense bargaining session ensued. Finally, the grinning Panamanian shook the sergeant's hand; a deal had been struck: $5,000 for the whole load.

By the time the program ended in the first week of January, 8,848 weapons (most of which had been distributed to the Dignity Battalions) had been collected. The total paid for these weapons was over $800,000. When a reporter commented to

Southcom officers that this was an expensive operation, he was told that paying for guns with twenty-dollar bills was a lot cheaper than buying them with blood.[3]

Up in the Quarry Heights tunnel the initial euphoria and anxiety of D-day had ground down to the exhausting routine of coordinating endless troop movements, complex logistics, and the frustrating task of restoring order in the country's cities without unnecessarily resorting to deadly force. But at least Jerry Murguia and the other tired officers in the Southcom J-3 shop had the satisfaction of knowing that the complex Blue Spoon OPLAN they had hammer-and-tonged together—under the incessant chiding of General Max Thurman and the meticulous attention to detail that Lieutenant General Carl Stiner had demanded—had stood up in actual combat.

And Thurman, who haunted the Operations Center like a gaunt Carolina preacher at a wake, saying little, noting everything, had the satisfaction of knowing his superiors in the Pentagon had trusted him and Stiner enough to allow them absolutely free rein in commanding the operation. During the first critical twenty-four hours of Just Cause, Chairman of the Joint Chiefs General Colin Powell and Defense Secretary Dick Cheney had listened intently to the Southcom situation reports, which were broadcast by speakerphone in the Crisis Situation Room of the Pentagon's National Command Center. But neither Powell nor Cheney had tried to micromanage the show down here. And Thurman was especially gratified at the report that the president himself had only stayed awake for the first two or three hours of the operation; then, satisfied that the professionals were handling the job well, Bush had reportedly gone to bed and slept well.[4]

The single channel of vertical communications Thurman had established from JTF South, through Southcom, to Lieutenant General Thomas W. Kelly, then on to Powell and Cheney, had survived the onset of combat just as well as the detailed Blue Spoon OPLAN. There had been no breathless Jimmy Carter demanding unobtainable details from company-sized engagements—as had happened during the ill-fated Desert One hostage rescue attempt—nor anything analogous to the distinctive Mittel-Europa voice of Henry Kissinger booming directly into the earphones of combat pilots on a command override channel, which had been the most blatant White House interference during the disastrous *Mayaguez* affair in 1975.

The only DoD communication that managed to bypass this channel on D-day had been a phone call from the Pentagon J-6 Communications directorate straight to a lieutenant colonel in the 1190th Signal Brigade at Fort Clayton, requesting that the officer do everything possible to make sure the new government of Panama, particularly President Endara, could communicate directly with the outside world—without obviously resorting to U.S. military facilities.

"Do whatever you have to down there," the general told the colonel. "Be sure Endara can talk directly to the other Latin American heads of state."

"Yes, sir," the officer answered, "I understand." The two men were old friends, but there was nothing congenial in this conversation.

"I hope you do," the Pentagon Communications general replied. "I just came from a meeting with Chairman Powell in the president's office. The war phase of this thing is almost over, and from now on its politics. And you can't have politics without telephones."[5]

The brigade commander, Colonel Jorge Torres-Cartagena, had dutifully reported this breach of operational etiquette. General Thurman had accepted the lapse as inevitable. Naturally, politics would eclipse the military action as the operation progressed. He understood that everything possible should be done to enhance the bona fides of the new Endara government as an independent entity, not simply an extension of imperial American rule.

The "tunnel rats" in Jerry Murguia's J-3 shop noted that a new contingent of players—Civil Affairs officers—were increasingly absorbing General Thurman's attention. As a corollary to the Blue Spoon OPLAN, a contingency operation known as Blind Logic was being put into effect. The U.S. Southern Command was helping Panama dismantle Noriega's corrupt dictatorship. These specialists would appear at any hour of the day or night clutching their poster-board "wiring plans" (organizational charts) for the ministries of the new Panamanian government. And Thurman, following his viceregal responsibilities in the tradition of Eisenhower and MacArthur, would approve or veto the appointment of a director general in the Interior Ministry or deputy provincial governor. D-day had marked the beginning of Year One for democratic rule in Panama, and Southcom intended to be thoroughly, if invisibly, involved in the building of the foundation.

In Colon, the task of clearing the final pockets of resistance fell to the members of the 4th Battalion, 17th Infantry, and to Bravo Company, 3d Battalion, 504th Parachute Infantry Regiment. These paratroopers had successfully captured the PDF logistic base at Cerro Tigre at H-hour on D-day and had been repositioned to Colon and deployed at the bottleneck on the afternoon of December 21. Their objective in Colon was the two-story DENI station where PDF and Digbat holdouts had taken refuge. The technique the Bravo Company commander had elected to employ was brutally direct. Bravo Company would move forward and surround the building. Then a platoon of artillerymen would come up with two 105 mm howitzers and level the guns at zero elevation directly at the walls of the DENI station. If the PDF inside did not respond to the regular "Miranda rights" surrender request on the bullhorn, the howitzers would be fired.

While the troops waited for dark in their positions along the bottleneck, they ate their tepid MRE barbecued chicken and corned beef hash, watching a Cobra helicopter gunship duel with snipers in the streets around the DENI station. Captain Charles Dyer, the company commander, moved his troops forward by platoons after 2100 hours. The company's three platoons maneuvered well in the blacked-out streets, and were in position ahead of schedule. But several of the tired soldiers became lost in the dark, unfamiliar streets. Dyer had to personally escort one man to his correct assault position, accompanying the soldier with a vehement round of colorful expletives.

Once the perfunctory loudspeaker surrender message had been delivered, the howitzers cut loose. To the men crouched behind palm trees in their assault positions, the shock waves were literally stunning. The howitzers were firing from only fifteen yards away, and the impact of the high-explosive rounds seemed to suck the air from the street. A ragged burst of AK assault rifle fire replied to the first cannon rounds, but the PDF gunner quickly fell silent.

The concussion of the exploding 105 rounds was so strong that a sleeping bat fell from palm fronds and landed on the sleeve of Captain Dyer's radio operator. The man panicked, screaming, "It's a bat!" He thrust his arm in the air yelling for someone to pull it off.

Second Lieutenant Chris Bennett, his platoon leader, scowled at the man. "Shit," he said. "I got other things to worry about."[6]

After several howitzer rounds, a wide breach was blown in the DENI station wall. Just as the assault teams were poised to move forward by squad rush, men from the 3d Platoon came under fire from down the street. They took cover. Luckily no one was hit. Then they realized where the fire was coming from. The MP platoon that had been ordered to secure the approaches to the DENI station, was firing *toward* the assault troops of Bravo Company. Attempts to raise the MPs on a tactical radio net were unsuccessful.

Once the platoon was repositioned, the assault force went through the breach and cleared the building. Several of the PDF inside had successfully escaped, but the remainder were taken prisoner. When the company regrouped an hour later, 2d Lieutenant Sean Corrigan, the commander of the 3d Platoon, whose men had been fired on by the MPs, complained bitterly to Captain Dyer that the "MP son of a bitches were shooting at us."

A lieutenant from the 4/17 Infantry added that these same trigger-happy MPs had fired on his men on D-day, killing one and wounding several. Dyer gathered up several of his officers and burly NCOs and departed for the MP position, intent on "talking" to them about their terrible fire discipline. Luckily for the MPs, a senior officer from the 4/17th intervened. Although the MP lieutenant received a severe tongue lashing, he escaped far worse treatment from the outraged paratroopers.[7]

The last pocket of PDF resistance in Colon had been captured. And the worst threat to the assault force had come from the Military Police guarding their flank.

On the morning of December 22, the Panamanian government of President Guillermo Endara announced that it was forming a new national police force, the *Fuerza Publica,* to replace the PDF. Recruits for this force were to be sworn in at the DNTT station beneath Ancon Hill, which the 5/87th Infantry had captured only two nights before. The announcement over the resurrected national radio station stated that former members of the Defense Forces below field-grade rank, who had no history of criminal activity, nor connection to the Dignity Battalions, would be welcome to take the oath of allegiance to the legitimate government of Panama. Obviously, there wasn't time for a careful screening of these new police officers, although Southcom had compiled a "Black List" that included all known PDF officers and men who had taken part in abduction, torture, and other serious human rights abuses. Vice President Guillermo Ford, who had himself been savagely beaten during the spring election campaign (the election Noriega later annulled) while PDF riot police looked on, would officiate at the ceremony.

At the appointed hour, hundreds of men lined up in the hot sun, clutching their ID cards, eager to renew the sinecure of a government position in these uncertain times. They were processed from one table to another in the courtyard of the DNTT compound, and eventually formed into ranks before the shell-pocked central administration building facing the Gaillard Highway. The shattered glass and broken masonry had been swept up into tidy mounds in the corners of the parking lot. The bullet-scarred entrance of the building was decorated with Panamanian flags and bunting in the national colors.

Finally, the several hundred volunteers had been processed and stood in reasonably even formations on the hot asphalt parking lot, awaiting the vice president, who would administer the new oath of allegiance. American MPs stood beside machine-gun Humvees, nervously scanning the road, and the Diablo Heights housing district on the side of Ancon Hill. The civilian sedan with the vice president's party arrived, escorted by Humvees mounting .50-caliber machine guns, carrying combat-equipped soldiers from the 87th Infantry. There was the normal flurry of Latin protocol, with handshakes and embraces among the assembled civilian dignitaries, and sharp salutes from the American officers.

But when Vice President Ford mounted the steps to administer the oath, an 81 mm mortar round smacked down into the compound, exploding with a force of a thunderclap. The smoke had not cleared when two more rounds landed. Pandemonium ensued with the hundreds of new volunteers dashing for safety. But the only exit from the compound lay in a gauntlet of American Humvees blocking the driveway. Now small arms and automatic weapons fire raked the compound and the slopes of Ancon Hill. The mortar and automatic weapons fire was coming from the wasteland of dense elephant grass on Albrook Field beyond the tracks of the Panama railway and the huge abandoned aircraft hangar that served as a transshipment point for American household effects in plywood lift vans.

First Lieutenant Paul Freudenburgh, who had helped clear the DNTT compound at H-hour two days before, now found himself defending it. He ran his men through the humid midday heat and up the railroad embankment to find a secure position from which they could direct plunging fire on the PDF concealed in the kuna grass on Albrook Field. As his men maneuvered, they were followed by a walking mortar barrage. One of his men was hit in the back by either a shell fragment or an AK-47 round. He went down hard and didn't get up. All Freudenburgh could do was leave a medic with him and keep the platoon moving.

Despite the casualty, his soldiers, who had seemed confused and timid the night the operation began, now moved with clear professional purpose. But other elements of the battalion along the Gaillard Highway seemed in a state of near panic, uncertain where the fire was coming from. Freudenburgh positioned his men in the shelter of some buildings near the Christian Servicemen's Center and got them separated by teams so that they could lay down well-directed fire from their rifles, SAWs, and M-60 machine guns. But the PDF seemed determined to continue this fight. They returned the fire.

Now one of the PDF mortars was dropping rounds behind them, up the slope of Ancon Hill.

Overhead, two slow-moving A-37 Dragonfly attack jets appeared out of the dazzling midday sun. The lead pilot, 1st Lieutenant Kevin Manion, called JTF South directly and asked for priority weapons release. He could see the PDF mortar and automatic weapons positions in the grass below. General Stiner immediately authorized an air strike. The two jets rolled in, firing their nose-mounted 7.62 mm miniguns and 2.75-inch rockets from pods slung beneath their wings. The field below erupted in multiple rocket explosions and sparkled with the impact of hundreds of tracer rounds. The jets climbed back from their steep pass and rolled back into another gun run. Now the tall kuna grass was smoldering.

No more fire came from Albrook Field. When two platoons of the 5/87th Infantry maneuvered toward the PDF position, they began finding the shattered bodies of dead Panamanian soldiers who had tried to escape, a good 100 meters from the abandoned mortars and machine guns.

One weary, combat-cynical soldier turned to his sergeant. "Well," he said, "that's one way for the assholes to find out the difference between cover and concealment."

While the PDF gun positions were being suppressed, the large household effects storage site in the old Albrook hangar caught fire, probably from automatic weapons tracers. And there was no fire department functioning to extinguish the blaze. By the end of the afternoon, several hundred lift vans of incoming and outgoing American possessions had burned. Some Panamanians saw a strange symmetry in this fire: On one side of Ancon Hill, El Chorrillo, three blocks of the city's poorest barrio were reduced to ashes, while on the other side, a virtual treasure trove of gringo affluence—all the shiny white appliances, microwave ovens, linens, and silverware—was also reduced to a heap of sooty embers.

During the same period, General Stiner also authorized the use of fixed-wing air support for Marine Task Force Semper Fi. When Marines from the Fleet Antiterrorist Security Team and 2d Light Armored Infantry Battalion surrounded the multistory PDF barracks in the town of La Chorrera, west of Howard Air Force Base, they called in A-7 attack jets. After an observation aircraft marked the barracks with a smoke rocket, the A-7s rolled in and fired their 20 mm Vulcan cannons. The fire was aimed precisely, and fell completely within the PDF compound, missing nearby civilian buildings. This air support convinced the PDF garrison to surrender.

The attack on the DNTT compound had an unexpected repercussion. Although the goal of the PDF holdouts and Dignity Battalion members who unleashed the mortar and automatic weapons fire had obviously been to disrupt the formation of the new Public Force—and possibly even kill Vice President Guillermo Ford—many of the reporters gathered up on Quarry Heights saw the episode as an attack on Southcom itself. Several mortar rounds did in fact land on the northern slopes of Quarry Heights. And a number of television correspondents were able to conduct rather colorful "under fire" live feeds to their networks. The fact that the PDF gunners were concealed in kuna grass at least a kilometer away from Quarry Heights, however, was not a prominent feature of these reports.

Ironically, the incident that permitted these fledgling war correspondents to cover actual *combat* also served to collectively scare the hell out of some of them. Combined with the ongoing looting, the persistent sniper attacks and drive-by shootings, and the somber casualty toll from the Marriott friendly-fire incident, the mortar attack on December 22 served to dampen the enthusiasm for firsthand investigation by some reporters.

Many elected to continue covering the war from the relative comfort of the Southcom media center that had been established in the Quarry Heights Officers' Club. Although the center became increasingly crowded, it offered all the amenities—electricity, flush toilets, and air conditioning—as well as the television satellite uplink dishes so essential to the electronic media. Southcom even provided food. On D-day, these were simply MRE rations, but the press did not have to put up with green plastic pouches of corned beef hash or chicken a la king for long. Within thirty-six hours, the Officers' Club kitchen was serving simple meals around the clock. As the reporters descended on Panama they had to process through Howard Air Force Base, the only operating airport. They soon discovered that there were no hotels or restaurants open in Panama City and that there were no rental cars, taxis, private limousines, or buses available. Most migrated to the media center atop Quarry Heights.

There the hard-pressed Southcom public affairs staff worked literally day and night trying to provide telephone lines, more satellite uplinks, and fax machines. Lieutenant Colonel Jim Swank, a decorated combat veteran of Vietnam, became one of the main "points of contact" for the news media. Although he had not seen his wife (six months pregnant) and children, who were down at Fort Amador, since H-hour, Swank was obliged to stay on duty, answering every petty complaint and demand of the reporters up on Quarry Heights. His civilian counterpart, Bill Ormsbee, a longtime resident of Panama, found himself providing endless fundamental historical briefings: "No, sir, Panama was never officially an American colony. . . ."

By December 22, more than 275 additional correspondents had streamed into Howard aboard chartered aircraft. A Lockheed 1011 arrived low on fuel, carrying fifteen tons of equipment for the electronic media. The correspondents demanded immediate offloading, despite the fact that the incoming airlift of 7th Light Infantry Division MPs was a priority. (These soldiers were desperately needed to help restore law and order in Panama City and the suburbs.) And, of course, the aircraft crew requested refueling as soon as possible.

One hard-pressed Air Force public affairs sergeant who met

a flight late on December 21 had managed to borrow a school bus and a deuce-and-a-half truck. She was well pleased with her logistical arrangements, given the shortage of transport at that stage of the operation.

But this transport, and the other support the Air Force provided was simply not good enough for a woman television journalist who stepped off the plane dressed in a tailored winter suit, nylons, and high heels. She demanded an air-conditioned car to take her to air-conditioned quarters where she could shower and wash and set her hair. She had a live feed scheduled to her station for the eleven-o'clock news. This journalist was a "Barbie," public affair parlance for a local station's star correspondent, the female counterpart of the male local-market talking head, "Ken." With the advent of portable satellite uplinks, these universally attractive, often vapid news presenters have become fixtures at hurricanes, major plane crashes, and of course wars. Local television stations discovered having their own correspondent reporting live from the scene of such tragedies was good for ratings. And, just as the parking lot of NASA's Cape Canaveral media center filled up with satellite vans from St. Louis, Atlanta, and Baltimore, after the *Challenger* exploded, the apron at Howard Air Force Base became crowded with Kens and Barbies and their overburdened production crews.

When the Air Force public affairs sergeant finally convinced the correspondent in high heels that her demands were impossible to meet, the woman replied coldly that the owners of her station, who had powerful connections in Washington, would not be happy. At least, she said, there had to be some "soldiers" available to help her with her bags.

"No, Ma'am," the sergeant replied. She herself had not had a shower for thirty-six hours. "The *airmen* are kind of busy right now."

She pointed down the ramp to the MASH where volunteer airmen who had already worked eighteen-hour shifts were carrying stretchers from the dust-off helicopters. The correspondent peered toward the wounded, but did not seem to fully comprehend what was going on down there.

With almost 200 reporters living and working in the Quarry

Heights media center by the night of December 22, herd journalism in its most egregious form was probably inevitable.

But there were some courageous and resourceful journalists who did overcome the danger and hardships of reporting in Panama City. Lindsey Gruson of the *New York Times* was certainly one of the best. Although he had been taken hostage by Digbats at the Marriott Hotel and brutalized at H-hour, he was back on the street reporting as soon as this first group of hostages was released before dawn on D-day. Gruson continued to file vivid accounts of the fighting, and was the *Times'* chief reporter on the scene for several days.[8]

The *Washington Post*'s stringer, Berta R. Thayer, held down the reporting for her paper before D-day. But the *Post* had to depend on Associated Press correspondent Eloy O. Aguilar for eyewitness coverage of the first day's fighting. Veteran correspondent William Branigin of the *Post*'s Foreign Service managed to slip into Panama the night of D-day, check in with the Southcom Public Affairs Office (PAO) on Quarry Heights, then move out into the barrios to write a hard-hitting and accurate account of the confused fighting. Branigin also reported on the friendly fire engagement at the Marriott Hotel.[9]

And some news magazine correspondents in Panama City also avoided herd reporting. David Adams and John Contreras of *Newsweek* and *Time*'s Wilson Ring and Dick Thompson produced accurate firsthand reports under tight deadline pressure.

However, this relative handful of resourceful reporters was not enough to fully cover a story of this magnitude. There was no direct reporting on the fierce fighting around Panama City, along the east bank of the Canal, or in Colon during the first crucial forty-eight hours of the operation. Instead, most journalists dug in at the Quarry Heights Officers' Club and poached each others' leads.[10] A prime example of mob journalism was the "Women In Combat" story centered on Military Police Captain Linda Bray, who led the 988th MP company in securing the PDF dog kennel in Curundu at H-hour. There had been a skirmish before the PDF guards fled. But erroneous reports that a major firefight, during which Captain Bray led her troops in heavy combat, were quickly exaggerated. It was reported that three enemy soldiers were killed and many wounded. Soon, the story acquired almost legendary proportions: a young woman officer standing tall in a deadly crossfire, coolly issuing orders to her male soldiers.

Although Southcom PAO had arranged a press conference for Captain Bray soon after her name emerged, only four reporters signed up to interview her. But when the original story triggered what the PAOs later described as a "feeding frenzy" on the subject of women in combat, scores of reporters demanded follow-on interviews with Captain Bray. The pack was hungry and had to be fed. Captain Bray was again paraded before the press and eventually interviewed by all four morning talk shows. The media seemed to think that an MP company commander in a war zone should be made available to them on an on-demand basis. When she wasn't, some reporters claimed Southcom was trying to cover up something. Then part of the media pack swung against the story, stating that Southcom had purposely exaggerated Captain Bray's combat role. For her part, Captain Bray tried to get on with her job, and her superior officers eventually objected to her long absences from duty to meet the news media.

The issue quickly became a political cause celebre in Washington. Colorado Congresswoman Patricia Schroeder used Captain Bray's story to press for a reversal of the laws and military regulations restricting women from assignment to combat arms units: Infantry, Armor, and Artillery. Ms. Schroeder noted that Captain Bray had carried an M-16 rifle, "not dog biscuits." Soon Congresswoman Schroeder had gathered several political allies who joined her demand that women soldiers in Panama be awarded the Combat Infantryman's Badge. When the Army pointed out that this coveted badge was only presented to Infantry soldiers who had been in close combat with armed enemy combatants, and that there were literally thousands of male soldiers from Armor, Artillery, and Engineer units who had seen combat in Panama but would not receive the CIB, the politicians refused to accept this explanation. They continued to press for CIBs for the women soldiers of Operation Just Cause.[11]

By the time the story played itself out, some reporters

were implying that Southcom had engineered a cover-up. Philip Shabecofs of the *New York Times* stated: "Today an Army Spokesman in Panama, Col. James C. Swank, said Captain Bray and all other female officers are currently unavailable for comment until authorized by the Secretary of the Army."[12]

During all the hoopla about Captain Linda Bray, who was after all just a hardworking young professional soldier who had carried out a relatively mundane assignment, very little media attention was given the Task Force Aviation women helicopter aircrew who had flown an unprecedented four multilift air assaults into heavily defended landing zones during the long hours of combat on D-day.

The restrictions on effective press coverage of Operation Just Cause, self-imposed and otherwise, eventually rebounded on the emotional issue of civilian casualties. The related issue of ostensibly unrestricted use of American firepower—"overkill"—was also badly handled by the press. Although Father Javier Arteta gave his eyewitness account of the El Chorrillo fire soon after the disaster, few major American publications picked up his story. Instead, it became an article of faith that somehow American "firepower" had destroyed the poor barrio. And when the 5,000 evacuees of El Chorrillo were housed in canvas cubicles in another unused Albrook hangar, some news commentators saw this squalor as a tacit admission of responsibility for the fires by the U.S. government.

Further, two deadly incidents during the follow-on military operations after D-day served to solidify the view that the American military had acted with brutal disregard for human life.

In Colon, on the afternoon of December 22, PDF stragglers and Dignity Battalion snipers were still harassing the American troops spreading out through the city. At 1604 hours, an American AH-1 Cobra helicopter gunship was escorting an OH-58 observation helicopter, overflying the city on a reconnaissance mission. The two aircraft came under heavy-caliber automatic weapons fire from a landmark high-rise apartment, the Quince Piso Building. The OH-58 immediately swung away, trailed by the Cobra, but the stream of fire followed them. Then the Cobra took a hit, with a heavy 12.76 mm or 14.5 mm round smashing a fist-sized hole through the canopy between the tandem pilot and copilot/gunner's cockpits. The Cobra's crew saw the enemy gunner firing from a window near the corner of an upper floor.

Swinging back toward the building, the Cobra pilot told his gunner to fire a burst of cannon fire to suppress the machine gun long enough for the two helicopters to escape. But the Cobra's 20 mm cannon jammed; a pin had been sheared by the force of the round that had hit the aircraft. The gunner, staring down the muzzle of the PDF gun, was forced to fire a 2.75-inch rocket, the Cobra's only remaining weapon. The gun position was destroyed. Tragically, however, the apartment next to the sniper was also struck by the rocket. José Salas Galindo and his wife Dionicia and their two children were in this apartment. Dionicia Galindo was killed instantly, her body literally blown into pieces. Both children were wounded.[13]

José Galindo later became the visible symbol of a Panamanian group whose attorneys led a vigorous campaign for financial compensation for civilian casualties of the operation. In most of the press accounts of this tragedy, the account of the helicopter attack was rendered as an unprovoked, indeed gratuitous, misuse of firepower. The fact that a machine gunner was firing from the building was rarely mentioned. But the incident was used as an example of indiscriminate bombardment during Operation Just Cause that had caused the death of thousands of civilians.[14]

The other major incident that fueled the civilian casualty—overkill controversy occurred near the Madden Dam. The troops of Delta Company, 3d Battalion, 504th Parachute Infantry Regiment, who had secured the dam at H-hour, had maintained a roadblock on the Trans-Isthmus Highway since D-day. On the afternoon of December 23, a Toyota Land Cruiser with five men in civilian clothes rolled up to the concertina wire. The men had the short hair and muscular appearance of PDF soldiers. A Spanish-speaking paratrooper ordered all five men out of the car. As they came out, a cylindrical green CS gas grenade fell off the front passenger seat. The American soldiers shouted at the men to get down flat on the ground and spread their arms and legs.

The five Panamanians began to grumble, but reluctantly complied. But one man rose again and ignored the shouts of a young sergeant beyond the wire. Now a full squad of paratroopers had formed up around the roadblock, their M-16 rifles leveled at the Panamanians on the ground. First Sergeant Roberto Enrique Bryan, a Panamanian-born veteran paratrooper, was Delta Company's senior NCO. He was at a sandbag gun position seventy meters down the road when he heard the confrontation. He immediately came running to the roadblock.

But before he arrived, the Panamanian who had been reluctant to lie down spread-eagled pulled the pin from a fragmentation grenade and lobbed it bouncing through the concertina wire to the feet of the standing Americans. The grenade exploded with a savage blast. As ten Americans went down wounded, the Panamanians across the wire rose to sprint away. But the uninjured American soldiers opened fire with their M-16s. All five Panamanians fell, four dead and one badly wounded.

Sergeant Bryan arrived to see his troops sprawled by the wire; there was blood everywhere.

"Cease fire," Bryan ordered.

He bent to help the wounded troops. One man's leg was practically severed below the knee. Another man's intestines and liver spilled from his ripped abdomen like some kind of a bizarre anatomy display. Sergeant James Miller, a company medic, dashed up behind Bryan to administer what aid he could. But before he could begin his grim task, Miller spotted the surviving Panamanian sprawled on the ground bring his two fists together in a jerking motion, as if the man were pulling the pin from another grenade.

"He's alive!" Miller yelled. "He's alive!"

Bryan did not hesitate. He leveled his M-16 and fired three, three-round bursts into the Panamanian. The man fell dead.

Moments later, 1st Lieutenant Brandon Thomas, a Delta Company officer, arrived and began berating Bryan for killing an unarmed man. Bryan ignored the reprimand and got to work with the medics, rendering aid to the wounded.

Three months later at Fort Bragg, North Carolina, the Army formally filed charges of unpremeditated murder against First Sergeant Bryan. First Lieutenant Thomas, who had not actually witnessed the shooting, became the prosecution's chief witness. In the ensuing months, Bryan's action at the Madden Dam became the subject of continuing press scrutiny of the rules of engagement for the American forces in Panama. A general impression formed that Bryan had arbitrarily executed a wounded prisoner. But during the eventual court martial in August 1990, the facts of the incident emerged. Bryan was acquitted of all charges. His delayed promotion to sergeant major was put into effect.[15]

The court martial jury that acquitted Sergeant Bryan of all charges deliberated less than two hours, just enough time to review the formal indictment and to vote on each count. There was no question that the veteran NCO had acted properly under the rules of engagement.

During this period, the emotional issue of Panamanian civilian casualties of the invasion became muddled and politicized. Some Panamanian groups and individuals alleged that thousands of civilian dead had been dumped in unmarked mass graves within hours of the invasion. On September 23, 1990, the CBS News magazine program "60 Minutes" gave air time to allegations that the civilian death toll was as high as 4,000. Former Attorney General Ramsey Clark charged that there was a "conspiracy of silence" to cover up the death toll, which he said totaled more than 3,000. Former officials of the Noriega government fanned the controversy by claiming 8,000 Panamanian civilians had died in the invasion. Again they cited unmarked mass graves as evidence of this death toll.

U.S. Southern Command had originally estimated total Panamanian fatalities as 516 (314 military and 202 civilian); this estimate was based in part on data reported by combat units, and on some medical units, which had actually counted bodies before turning them over to Panamanian authorities. It was the Panamanian government's Institute of Legal Medicine that continued the official investigation into the numbers of military and civilian dead. As of November 1990, "the Institute stated that it had identified 65 military and 155 civilian remains. Another 50 bodies had not yet been identified. In addition to these 270 confirmed fatalities, the Institute holds 75 unresolved reports of missing persons. Since some of the 50 unidentified remains could account for some of the missing persons, the Institute's figures suggest a range of between 270 and a maximum of 345 possible deaths (military and civilian)."[16]

The issue of mass graves was eventually clarified. U.S. forces had temporarily interred the remains of twenty-eight Panamanians, military and civilian, in shallow, *individual* graves in Corozal Cemetery. These remains, many burned beyond recognition, were disinterred one week later and turned over to the Panamanian government. In late December 1989, Panamanian health officials had buried 123 dead Panamanians in a common grave in the Jardin de Paz Cemetery in Panama City. These remains were later exhumed and many were identified by dental records and turned over to individual families for private burial. Panamanian authorities buried eighteen bodies in a common grave at Colon's Mt. Hope Cemetery. When these remains were later exhumed, it was determined only eight had died during military operations; the other ten were taken from hospital mortuaries after power cuts shut down the refrigeration.

After thorough investigation by mainstream human rights and religious groups, including Physicians for Human Rights, Americas Watch, and Panama's Roman Catholic church, representatives of these organizations agreed that there were no grounds for claims that "thousands" of civilians had died and were secretly buried in unmarked mass graves.[17]

(When the author interviewed Panamanian officials on this matter in December 1990, they noted that Panama's population is only 2,300,000. Moreover, all adults in Panama are required to carry identity cards (the *Cedula*) that are renewed at regular intervals. When these cards were renewed in the year following the invasion, there was no mass discrepancy of several thousand individuals—the ostensible number of uncounted civilian casualties.)

CBS News producer Jon Meyersohn and Doug Mullen, an executive of GTE Corporation, who had been taken from the Marriott as hostages after H-hour, were finally released on December 23. They were rattled and exhausted, but not seriously injured. However, Raymond Dragseth, the Defense Department school teacher who gunmen had abducted from his Punta Paitilla apartment the morning of December 20, was not so lucky. His body was identified among those buried by Panamanian officials in the Jardin de Paz Cemetery. He had been shot once in the back of the head.

Other American civilians had escaped similar vengeance by successfully hiding from Dignity Battalion kidnap squads or by seeking refuge with anti-Noriega Panamanian friends. But nine employees of the U.S. Evergreen Company had been seized at the Caracol Apartment Hotel near the city center before American troops could secure the building. They were later released. One couple, Terry and Karen Olson, managed to hide in the building with a colleague, Jim Ritter. For two days, they remained barricaded in an apartment while drunken Digbats and looters roamed the building pounding on doors, screaming for vengeance against the gringos. Finally, after 2:00 A.M. on December 22, troops from the 1st Ranger Battalion, who had helped capture the Comandancia, secured the apartment building.

An interesting coincidence of this rescue was the fact that Karen Olson's father, Roderick Gambrell, Jr., a World War II artillery officer, had taken part in an ill-fated attempt to rescue the isolated 1st and 3d Ranger Battalions being decimated by German forces on the Anzio beachhead. He later wrote Lieutenant Colonel Robert Wagner, commander of the 1st Ranger Battalion: "It is rather ironic that in the Panama action the 1st Rangers rendered a service to me that, despite a maximum effort, we were not able to render to them at Anzio forty-six years ago."[18]

\*     \*     \*

While multiple American Special Operations teams and regular military units searched for Manuel Noriega, he remained hidden in the modest Campo Lindbergh home of Ulysses Rodriguez's sister. Soldiers of the 2d Battalion, 504th PIR, did raid Jorge Krupnik's villa, acting on the tip of an informant eager to receive the million-dollar reward for Noriega's apprehension. A frustrated Lieutenant Colonel Harry Axson, the battalion commander, told reporters that there was "no doubt" that Noriega had recently been in the villa. But there were no new tips as to the fugitive general's whereabouts.

In his Campo Lindbergh hideout, Noriega was reduced to listening to Ulysses Rodriguez's drunken ramblings about how he and Noriega should flee to the hills where an army of campesinos and Dignity Battalion stalwarts would eventually defeat the gringos. Noriega told him that they would probably both die of heart attacks if they tried to lead troops in the jungle.

Meanwhile, the Army's Delta Force had become increasingly desperate, chasing one spurious tip after another. On December 23, Lieutenant Colonel Lynn Moore was inspecting his battalion's positions east of the Canal. He met with the commander of Delta Company at the Madden Dam, then departed aboard his OH-58 command-and-control helicopter. Once airborne, Moore sighted three MH-60 Pave Hawk Special Operations helicopters flying parallel to his aircraft. One of the Pave Hawks crossed sharply in front of Moore's helicopter.

"There's a Special Op going down," Moore told his pilot. "Let's not get in their way."

But when they turned west, another Pave Hawk flew menacingly close to them. "We better set back down," Moore now told the pilot. "Whatever they're doing, they don't want us airborne."

Moore's pilot headed back to the grassy peninsula on the edge of Lake Madden just south of the dam, where they had earlier landed to meet Delta Company's officers. As they settled on the grassy bank, Moore craned his neck out the open door to see two Pave Hawks circling above, but he couldn't find the third Special Ops helicopter. Then he looked back. The Pave Hawk had landed directly behind the smaller helicopter. Delta Force operators in their unmistakable black "Ninja" uniforms, clutching their distinctive weapons, spilled from the helicopter.

Moore slid his feet out the door and raised his hands. Damn it, he thought, they're after Noriega and they think this is his chopper. Moore pointed to his large 1st Cavalry Division Vietnam combat patch on the right shoulder of his BDU blouse. It was unlikely any PDF impostor would have been astute enough to add such a detail to a purloined American uniform.

Further up the bank, the soldiers from Moore's Delta Company saw their battalion commander, his hands in the air, menaced by strange black gunmen. Noriega's UESAT special forces wore such uniforms. The Old Man was about to be taken hostage. A sergeant barked a command and a soldier cranked back the operating lever of a .50-caliber machine gun. Another NCO fired a single warning shot from his M-16.

The bullet whizzed past Moore, struck the instrument panel of the helicopter, and ricocheted back, almost hitting Moore again.

After some shouted invective from all sides, a potentially bloody friendly firefight was avoided. The chagrined Delta Force operators climbed back aboard their helicopter and continued their pursuit of the fugitive dictator.[19]

Although Lieutenant Colonel Lynn Moore never became a PDF hostage, eleven workers from the Smithsonian Tropical Research Institute stationed in the San Blas islands were captured and held hostage by the PDF. Given the isolated location, their fate remained unknown for several days. The group was taken to a larger island near the research station and forced to march into the jungle. Apparently the PDF originally felt they could trade the hostages for their own freedom. But after several days, it became clear no American invasion of the islands was imminent. Eventually the PDF took the hostages to a farm that had a radio, and they managed to contact American officials, who sent a helicopter to rescue them.

At Rio Hato, Captain Tomas Garcia, commander of the 6th Infantry Company (Macho de Monte), and his subordinate, Lieutenant Henry Cedeno, approached the Ranger perimeter carrying a white flag. They controlled almost 150 survivors of the 6th and 7th companies who had taken refuge in nearby villages. These soldiers were ready to surrender, they said, on the proviso that they would be treated as prisoners of war, not criminals. The officers of the 75th Ranger Regiment assured them that they would be offered fair treatment.

"Your men fought well, Captain," an American major told Garcia.

The young captain nodded bitterly; the bravery of his men was not in question. "*They* fought well, yes," he agreed. "But our leaders abandoned us."[20]

The beginning of the end for General Manuel Antonio Noriega came on the afternoon of December 24, 1989, Christmas Eve. For two days he had been shuttling between the modest home of Ulysses Rodriguez's sister in Campo Lindbergh and the luxurious villa of Jorge Krupnik in San Francisco. But the raid by the 2/504th on the Krupnik villa made it clear that the American ring was closing tight.

There was other somber news as well. One of Noriega's most trusted PDF associates, Lieutenant Colonel Luis del Cid, commander of Military District 5 in the western province of Chiriqui, had surrendered to the gringos. Del Cid was the other senior Panamanian officer named in the 1988 federal drug-trafficking indictments. The fact that he had voluntarily surrendered, offering no armed resistance, and then was paraded before a Southern Command press conference, was a crushing blow to Noriega, who heard the news over the resurrected Radio Nacional. But the surrender was only one blow. Del Cid had then been turned over to American Drug Enforcement Administration officers at Howard Air Force Base, stripped of his dress uniform, and flown off to Miami bound in handcuffs, wearing a rumpled orange prisoner's jumpsuit.

As the details of del Cid's surrender filtered in, Noriega began to realize the scope of his dilemma. Military District 5 had represented his last hope of resistance. The mountains of Chiriqui held a strong and well-armed PDF and Dignity Battalion contingent. And del Cid had acted decisively after the American invasion, mining the airfield at the provincial capital of David and retreating with his headquarters staff to the fortified mountain village of San Andres. But then del Cid had second thoughts. Through intermediaries he made contact with Major General Marc Cisneros, Southcom's Army commander. Cisneros had employed a carrot-and-stick approach on del Cid, offering vague promises of leniency, coupled with an unmistakable threat of annihilation if he did not surrender. During several telephone conversations, Cisneros outlined his demands: Del Cid had to muster not only the PDF, but also the disarmed provincial Dignity Battalion for surrender. And he had to prominently display a large, white flag from the PDF's David *cuartel*. As a tangible symbol of American power, General Cisneros arranged for an AC-130 Spectre gunship to overfly the David headquarters. The message could not have been clearer: surrender or die. Del Cid surrendered.

And Cisneros continued this process elsewhere in the western provinces. The American military dispatched a helicopter task force commanded by Special Forces Major Gilberto Perez, who flew from one military district headquarters to another, accompanied by a small combat force and the omnipresent Spectre gunship overhead. One by one the western PDF contingents lined up on the parade ground of the provincial capitals to lay down their arms.

In the Atlantic coast provinces, the seasoned NCOs of the Jungle Operations Training Battalion, led by Lieutenant Colonel Donald W. Richardson, began their own sweep operation to secure the isolated PDF contingents and subdue the Dignity Battalions in the coastal towns and villages. As in the western provinces, most of the armed garrisons surrendered without resistance. Many of those who surrendered in the West and on the Atlantic coast were quickly mustered into the new *Fuerza Publica* police force and sent out to restore order.

General Cisneros orchestrated most of the western province surrenders, using his most potent weapon, the telephone. This approach was quickly dubbed, the "Ma Bell Campaign."

The campaign not only effectively removed a credible military threat, it undoubtedly helped complete Noriega's demoralization.

On the morning of Christmas Eve, his trusted bodyguard Captain Ivan Castillo, left to look for "PDF loyalists," who might help hide the general. Castillo never returned. Ulysses Rodriguez also abandoned him. Noriega was left with two enlisted bodyguards. He knew that several senior PDF officers had already sought asylum in the Vatican Embassy, the Nunciatura, a handsome two-story villa with an old walled garden, just off Avenida Balboa in Punta Paitilla. The papal nuncio, Monsignor José Sebastian Laboa, had been an outspoken critic of Noriega and the corrupt PDF. But Laboa, a brilliant and worldly Spanish Basque, apparently realized that granting asylum to the toppled PDF leadership might help prevent a protracted guerrilla war against the Americans. Noriega gambled that the Monsignor would extend this asylum to include the Maximum Leader, himself.

Moreover, Noriega's best hope of asylum leading to safe exile—the Cuban and Nicaraguan embassies—was no longer an option. U.S. forces had surrounded these two embassies.

After a hasty telephone negotiation with Monsignor Laboa, Noriega worked out an arrangement to rendezvous with the Nuncio's car in the parking lot of a Dairy Queen near San Miguelito. The cloudy afternoon of Christmas Eve, Noriega, dressed in a sweaty gray T-shirt and baggy Bermuda shorts, his face hidden beneath an oversize baseball cap, climbed into the back seat of the Nuncio's large Toyota sedan and identified himself to Laboa's colleague, Father Javier Villanueva. The car, flying the papal flag, was technically diplomatic territory. Noriega's brief period of limbo in the diplomatic sanctuary of the Nunciatura had begun.

\*     \*     \*

With General Manuel Noriega finally driven to ground, the tired Southcom staff officers who had executed Blue Spoon from OPLAN to Op Order, and their colleagues in the combat units stationed in Panama had the chance to see their families. Lieutenant Colonel Jerry Murguia, Colonel Jorge Torres-Cartagena, and Lieutenant Colonel Jim Swank finally managed brief visits to Fort Amador. They were shocked by what they saw. Although they knew full well the firing across the golf course had been heavy, they were unprepared for the extent of the damage to the former PDF barracks. Every building was badly pockmarked by heavy-caliber rounds. There were still heaps of shell casings in the backyards of the family quarters, and the lawns were crosshatched with the unmistakable pattern of armored vehicle treads.

But the lights twinkled on the Christmas trees, and the men had the chance to eat a plate of turkey, change uniforms, and head back to Quarry Heights. Emilio Torres-Cartagena proudly pointed out to his father where a PDF ZPU round fired across the bay from El Chorrillo had chipped off a corner of the family's house. The howitzer used in the firepower demonstrations, he added, had been "really cool." Maybe, he said, he'd be an artilleryman when he grew up.

As the officers left the fort to return to duty, they drove past the heroic concrete sculpture of the Macho de Monte soldier that Manuel Noriega had hastily commissioned after the crushed October coup attempt. The figure in jungle fatigues and booney hat still had his muscular right arm raised high. But the AK-47 he had once clutched in his fist was missing.

Major Wanda Bisbal, commander of the 6th Aerial Support Squadron at Howard Air Force Base, returned briefly to her quarters at Fort Clayton. The old post beside the Miraflores Locks had been relatively undamaged, despite a long-range PDF mortar barrage fired from Tinajitas beyond the hills to the east. But there was one spectacular casualty. An Army captain on temporary duty in the States had parked his cherished sports car near the Bachelor Officers' Quarters, and carefully draped the vehicle in a form-fitting vinyl cover to protect it from the tropical sun. One of the PDF mortar rounds had struck squarely in the center of the sports car's roof. All that was left was a scattered heap of charred metal.

Manuel Noriega's Nunciatura asylum was an austerely furnished second-floor bedroom, decorated with a wooden crucifix. There were no Hindu love goddesses here. And the picture on the small color television set was bleached and fuzzy. But there was a bed, and Noriega was exhausted. After meeting briefly with the Nuncio, Noriega drank a cold bottle of Soberena beer and fell onto the cot and into exhausted sleep. Earlier he had commented on the irony that this same spartan guest room had been used by Guillermo Endara, seeking asylum from the rabid Digbats after the failed October coup, and by Archbishop Marcus McGrath, Panama's senior Catholic cleric and Noriega's most bitter personal enemy. But Noriega was in company more to his liking now. Several of his senior PDF colleagues, including the infamous Colonel Nivaldo Madriñan and Captain Eliecer Gaytan, his chief UESAT officer, had bedrooms down the hall.

That evening, Monsignor Laboa called General Cisneros and announced that Noriega had been granted asylum. The Southcom commanders were not amused. General Max Thurman, a Catholic of unshakable faith, could hardly order Sheridan tanks to batter down the gates of the Vatican Embassy. Once more, Manuel Noriega had skillfully thwarted the senior American officer in Panama.

For the next eleven days, a bizarre diplomatic and military standoff ensued, a spectacle that was once more captured by the unblinking television eye of the world's assembled media. Before the tragicomic episode ended, America's relations with the Vatican, Spain, and several of its principal Latin American allies were badly strained. Simply stated, Noriega wanted to parlay his asylum into safe passage out of the country. President Bush, General Thurman, and his field commanders wanted Noriega's hide. Monsignor Laboa was caught in the middle.

In an ill-advised, and justifiably ridiculed, spurt of overenthusiasm by Psychological Operations forces, a high-decibel rock-music assault on the Nunciatura began the day after Christmas. General Carl Stiner's authorization of this "operation" was one of his few tactical errors in an otherwise brilliantly commanded campaign. U.S. troops, including infantrymen from the 82d Airborne and the 7th Division, armed for heavy combat, supported by Sheridan tanks and hovering Apache gunships, surrounded the Nunciatura. The entire block was cordoned off. Thousands of anti-Noriega demonstrators choked Avenida Balboa and swarmed up to the American roadblock across the Rio Mataznillo, beating pots and pans in the distinctive protest tattoo of the civic crusade. In a derisive parody of Noriega's grandiose patriotic slogan, *"Ni un Paso Atras,"* they chanted, *"Ni un Dia Mas,"* (Not One Day More). But their noisy demonstrations were drowned out by the high-powered U.S. Psy Ops loudspeakers. While the world's assembled press watched from the windows of the nearby Holiday Inn, the Americans blasted the Vatican Embassy with rock music. Noriega was known to love opera and the heroic classical works of Beethoven and Wagner. Supposedly, megadecibel renditions of Linda Ronstadt's "You're No Good" or the heavy-metal onslaught of Twisted Sister, not to mention such cleverly chosen works as "I Fought the Law and the Law Won," or "Somebody's Watching You," would deprive Noriega of sleep and convince him to surrender. But all this tactic accomplished was to trivialize an otherwise bravely fought and skillfully led military operation. Within three days, Monsignor Laboa brusquely told Major General Marc Cisneros, Southcom's principal negotiator, that all discussions were suspended until the rock music was stopped.

The bitter frustration gripping General Max Thurman and his task force commander, Lieutenant General Carl Stiner, at their inability to finally collar Noriega spilled over to the troops restoring order in Panama City. On December 29, soldiers of the 7th Infantry Division patrolling the affluent San Francisco neighborhood where many of Noriega's cronies had villas, battered their way into the residence of the Nicaraguan ambassador, Antenor Ferrey, despite the fact that the stucco entrance arch of the villa was emblazoned with a large diplomatic seal.

Intelligence reports had noted that wanted Dignity Battalion officers might have taken refuge there. There were also reports that Ambassador Ferrey, who had been Noriega's chief link to Sandinista *comandantes*, had a hidden arsenal in the villa, possibly including the SAM antiaircraft missiles that had so far eluded the Americans. Earlier, troops of the 82d Airborne Division had surrounded the Nicaraguan and Cuban embassy chanceries in the city center, but had avoided the ambassadors' residences. Now the American soldiers struck with a vengeance, even manhandling the ambassador during a shoving match on the front steps.

In Washington, Chairman of the Joint Chiefs General Colin Powell saw a CNN report documenting this blatant breach of diplomatic convention. The general was not amused. Between the fiasco of the rock music bombardment, the El Chorrillo fires, and now these strong-arm tactics, the smoothly executed military operation was being tarnished. He tried to telephone Max Thurman directly, one of the few command interventions. But Thurman was unavailable. He called Powell back later that day and offered a rather weak explanation that the troops had, in fact, unearthed a sizable cache of automatic weapons and rocket-propelled grenades in the ambassador's residence. And Thurman also presented the rationale that the soldiers hadn't understood the meaning of diplomatic immunity.

General Powell was not a man to accept such excuses. "I just saw it on CNN," Powell said, noting that the diplomatic seal was "the size of a manhole cover. It's undeniable. Stop bullshitting me."

"Yes, sir," Max Thurman answered through clenched teeth. He was an officer who prided himself on his personal honor and integrity. But when the chief called you on the carpet, you stood up and saluted.

Powell went on to remind Thurman that needlessly provoking the Sandinistas might have serious repercussions in the CINCSOUTH's other countries of responsibility. In fact, the Sandinistas were then in the process of expelling American diplomats, including important civilian and military intelligence officers.

To the men in the Operations Center, this angry reprimand was the only direct interference from the Pentagon that they witnessed during the entire execution of Blue Spoon.[21]

In Washington and Rome, the negotiations continued. The Bush administration was adamant. Noriega would be allowed no safe-haven exile. But U.S. forces would respect the diplomatic sanctity of the Nunciatura. In other words, Noriega was indefinitely suspended in this limbo.[22]

Noriega's increasingly desperate attempts to escape the American net sputtered down to an anticlimax on January 3, 1990. His originally grandiose demands, which included expunging all criminal charges against him and salvaging his personal fortune, now amounted merely to a request that he be allowed to wear his tropical dress uniform and be spared the indignity of a del Cid-type press conference circus when he surrendered. At quarter to nine that night, Noriega, dressed in a freshly laundered khaki uniform (delivered an hour before by his ever-faithful mistress Vicky Amado), left the wrought-iron gates of the Nunciatura and was taken into custody by grim-faced soldiers of the Delta Force. General Maxwell Thurman and Major General Marc Cisneros stood across the street staring silently at the spectacle. Twenty-three American military men had been killed in action and 347 wounded in the campaign to crush that miserable little dictator's hold on this country. Now his defeat was complete.

Hunched between three Delta Force operators, Noriega was duck-walked to an MH-60 Pave Hawk helicopter that had set down in a narrow vacant lot nearby. The helicopter thumped away into the hot night sky, en route to Howard Air Force Base.

The aircraft flew low over Panama Bay, and banked left to avoid the shattered hulk of Noriega's Comandancia. As he stared through the helicopter window, the former dictator could see the huge flag of his country, again floodlit, flying above the dark mound of Ancon Hill.

## Mopping Up

At Howard's Hangar 3, amid the pallets of Special Operations equipment and weapons, with the crackling din of the task force radio net in the background, General Noriega was read his Miranda rights by Drug Enforcement Administration officers in shiny blue windbreakers. Then he was stripped and searched for weapons and drugs. He was dressed in the same kind of floppy orange prisoner's jumpsuit that del Cid had been issued, handcuffed, and escorted onto the waiting MC-130 transport that would carry him to federal custody in Miami.

As the big transport taxied toward the end of the runway, incoming American aircraft whistled down through the humid night, carrying reinforcements. The tired troops stepping down onto the Howard ramp wore fatigue hats, not helmets. Their weapons were unloaded. The war was over.

# Epilogue

## Lessons Applied

*0238 Hours, 17 January 1991*

The two huge MH-53 Pave Low Special Operations helicopters trundled through the moonless night, only 100 feet above the desert floor, at a precise airspeed of 140 knots. They were flying parallel, separated by twenty-eight miles of featureless Iraqi sand. Behind each Pave Low, four AH-64 Apache gunships flew in tight formation, close enough to follow the winking infrared strobe on the Pave Low's tail boom. Each Apache carried a full load of sixteen Hellfire missiles.

The copilots and engineers seated on the noisy flight decks of the MH-53s carefully monitored their integrated avionics computers. The Pave Lows had the world's most advanced navigation capabilities, which combined laser ring gyro inertial systems with regular updates from Global Positioning System satellites and Terrain-Following Radar. Flight data were superimposed on the aircraft commander's rectangular forward-looking infrared (FLIR) display. The Pave Lows could safely fly through any weather, only a hundred feet above the nearest terrain feature, and reach an objective as small as a five-foot diameter circle at a precisely predetermined time.

Tonight their objectives were two Iraqi early warning radar sites guarding the frontier with Saudi Arabia, 400 kilometers west, northwest of Kuwait. These radar sites protected the southern approaches to Baghdad. They would be the first enemy targets of Operation Desert Storm. On this first night of the air war, it was essential that these two radar sites be destroyed at exactly the same moment to open an ingress lane for American EF-111 electronic jamming aircraft in the vanguard of the waves of bombers forming up over the empty desert of Saudi Arabia. Multiple two-plane flights of F-117A Stealth fighter-bombers would also use this lane, an extra precaution in the event the Iraqi's Soviet-supplied air defense radars were sensitive enough to detect their inbound passage.

The attack on the Iraqi radar sites had been carefully planned by Colonel George Gray III, commander of the 1st Special Operations Wing, which had contributed so much to the success of Operation Just Cause in Panama thirteen months before. Gray had presented the plan to General H. Norman Schwarzkopf, commander in chief of U.S. Central Command in Riyadh, in October 1990. Based on his experiences in Panama, Gray knew that precisely guided high-technology weapons systems striking simultaneously with overwhelming firepower offered the best promise of achieving complete tactical surprise in the initial air attack. He had seen firsthand what the Apaches' devastatingly accurate Hellfire missiles could accomplish. He proposed that his Pave Lows lead Apaches right to the front gates of these two key Iraqi radar sites, so that the Hellfires could destroy the electrical generators and antennas in a single barrage.

Gray had spread his aerial charts and satellite photographs on the floor of Schwarzkopf's modest personal office in the basement of the Saudi Ministry of Defense and Aviation in downtown Riyadh. The big, gruff CINC studied the charts, frowning deeply. Finally he spoke.

"Colonel," Schwarzkopf growled, "before I authorize a plan like this, can you guarantee me *one hundred percent* success?"

Gray knew he was being tested. Losing six expensive helicopters and their crews to Iraqi groundfire or missiles while failing to open the door to Baghdad for the bombers would not improve the chances of his name appearing on the promotion list to brigadier general. But Gray had learned in Panama to trust high technology enough to use it audaciously.

"Yes, Sir," Gray said, "as long as you give me the Apaches

and some good crews so that we can rehearse this thing."

Schwarzkopf frowned again. "Okay, Colonel. You've got them. Just don't use up all my goddamn Hellfires." He smiled now. "I'm eventually going to need them against the Republican Guard."

George Gray had rehearsed his crews out in the empty wilderness of the King Khalid Military City, a base the size of Maryland. Night after night, the three-helicopter flights had roared across the gravel flats below 100 feet, then flared to a hover 1,200 meters from plywood replicas of the Iraqi radar sites. Most of the training had been dry-fire exercises. But in the final days leading up to Desert Storm, the Apache crews had indeed used up several of Schwarzkopf's precious Hellfire missiles.

At precisely 0238 hours, the two assault flights dropped below fifty feet and spread to a fingertip hover formation near the Iraqi early warning sites. Lights burned brightly in the prefab concrete buildings. The big radar antennas rotated with ponderous grace. Each of the four Apache pilot/gunners aligned his laser target designator on a predetermined generator or antenna. The silent digits of the countdown to weapons release blinked on their FLIR scopes.

The missile barrage began. One by one the white-hot rocket plumes slashed through the night. The first explosions detonated at both sites within two seconds of each other.

In the Iraqi Air Force Integrated Air Defense System control room in downtown Baghdad, the data from the two radar sites on the southern frontier dropped off the scopes at almost the same second. As Colonel Gray had hoped, the Iraqi Air Defense officers naturally assumed this simultaneous data drop had to be due to a computer failure, not enemy action.

The officers and technicians in the control room were still working to reacquire the sites when the first GBU-28 laser-guided 2,000-pound bomb, dropped by an F-117A Stealth flying undetected 8,000 feet above the city center, crashed through the roof of the building and blasted the Air Defense center and its occupants into small pieces.

# NOTES

## Prologue

**1.** To reconstruct the events of October 3, 1989, the author relied on interviews with former and currently serving American military and civilian intelligence officers in Panama and Washington. These officers also confirmed the validity of certain published accounts of these events, most notably: "The Yanquis Stayed Home," *Time,* October 16, 1989, pp. 24–28; and Frederick Kempe, *Divorcing the Dictator* (New York: G.P. Putnam's Sons, 1990), ch. 21, "Unfinished Business," pp. 369–93.

**2.** The term "gringo" is commonly used in everyday Panamanian speech, and does not carry the pejorative connotation it has elsewhere in Latin America.

**3.** Interview with a former member of the PDF 4th Company, now a member of Panama's Public Force, December 11, 1990. This officer was a witness to the events inside the Comandancia and confirms published accounts, including those of *Time* and Frederick Kempe in his well-researched book, *Divorcing the Dictator.*

**4.** Frederick Kempe summarizes this intrigue well in *Divorcing the Dictator,* p. 420:

What Noriega recognized was that American foreign policy most often is a complex result of individuals' ambitions and competing bureaucratic agendas. So Noriega fed American agencies and their representatives. He gave intelligence and a listening post to the CIA; ... he turned narco-traffickers (often his own competition) over to the Drug Enforcement Administration, and he shipped off criminals to the FBI, despite lack of any extradition treaty. In short, he consistently served America's narrowest interests, all the time satisfying his own agenda, which included facilitating money laundering, the sale of intelligence and high technology to the Cubans, and the transfer of arms to guerrilla movements throughout the region.

**5.** "Donald Jones" is a pseudonym of a field-grade U.S. military intelligence officer who served in Panama in 1989 and 1990. He agreed to be interviewed on the condition he remain anonymous. The interviews were conducted in April and December, 1990.

**6.** According to the American intelligence officers cited in note 1 above, the actual chain of events that occurred inside Noriega's office closely resembled the published accounts in *Time* and in Kempe, *Divorcing the Dictator*.

**7.** Interview, December 14, 1990, with members of the U.S. Army's 1st Battalion, 508th Parachute Infantry Regiment, who captured Noriega's Fort Amador headquarters on 20 December 1989. A quantity of the sadistic so-called snuff videos (with scenes of women tortured and eventually killed) was discovered, some still in the envelopes of Panamanian diplomatic missions in the United States. Investigative journalist Bob Woodward confirms the discovery of this sadistic pornography (as well as witchcraft and Nazi materials) in Noriega's quarters. This material was used to help convince the Catholic church to force Noriega from the sanctuary of the Vatican Embassy in Panama City. See Bob Woodward, *The Commanders* (New York: Simon and Schuster, 1991), p. 191.

**8.** Since Operation Just Cause, critics have charged that the Bush administration overreacted to the Panamanian National Assembly resolution on the "state of war" existing with the United States and the related "maximum leader" resolution. The exact text of the resolution was transcribed and translated into English by the CIA's Foreign Broadcast Information Service. The two pertinent resolutions are:

1. To declare the Republic of Panama in a state of war for the duration of the aggression unleashed against the Panamanian people by the U.S. Government.

2. To face this state of war, the position of head of government of the Republic of Panama is created, and General Manuel Antonio Noriega Moreno, commander in chief of the Panama Defense Forces [FDP], is appointed to occupy this position as maximum leader of the struggle for national liberation.

Clearly, this resolution put Panama on a war footing, and gave General Noriega unprecedented power. See Foreign Broadcast Information Service-LAT-89-241, 18 December 1989 (Central America), pp. 19–21.

## *Chapter 1*

1. The details of this conversation have been verified with Military Intelligence sources. Also see "Debriefing Report: On the Run with Manuel Noriega," *Harper's Magazine,* November 1990, pp. 20–24.

2. Interview with Lt. Col. Jerry Murguia, Southcom, Panama City, December 3, 1990, transcribed notes, pp. 3–4.

3. Murgia interview notes; pp. 4–5.

4. The actual call signs used by F-117A Stealth aircraft in Panama are still classified and have been replaced by the generic call sign Gander. At the time this book was in the editing stage, (F-117A) Stealth fighters were still deployed in the Persian Gulf; divulging any of the 37th Tactical Fighter Wing's call signs, which are used on open radio frequencies during tanker refuelings and other operations, might endanger those crews still overseas.

5. For a reasonably detailed unclassified explanation of the Airborne Command and Control, AWACS coverage, and secure communications network involved in the initial Airborne assaults of Operation Just Cause, see "Historical Summary of OPERATION JUST CAUSE, 17 December 1989–12 January

1990," Headquarters 82d Airborne Division, Fort Bragg, North Carolina, 22 January 1990, pp. 9–11, 13–15. Also see diagram/briefing slide "Enroute Communications," OPERATION JUST CAUSE, 82d Airborne Division, available through Division History Office, Ft. Bragg.

**6.** Debriefing of PDF Major Gonzalo Charlo Gonzales, by Major General Marc Cisneros, February 1990, as reported by Lt. Col. Jerry Murguia; Murguia interview, December 3, 1990. Also, interview with Maj. Gen. Marc Cisneros, June 3, 1991.

## Chapter 2

**1.** The author was fortunate to be able to interview one currently serving staff officer and one senior NCO assigned to Navy Special Operations at Little Creek. Both men jeopardized their careers to discuss the controversial details of the Paitilla Airport operation, and both spoke with the understanding that they would remain anonymous. The information they provided supplemented on-the-record interviews the author conducted with Commander Tom McGrath and Lieutenant (j.g.) Michael Phillips on April 17, 1990, with follow-up interviews over the next month.

**2.** Interview with Col. William "Buck" Kernan, Commander, 75th Infantry Regiment (Airborne), November 15, 1990.

**3.** Bob Woodward, *The Commanders* (New York: Simon and Schuster, 1991), pp. 163–65. Woodward notes that both Marine Commandant General Al Gray and Chief of Naval Operations Admiral Carl Trost regretted not having a larger role in Operation Just Cause. In fact, they lobbied Chairman of the Joint Chiefs of Staff General Colin Powell for a greater Marine and Navy role, even up to the eve of the operation.

**4.** Interview with former senior Special Operations Forces and Military Intelligence officer, November 3, 1990. This retired officer is now an executive of a consulting firm under contract to review American Special Operations doctrine and critique actual operations. He granted the interview on the condition that he remain anonymous.

**5.** After Operation Just Cause, a myth developed that the

SEALs at Paitilla Airport had encountered PDF armored cars that had decimated the American ranks with automatic-weapons fire. There were no PDF armored vehicles at Paitilla on December 20, 1989. The origin of this myth was an erroneous report issued by U.S. commanders during a press conference. This report was later widely disseminated in the press. See Patrick E. Tyler and Molly Moore, "Invasion of Panama Reflected General Thurman's Gung-Ho Style," *Washington Post,* January 7, 1990, p. A1.

**6.** These apprehensions were independently confirmed by the anonymous sources cited in note 1 above.

**7.** Interview with Col. George Gray III, USAF, Commander, 1st Special Operations Wing, April 10, 1991.

**8.** Gray interview transcript, p. 2.

**9.** Lieutenant (j.g.) John Connors' boat landed at approximately 0059 on December 20, 1989. The tide at Paitilla Point at that time was between slack and ebb, with ample water near the bluff, the previous high tide having been at 2107 hours; the next low would occur at 0323, as calculated by Mr. Elmo Long, Tides and Current Predictions Branch, National Oceanic and Atmospheric Administration, Rockville, Maryland. Commander Tom McGrath flatly stated to the author: "Tide was no problem that night." But some journalists later confused television images of paratroopers from the 82d Airborne Division stranded in mud flats off Panama Viejo at dawn by low tide with the SEALs at Paitilla. See F.A. Wright, "Invasion of Panama Not the Textbook Operation Planners Say it Was," *U.S. Veteran News and Report,* January 24, 1990, p. 6.

**10.** Interview with Lt. (j.g.) Michael Phillips, April 17, 1990, transcript, p. 3.

**11.** Later evidence clearly established that many of these light aircraft had been used to fly illegal drugs. See David Hughes, "Panamanians Work to Restore Airline, Airport Services," *Aviation Week & Space Technology,* January 29, 1990, pp. 70–71. According to Hughes, Air Force security police under the command of Col. Edward Harrow used drug-sniffing dogs to find traces of narcotics aboard the light planes these watchmen had been guarding on the night of the invasion.

**12.** Gray interview transcript, p. 1. After the tragedy at Paitilla Airport, a senior Navy official told a defense journalist that the SEALs at Paitilla tried calling the AC-130 Spectre gunship on "every possible frequency," but received no response from the aircraft. See Barbara Starr, "Comms Failure Blights SEAL Operation," *Jane's Defense Weekly,* 5 May 1990, pp. 834–835. A former Air Force Special Operations officer serving in Saudi Arabia later confirmed other reports that the crew of the Spectre observed the entire bloody encounter at the PDF hangar, using sensors and night-vision devices, but that they were unable to provide fire support without a proper request from the men on the ground. This officer also concurred that the Spectre was probably not the best suited fire-support platform for the SEALs at Paitilla.

## Chapter 3

**1.** The author is grateful to members of the 37th Tactical Fighter Wing who briefed him on the F-117A Stealth fighter at Nellis Air Force Base, Nevada, on May 21, 1991.

**2.** Interview with Col. Anthony J. Tolin, USAF, May 24, 1991, transcript, p. 3. Colonel Tolin, commander of the 37th Tactical Fighter Wing during Just Cause, patiently explained all the relevant planning and execution details for the Rio Hato mission to the author. Within the constraints of security, he was unusually open about the role of the F-117A during Operation Just Cause.

**3.** Bob Woodward, *The Commanders* (New York: Simon and Schuster, 1991), pp. 176–77. Woodward, who was thoroughly briefed by members of the Joint Chiefs of Staff, makes it clear that distance from the PDF barracks, not a specific set of crosshair coordinates in the grass, was the critical factor for the F-117A Stealths at Rio Hato.

**4.** Tolin interview transcript, p. 5.

**5.** The bombing of Rio Hato triggered one of the fiercest controversies of the Panama invasion. Soon after Operation Just Cause, Defense Secretary Dick Cheney stated that the Stealth aircraft had delivered their bombs with "pinpoint accuracy" at Rio Hato. This statement did not include the information that the F-117As had been ordered to drop their bombs in open ground seaward from the barracks. Cheney gave the impression that the Stealths had struck *exact* aiming points, which, of course, was not the case.

Michael R. Gordon, the Washington-based military correspondent of the *New York Times,* raised this issue to initiate a press campaign against the Stealth's reputed precision weapons delivery and alleged Air Force duplicity. Gordon visited Rio Hato after the invasion, photographed the crater of the second Stealth's bomb, which straddled the seaside bluff near the 6th Company's cantina, and confronted the Air Force with this evidence of inaccuracy. The Air Force denied that the Stealths had not met their mission objective and noted that the planes' precise navigation system had worked perfectly—as had their weapons delivery systems. But the Air Force did concede that there had been some initial confusion as to the exact target coordinates. Gordon downplayed the primary mission objective of stunning but not killing the enemy and stressed the Stealths' lack of accuracy. The second Stealth's bomb, he wrote, had landed "way off target."

He politicized the issue by noting that the use of the Stealths in Panama was possibly an Air Force ploy to "buttress the case" for buying B-2 Stealth bombers, which Congress was reluctant to fund. See Michael R. Gordon, "Stealth Jet's First Mission Was Marred, Pentagon Says," *New York Times,* April 4, 1990, p. A11.

Under media pressure, Secretary Cheney was obliged to order an inquiry into the Air Force's original report on the Stealth's performance in Panama. Gordon then used this event to note that one of the F-117s "had missed its target by more than 300 yards." The implication here was obvious: that the F-117A's "pinpoint" bomb guidance system was deeply flawed—or at least it had been in Panama. Another obvious implication of his articles was that the Air Force had carried out a cover-up, hoping to deceive Secretary Cheney. Gordon again brought up inside-the-Beltway politics, noting that the F-117A is "an aeronautical cousin of the B-2 bomber." By now, other media commentators were echoing the allegations that the only reason the Air Force had used the dubiously accurate F-117A Stealth fighter-bombers was to promote the equally dubious B-2 Stealth bomber. See Michael R. Gordon, "Inquiry Into Stealth's Performance In Panama Is Ordered by Cheney," *New York Times,* April 11, 1990, p. A8.

The *Times* editors wholeheartedly endorsed Gordon's thesis in a mocking editorial that disparaged the worth of Stealth technology and lambasted the honesty and motives of Air Force officials. By this point, many in the media were convinced the Stealth was just another expensive Pentagon toy that would not perform as advertised. See the editorial "Air Force Accuracy in Panama," *New York Times,* April 13, 1990, p. A30.

The Air Force was in a double bind here, according to Colonel Ron Sconyers, the Tactical Air Command public affairs officer who handled the Stealth controversy. Sconyers told the author [Interview with Col. Ron Sconyers, USAF, May 13, 1991, transcript, pp. 2–3] that he was constrained by security considerations from detailing the Stealths' bombing procedures, and thus clarifying the impression left by Gordon that the F-117A was a technical failure. To this day, the Air Force has not officially released details of a typical Stealth bombing-mission "profile," for fear that so doing would permit potential foes to develop effective countermeasures, including barrage antiaircraft fire at critical altitudes and ground disruption of laser guidance.

Colonel Anthony J. Tolin, commander of the 37th Tactical Fighter Wing during Operation Just Cause, spoke with great bitterness about Gordon's articles. The original article, Tolin noted, was replete with errors: Gordon left the impression that there had been a muddle in targeting orders "at the last minute," even as the aircraft "approached their targets." This simply was not true, Tolin states. The decision for Lead and Two to swap targets had been agreed on before the planes left the Tonopah Test Range. The two pilots had, in fact, delivered their bombs with "zero-meter" accuracy: each bomb struck precisely on the spot where the pilots held their laser target designators. And Tolin angrily dismissed press allegations that the Air Force, beginning with his command, had engaged in a cover-up, as nothing but "a crock." [Tolin interview transcript, p. 5.]

Gordon further charged that there had been "a major breakdown in communications" among Ranger commander Buck Kernan, JTF South commander Lieutenant General Carl

Stiner, and the Air Force as to the nature of the air support at Rio Hato. Gordon stated in his original April 4, 1990, article (which launched the controversy) that Kernan had the impression the barracks were going to be bombed and was never told of the plans for offset bombing. Yet Colonel Kernan told the author [interview with Col. William "Buck" Kernan, notes, p. 3] that he had submitted a fire-support request for an air attack that would leave the PDF "dizzy and shaken up" just before the Rangers' airdrop. Kernan said he felt Gordon had manipulated the information he provided the journalist in an interview for his own purposes.

The overall impression left by the articles and editorial was that the F-117A was a badly flawed weapons system that was used in Panama principally for political reasons. And that was where the matter stood until the Persian Gulf War.

Eleven months later, however, when the military value and incredible—indeed "pinpoint"—accuracy of the F-117A Stealth fighter had been amply demonstrated in Iraq, the same Michael Gordon commented that the Stealth's performance in the war had "validated a new Air Force maxim: precision counts." He noted that the F-117A Stealth aircraft had dropped laser-guided bombs with unerring precision to destroy key Iraqi bridges which conventional fighter-bombers had missed. He did not apologize for his earlier vindictive campaign against the Stealth and the Air Force. See Michael R. Gordon with Eric Schmitt, "Radios and Mine Sweepers: Problems in the Gulf," *New York Times,* March 28, 1991, p. A19.

**6.** For a full description of the role of the Apaches in Operation Just Cause, see Frank Colucci, "Rehearsal Reaps Rewards," *Defense Helicopter World,* June–July 1990, pp. 18–24; and Robert R. Ropelewski, "Planning, Precision, and Surprise Led to Panama Successes," *Armed Forces Journal International,* February 1990, pp. 26–32.

**7.** "Historical Summary of OPERATION JUST CAUSE, 17 December 1989–12 January 1990," Headquarters 82d Airborne Division, Fort Bragg, North Carolina: Summary for 10 December 1989 (D-Day), p. 6.

**8.** Interview with Col. George Gray III, April 10, 1991, notes, p. 1

## Chapter 4

**1.** Interview with Brig. Gen. (P) William Hartzog, Fort Clayton, Republic of Panama, December 7, 1990. Also see: "Task Force Bayonet Summary of Operation Just Cause," Headquarters 193d Infantry Brigade (Light), Fort Clayton, Republic of Panama, 1 March 1990, p. 3.

**2.** Headquarters, 82d Airborne Division, "Historical Summary of OPERATION JUST CAUSE, 17 December 1989–12 January 1990," dated 22 January 1990, pp. 10–11.

**3.** See Lee Hockstader, "Sandinistas Charged in Missiles Sale," *Washington Post*, January 1, 1991, p. A15. After the election defeat of the Sandinistas, the Nicaraguan government was eventually forced to admit its role in distributing modern Soviet SAMs (transshipped by the Cubans) to the FMLN.

**4.** Interview with Lt. Col. Jerry Murguia, United States Southern Command, Panama City, December 3, 1990, transcript, p. 4.

**5.** Interview with U.S. Air Force operations officer, Howard Air Force Base, Republic of Panama, December 7, 1990, transcript, pp. 1–2. This officer discussed the incident with the Panamanian air controller after the invasion.

**6.** Confirmation of this bizarre close encounter came from congressional sources quoted by the *Washington Post*. See William Branigin, "U.S. Paratroopers May Have Seen Noriega Escape During Invasion," *Washington Post*, January 7, 1990, p. A1.

**7.** On January 31, 1990, President George Bush delivered his first State of the Union address. He read from the letter James Markwell had sent his mother in Cincinnati, the night before the 1st Battalion left for Panama. The twenty-year-old Ranger frankly revealed that he was afraid of dying in the coming combat. But he added: "Remember, I joined the Army to serve my country and insure that you are free to do what you want and to live your lives freely."

**8.** Interviews with members of the 1st and 3d Battalions, 75th Ranger Regiment, Fort Benning, Georgia, November 1990; briefing by Lt. Col. Robert Wagner, Commander 1st Battalion, 75th Ranger Ranger Regiment, Hunter Army Airfield, Georgia, April 9, 1991.

**9.** Interview with Col. Jorge Torres-Cartagena, USA, December 3, 1990, notes, p. 4.

**10.** Interview with Maj. Kevin Higgins, Fort Bragg, North Carolina, July 11, 1991. Higgins' firsthand account of the mad dash to stop the Battalion 2000 convoy at the Pacora River bridge is more exciting than the official Army account of the engagement. This account notes that Higgins set up a "blocking force" on the bridge, which fired on the enemy convoy as it approached the span. The official published version does not note that Sgt. McDonald's decisive action stopped the lead enemy vehicle on the bridge itself only moments after the three helicopters landed. See: Headquarters, Department of the Army, Chief of Public Affairs, "Taking the Pacora River Bridge," *Soldiers in Panama: Stories of Operation Just Cause,* Washington, DC, 1990, pp. 14–15.

## Chapter 5

**1.** Interview with Capt. John H. Hort, Jr. and members of his company, Fort Kobbe, Republic of Panama, November 30, 1990, transcript, pp. 2–5.

**2.** The author was unable to interview Kurt Muse concerning his imprisonment and rescue. Therefore, the author drew extensively on the vividly written account of Neil Livingstone, the only journalist to whom Muse granted an interview. See Neil C. Livingstone, "Danger in the Air," *The Washingtonian,* June 1990, pp. 92–206. The author was, however, able to supplement this published account with further information obtained from Special Operations Forces familiar with the courageous rescue. For another interesting published account of Kurt Muse's rescue, see William Branigin, "U.S. Agent Rescued From Panama Cell Minutes Before Anti-Noriega Offensive," *Washington Post,* January 1, 1990, p. A12.

**3.** Livingstone, "Danger in the Air," p. 202. For a chilling view of La Modelo Prison through the perspective of a political prisoner, see R.M. Koster and Guillermo Sanchez Borbon, *In the Time of the Tyrants: Panama, 1968–1989* (New York: W.W. Norton, 1990), pp. 40–42.

**4.** The Delta Force is the Army's most secret Special Operations unit. Based at Fort Bragg, North Carolina, Delta is reportedly battalion-size. Like its Navy counterpart, SEAL Team 6, Delta's principal mission is counterterrorism. Rescuing hostages and other Americans held captive in fortified prisons such as La Modelo is an integral part of the Delta Force mission. Despite the popular Chuck Norris action films, however, very little is known about Delta's actual training, equipment, or methods. One knowledgeable Washington Special Operations executive told the author, "The only published unclassified stuff on Delta is rumor or inaccurate speculation. They're as secret as you can get, and that's the way they like it."

But it is known that Delta troops wear special nonreflective black "Ninja" uniforms and fight with specially designed laser-sighted submachine guns. They are also world-class explosives experts. After observing Delta operators preparing for Operation Just Cause in Hangar 3 at Howard Air Force Base, one pilot told the author, "They were doing things with C-4 that I didn't think were possible."

For a brief but accurate description of Delta Force, see John M. Collins, "U.S. and Soviet Special Operations," Congressional Research Service Report 87-398 S, December 23, 1986, pp. 21–23, 32–33. Also see "The Secret Army," *Time,* August 31, 1987, pp. 12–14.

**5.** Livingstone, "Danger in the Air," pp. 205–206. The author was able to confirm this portion of Neil Livingstone's *Washingtonian* account of Muse's rescue with a knowledgeable officer during an interview at Special Operations headquarters, U.S. Central Command (SOCENT), King Khalid Military City, Saudi Arabia, January 30, 1991.

**6.** Corporal Ivan D. Perez of Pawtucket, RI, was the first American soldier killed in Panama City. He was posthumously awarded the Silver Star. For excellent published accounts on the M-113 APCs at the Comandancia, see John B. Treaster, "It Was Worse than Anyone Could Imagine," *New York Times,* December 26, 1989, p. A3; and Ross Simpson, "Heroes of Panama," *Soldier of Fortune,* September 1990, pp. 40–90. Another accurate account can be found in the booklet issued at the Review Honoring Task Force Regulars, 5th Infantry Division (Mechanized), Fort Polk, Louisiana, 9 February 1990, pp. 8–13.

**7.** For more information on this incident, see Frank Colucci, "Rehearsals Reap Rewards," *Defense Helicopter World,* June–July 1990, p. 23; and Office of the Chief of Public Affairs, U.S. Army Command Information Division, Washington, D.C., "A Night at the Comandancia," *Soldiers in Panama,* pp. 18–19.

**8.** Interview with Lt. Col. Billie Ray Fitzgerald, Capt. Timothy Flynn, 1st Lt. Michael Mellor, and soldiers of the 1st Battalion, 508th Infantry (Airborne), Fort Kobbe, Republic of Panama, December 6, 1990. Other details of Charlie Company's assault on the Comandancia came from, "Extracts From After Action Report 1-508th INF BN (ABN) [Classified TOP SECRET; Declassified, December 1990] APO Miami 34006, dated 7 July 1990.

Another excellent source for this engagement is Robert K. Brown, "U.S. Warriors Topple Panamanian Thugs," *Soldier of Fortune,* April 1990, pp. 57–96. Brown, the magazine's publisher, "debriefed" Charlie Company troops immediately after the action. "I decided to play S.L.A.M. Marshall," Brown told the author, referring to America's foremost military historian, "so I let each guy tell his part of the story in his own words." What emerged was one of the most gripping firsthand accounts of the entire Panama invasion.

## *Chapter 6*

**1.** For an authoritative overview of the SEALs and Naval Special Operations Forces, see Norman Polmar, "SOF—The Navy's Perspective," *U. S. Naval Institute Proceedings,* August 1987, pp. 136–138. The author was fortunate to be able to review course material on U.S. Naval Special Warfare issued at the U.S. Special Operations Command training center, Hurlburt Field, Florida.

**2.** First Lieutenant Clarence E. Briggs III, *Operation Just Cause* (Harrisburg, PA: Stackpole Books, 1990), p. 59. Also: After Action Report, 3d Battalion, 504th Parachute Infantry Regiment.

**3.** Interview with Lt. Col. Lynn D. Moore, USA, U.S. Army War College, Carlisle, Pennsylvania, November 9, 1990, transcript, pp. 2–5.

**4.** Interviews with air crew of the 1st Battalion, 228th Aviation Regiment, Fort Kobbe, Republic of Panama, December 3, 1990, transcript, pp. 5–7.

**5.** The author was fortunate to review the videotaped After Action Report presentation of 3d Battalion, 504th Parachute Infantry, delivered at Fort Sherman, Republic of Panama, January 8, 1990. This report was declassified earlier that year.

## Chapter 7

**1.** Pentagon spokesman Lt. Col. Rick Oborn later confirmed that two of the four Rangers killed at Rio Hato were friendly fire casualties. See Eric Schmitt, "Army Says U.S. Fire Killed 2 GIs in Panama Invasion, *New York Times,* June 19, 1990, p. A3.

**2.** Neil C. Livingstone, "Danger in the Air," *The Washingtonian,* June 1990, p. 205. The successful rescue mission carried out by the Army's Delta Force marked a turning point for that unit. In 1983, a hastily organized Delta Force helicopter rescue mission in Grenada had been repulsed with heavy casualties. See Major Mark Adkin, *Urgent Fury: The Battle for Grenada* (Lexington, KY: Lexington Books, 1989), pp. 186–90.

**3.** Extracts from After Action Report 1-508th Infantry Battalion (Airborne), pp. 74–79; interviews with members of Company C, 1st Battalion, 508th Infantry, Fort Kobbe, Republic of Panama, December 6, 1990, transcript, pp. 4–6; also see Robert K. Brown, "U.S. Warriors Topple Panamanian Thugs," *Soldier of Fortune,* April 1990, pp. 59–60, 87–88.

**4.** The use of the 105 mm howitzer in firepower demonstrations at Fort Amador spawned one of the many news media myths about Operation Just Cause. Because the artillery piece appeared on the first televised news accounts, which also included footage of the El Chorrillo fires, it was assumed that indiscriminate American artillery fire had caused the devastation in El Chorrillo. This assumption became an article of faith for critics of the invasion, many of whom had only a confused understanding of the operation. One critic, National Public Radio Foreign Editor John Dinges, stated: "Just after midnight, the U.S. forces opened an artillery barrage from the headquarters of the 193d Brigade in Fort Amador across the small bay separating Fort Amador from PDF Command Headquarters." There are several things wrong with that statement. The howitzer did not fire until 0310 hours; no "barrage" (two or more artillery tubes) was ever fired; and no artillery fire was ever directed from Fort Amador elsewhere. In fact, Lieutenant Colonel Fitzgerald ordered that the gunners had to be certain no rounds would fly beyond Fort Amador and menace the Bridge of the Americas or Rodman Navy Station.

## Chapter 8

**1.** Lorenzo Crowell, "The Anatomy of *Just Cause:* The Forces Involved, the Adequacy of Intelligence, and Its Success as a Joint Operation," in *Operation Just Cause, The U.S. Intervention in Panama,* ed. Bruce W. Watson and Peter G. Tsouras (Boulder, CO: Westview Press, 1991), p. 91.

**2.** Interview with Brig. Gen. James Kinzer, Deputy Commander, 82d Airborne Division, Fort Clayton, Republic of Panama, December 6, 1990, transcript, p. 3. General Kinzer noted that the XVIII Airborne Corps Inspector General conducted a careful analysis of the airdrop and found "no dogs' breakfasts."

**3.** For a typical example of this criticism, see F.A. Wright, "Invasion of Panama Not the Textbook Operation Planners Say It Was," *U.S. Veteran News and Report,* January 24, 1990, p. 7. According to Wright, the decision for a night airdrop on a "secure air strip," was "risky at best, deadly at worst." Yet veterans of the Grenada operation remember the mass confusion and uncertainty connected with the air landing at Point Salines. One, Sergeant Peter Roderick, Jr., an M-60 gunner in the 2d Battalion, 508th Parachute Infantry Regiment, recalls that on October 24, 1983, his chalk was first rigged for an airdrop, then told to derig for an air landing, then ordered to rig again for a jump, and at the last minute, told to derig for a combat air landing.

When questioned about the Torrijos airdrop in Saudi Arabia during Operation Desert Storm, veteran NCOs and officers of the 82d Airborne unanimously concurred with one sergeant major's opinion: "No one wanted to repeat the fucking snafu we had at Point Salines." Over a warm Barbican near-beer at a cafe table in Rafha, Saudi Arabia, the sergeant major added that he would happily "punch the lights out of any straightleg liberal asshole" who had a different opinion. The fact that the 82d Airborne was about to go into combat in Iraq the next morning might have contributed to the sergeant major's vehemence.

**4.** Juan Vasquez, "Panama: Live From the Marriott!" *Washington Journalism Review,* March 1990, pp. 44–48. Vasquez's account is vivid, accurate, and above all honest. He makes it clear that the bloody anarchy and savage military operations in the streets of Panama City discouraged all but a few intrepid reporters from covering the story.

**5.** For a full account of the media pool in Panama, see Steven Komarow, "Pooling Around In Panama," *Washington Journalism Review,* March 1990, pp. 45–53. Also see "DoD Media Pool, Lessons Learned," United States Southern Command, Public Affairs After Action Report, pp. 1–10. In its own defense, Southcom Public Affairs accurately noted in this report that the street fighting in Panama City was more intense than had been anticipated, which precluded a safe and practical escort mission of this large, unwieldy pool to the still-contested points of combat around Panama City. In many ways, the failure of the Defense Department media pool during Operation Just Cause foreshadowed the similar frustrations encountered by "combat" media pools during Operation Desert Storm in the Gulf War.

**6.** Juan Vasquez, "Panama: Live From the Marriott!" p. 46.

**7.** For a detailed perspective on Marine Corps operations in Panama, see Maj. Bron N. Madrigan, "The Attack on the DNTT Station," *Marine Corps Gazette,* April 1990, pp. 9–10.

**8.** Interview with officers and men of the 1st Battalion, 508th Parachute Infantry Regiment, Fort Kobbe, Republic of Panama, November 30 and December 7, 1990. Also see Extracts of After Action Reports, 1st Battalion, 508th PIR, "Narrative of Team Red Operations," pp. 6–17.

**9.** Padre Javier Arteta, "El gran incendio de El Chorrillo vino a las siete de la manana del dia 20," (The great fire of El Chorrillo began at seven in the morning on the 20th [of December]), *La Prensa,* Panama City, August 31, 1990, pp. 12–13. The destruction by fire of the southwest quadrant of the El Chorrillo barrio has remained a point of contention. Many critics of the U.S. invasion believe the massive fire storm was sparked during the H-hour bombardment of the Comandancia. Some even state that American soldiers using flame-throwers deliberately set the blaze.

However, Father Arteta carefully documented the burning of the barrio with his 35 mm camera. His pictures reveal that the wooden tenements, which some critics maintain were destroyed by American "bombs," were still standing—untouched by fire—well after daylight. Father Arteta's photographs show the wall of fire advancing south and west from Avenida A during daylight hours on the morning of December 20, 1989.

In his *La Prensa* interview Father Arteta makes it clear that the buildings that had caught fire from the combat around the Comandancia were "isolated fires that did not keep burning. It's clear that the fire went out and did not pass to El Chorrillo." But he states that the fire started by the Dignity Battalion members was completely separate from the fires near the Comandancia. "The big El Chorrillo fire began at seven in the morning of the twentieth," he states. "I saw that. I left the church at 6:30 A.M., and El Chorrillo was okay. Cars were shot, there were houses with bullet marks, not bombs; and the houses were all intact, all except for some isolated fires."

Other eyewitnesses have also revealed that it was Dignity Battalion members, not U.S. shelling, that ignited the largest of the El Chorrillo fires. For more details, see James W. Nash, "Misconceptions Remain About Panama Invasion," *Houston Post,* May 4, 1990, p. 36.

Nevertheless, the myth that the crowded El Chorrillo barrio was shelled into ashes by U.S. forces has become one cornerstone of the "mass grave" theory, which contends that thousands of unnamed Panamanian civilians died in the invasion and were secretly buried in unmarked graves.

**10.** Interview with Col. Douglas Terrell, Commander, Task Force Aviation, Operation Just Cause, Fort Clayton, Republic of Panama, December 6, 1990, transcript, p. 3. Also see Frank Colucci, "Rehearsals Reap Rewards," *Defense Helicopter World,* June–July 1990, p. 23.

**11.** Interview with Lt. Col. D.I. Smith, Commander, 1st Battalion, 228th Aviation, Fort Kobbe, Republic of Panama, December 3, 1990, transcript, pp. 3–4; also, Terrell interview transcript, p. 4.

## *Chapter 9*

**1.** Interview with Maj. Kevin Higgins, Fort Bragg, North Carolina, July 24, 1991. It is interesting to compare the treatment of this PDF soldier with the charges by critics of the invasion that U.S. forces universally acted with gratuitous brutality toward Panamanian military personnel and civilians.

**2.** Interviews with members of 1st Battalion, 228th Aviation, Fort Kobbe, Republic of Panama, December 3, 1990, transcript, p. 7.

**3.** Interviews with serving and former members of SEAL Team Four, Norfolk, Virginia, December 1990. These men spoke on the condition that they remain anonymous.

**4.** A year after Operation Just Cause, Major General Marc Cisneros told the producers of the Public Television series "Frontline" that the U.S. command in Panama had not anticipated such widespread looting. The Blue Spoon OPLAN, however, assigned the 2d Brigade of the 7th Infantry Division (Light) an antilooting role. Inadvertently, they arrived too late to carry out this mission. See: "War and Peace in Panama," Public Television "Frontline," April 9, 1991.

**5.** Interview with soldiers of Charlie Company, 1st Battalion, 508th Infantry, Fort Kobbe, Republic of Panama, December 6, 1990, transcript, pp. 5–6. Also; Operation Just Cause Sequence of Events, C Company 1-508th Infantry, Extracts from After Action Report 1-508th Infantry (Airborne), pp. 26–27.

**6.** R.M. Koster and Guillermo Sanchez Borbon, *In the Time of the Tyrants: Panama, 1968–1989* (New York: W.W. Norton, 1991), pp. 377–378. And interview with Professor Richard M. Koster, Washingon, DC, July 17, 1991. Koster was an eyewitness to this strike by the Delta Force.

**7.** Neil C. Livingstone, "Danger in the Air," *The Washingtonian,* June 1990, pp. 92–93, and Neil Livingstone, "Just Cause Jailbreak," *Soldier of Fortune,* October 1990, pp. 45–47, 108–110. Neil Livingstone has published the most vivid and accurate accounts of Kurt Muse's rescue. The author was able to supplement Livingstone's accounts with background interviews with Special Operations personnel during the Gulf War. For more information, see Saundra Torry, "Va. Man Freed After Months In Panama Jail," *Washington Post,* December 22, 1989, p. A31.

**8.** 1st Lieutenant Clarence E. Briggs III, *Operation Just Cause* (Harrisburg, PA: Stackpole Books, 1990), p. 79.

## Chapter 10

**1.** For a detailed account of Chauvel's ordeal, see Patrick Chauvel, "Too Close to Combat," *Soldier of Fortune,* May 1990, pp. 62–76. The circumstances surrounding the death of Spanish photographer Juan Rodriguez have become a major point of contention between his family, which seeks compensation, and the U.S. government, which refuses to acknowledge the man was killed by American forces. See Alan Riding, "U.S. Sued in Death of a Journalist in Panama," *New York Times,* June 24, 1990, p. A15.

**2.** After Action Report of the Unit Ministry Team, 1st Battalion, 508th Infantry (Airborne), p. 3.

**3.** Interview with Col. Michael Snell, Commander of Task Force Bayonet, and members of the 193rd Light Infantry Brigade, December 3, 1990, Fort Clayton, Republic of Panama.

**4.** For a fast-paced, colorful account of the relationship between General Max Thurman and the Pentagon during Operation Just Cause, see Bob Woodward, *The Commanders* (New York: Simon and Schuster, 1991), ch. 15, pp. 175–196.

**5.** Interview with field-grade officer, 1190th Signal Brigade,

Fort Clayton, Republic of Panama, December 3, 1990, transcript, p. 6.

**6.** 1st Lieutenant Clarence E. Briggs III, *Operation Just Cause* (Harrisburg, PA: Stackpole Books, 1990), p. 83.

**7.** Ibid., pp. 84–85.

**8.** Gruson showed his true professional caliber by filing an exciting and complete account of the hostage ordeal within hours of his release on the morning of December 20. He then proceeded to change clothes and head right back out to the dangerous streets of Panama City. See Lindsey Gruson, "Threats and Dark Streets For Reporters in Captivity," *New York Times*, December 21, 1989, p. 1.

**9.** William Branigin, "U.S. Troops Surround Two Embassies," *Washington Post*, December 22, 1989, p. A1.

**10.** The author is familiar with the problems of herd coverage of a war. As a member of the international news media in Saudi Arabia, he personally witnessed many of his colleagues who were content to rewrite Central Command's Joint Information Bureau news releases and cover the war from the comfort of the Hyatt Regency Hotel in Riyadh or the Dhahran International Hotel. As in Panama, however, there were a number of brave and resourceful journalists who bucked the restrictive Defense Department press-pool system and conducted forbidden "unilateral" coverage of the fighting. The author encountered a few such individuals while driving his rented red Mitsubishi Gallant smack into a firefight between Marines of the 2d Division and some Iraqi holdouts off the Fifth Ring Highway in the suburbs of Kuwait City on February 27, 1991, the day the capital was liberated. One of the more colorful of these renegade journalists was *Soldier of Fortune* publisher Robert K. Brown, who had hidden out with Bedouins on the edge of the mine fields waiting for the ground war to begin.

**11.** "Invasion Revives Debate About Women," Reuters Dispatch, January 11, 1990; "Fire When Ready, Ma'am," *Time*, January 15, 1990, p. 29.

**12.** Philip Shabecofs, "Female Captain's Role is Called Into Question," *New York Times*, January 8, 1990, p. A3. Also see United States Southern Command Public Affairs After Action Report, Operation Just Cause, pp. 51–53.

**13.** Interview with copilot/gunner of the AH-1 involved in the Colon incident, April 25, 1991. This officer cited the official mission narrative as well as notes from the follow-on Southern Command investigation.

**14.** Colman McCarthy, "The Price of a 'Just Cause,'" *Washington Post,* May 20, 1990, p. F2. In his column, McCarthy states that Just Cause was an invasion, "in which, by conservative count, 2,000 Panamanian citizens were killed and thousands more injured." McCarthy does not reveal his sources for this casualty estimate.

**15.** Michael R. Gordon, "GI Accused of Murder in Panama Invasion," *New York Times,* April 12, 1990, p. A9; Patrick E. Tyler and Molly Moore, "Citing Rules of Engagement, GI Denies Murdering Panamanian," *Washington Post,* April 13, 1990, p. A10; "U.S. Paratrooper Acquitted in Killing in Panama Invasion," *Washington Post,* August 31, 1990, p. A4.

**16.** Information Paper, "Facts on Panamanian Casualties," issued by U.S. Southern Command Public Affairs Office, November 15, 1990, p. 1.

**17.** Mark A. Uhlig, "In Panama, Counting the Invasion Dead Is a Matter of Dispute," *New York Times,* October 28, 1990, p. E2.

**18.** Letter from Roderick Dhu Grambell, Jr., to Lt. Col. Robert W. Wagner, January 9, 1990.

**19.** Interview with Lt. Col. Lynn Moore, U.S. Army War College, Carlisle, Pennsylvania, November 9, 1990.

**20.** Interview with Lt. Col. Jerry Murguia, December 3, 1990, transcript, pp. 3–4. Capt. Tomas Garcia is now a precinct police chief in the new Public Force (Fuerza Publica) and Lt. Henry Cedeno commands a Public Force company in the western provinces.

**21.** Murguia interview transcript, p. 6. Also see Bob Woodward, *The Commanders,* pp. 192–193, and William Branigin, "Nicaragua Orders Americans Out; GIs Enter Managua Envoy's Home," *Washington Post,* December 30, 1989, p. A1.

**22.** One of the best descriptions of this unusual episode is found in Frederick Kempe, *Divorcing the Dictator* (New York: G.P. Putnam's Sons, 1990), ch. 22, "Noriega and the Nuncio," pp. 398–417.

# Index

AC-130 Spectre gunships, 31, 59, 61, 76, 77–78, 80, 82–83, 100, 112, 132, 198–99, 220
Adams, David, 257
Aguilar, Eloy O., 257
AH-1 Cobras, 132, 204
AH-6 Little Bird gunships, 78, 80–81, 100, 132–34
AH-64 Apache attack helicopter, 31, 78–83, 204, 206, 210–11, 214, 276, 277–78
Airborne Artillery, 8
Airborne Command, Control, and Communications (ABCCC), 36–37, 101
Airborne Warning and Control System (AWACS), 36, 281n5
Air Force, U.S., 54
Air Force Combat Control Team (CCT), 60, 61, 63, 66, 99; "Colt," 83, 167, 169
Albrook Air Force Station, 112, 128, 135, 252–53
Alexander, Sgt. Michael, 207–8
Almeda, Sgt. 1st Class Jim, 174
Alto del Golf neighborhood, 113
Amado, Vicky, 186, 274
Americas Watch, 264
Ancon Hill, 2–3, 4, 5, 35, 135, 144, 244, 252
Antiaircraft artillery (AAA), 96
Anti-Noriega demonstrations, 124–25, 212, 272
Arias Calderón, Ricardo, 93
Army, U.S., 54, 55

Army Training and Doctrine Command, 8
Arrijan, 146
Arteta, Father Javier, 201–2, 259, 295n9
A-7 and A-37 fixed wing attack jets, 94
Atlantic coast provinces, 268–69
Avenida Central, 232, 246
Avenida de los Mártires. *See* Fourth of July Avenue
Axson, Lt. Col. Harry, 265

Baghdad, 276–77
Balboa Harbor, 144
Balboa neighborhood, 129–30, 138, 184, 246
Bennett, 2d Lt. Chris, 250
Berry, Specialist Charles E., 132
Bisbal, Maj. Wanda, 189–90, 270
Blind Logic operation, 248–49
Boatright, Capt. Allen, 179, 245
Branigin, William, 257
Bratten, Col. Bill, 29
Bray, Capt. Linda, 257–58, 259
Brazil jungle training, 61
Bridge of the Americas, 10, 54, 143, 145
Broadus, Lt. Charles, 159
Brown, Sgt. Dan, 89–90, 168–71
Brown, Robert K., 291n8, 298n10
Bryan, 1st Sgt. Roberto Enrique, 261–62
Bush, George, 2, 13, 28, 98, 247, 271, 274, 288n7
Bushnell, John, 196

300

# Index

301

# About the Author

Malcolm McConnell is a former Foreign Service Officer and the author of fourteen books. As a journalist,
he has covered many of America's important military
operations during the last twenty-five years. He traveled twice to Panama and interviewed most of the key
participants in Operation Just Cause for this book.
During the Persian Gulf War in 1991, he spent two
months in the Middle East as a Roving Editor for
*Reader's Digest,* and was one of the few journalists to
report on Operation Desert Storm from Saudi Arabia,
Iraq, and Kuwait. McConnell lives on the Eastern
Shore of Maryland.